OTHER TITLES OF INTEREST FROM ST. LUCIE PRESS

The 90-Day ISO 9000 Manual and Implementation Guide
The Executive Guide to Implementing Quality Systems
Focused Quality: Managing for Results
Improving Service Quality: Achieving High Performance in the Public and
  Private Sectors
Introduction to Modern Statistical Quality Control and Management
ISO 9000: Implementation Guide for Small to Mid-Sized Businesses
Organization Teams: Continuous Quality Improvement
Organization Teams: Facilitator's Guide
Principles of Total Quality
Quality Improvement Handbook: Team Guide to Tools and Techniques
The Textbook of Total Quality in Healthcare
Total Quality in Higher Education
Total Quality in Managing Human Resources
Total Quality in Marketing
Total Quality in Purchasing and Supplier Management
Total Quality in Radiology: A Guide to Implementation
Total Quality in Research and Development
Total Quality Management for Custodial Operations
Total Quality Management: Text, Cases, and Readings, 2nd Edition
Total Quality Service

For more information about these titles call, fax or write:

St. Lucie Press
100 E. Linton Blvd., Suite 403B
Delray Beach, FL 33483
TEL (407) 274-9906 • FAX (407) 274-9927

$S_{\stackrel{t}{L}}$

CREATING PRODUCTIVE ORGANIZATIONS

Developing your work force

Manual

Elizabeth A. Smith

S^{t}L

St. Lucie Press
Delray Beach, Florida

Phone: (407) 274-9906
Fax: (407) 274-9927

S_L^t

Published by
St. Lucie Press
100 E. Linton Blvd., Suite 403B
Delray Beach, FL 33483

CONTENTS

PREFACE

The simple premise of this manual is that productive organizations are made up of productive people. High-performing organizations have leaders who plan for and anticipate the future. These leaders are expert in recognizing individual differences, managing people's feelings, and providing a supportive environment which reinforces and appropriately rewards individual and group effort.

This manual presents basic information about people, jobs, and the workplace using simple descriptions, methods, and contemporary examples and illustrations. Major threads woven throughout the material are (1) the need to develop a vision of what you want to become, both on the job and personally; (2) the many faces of productivity; (3) focus on the internal and external customers and others in the supply–end user chain; and (4) the specific sequence and nature of work processes leading to accomplishment.

The author's conceptual model will help you develop a method to identify, describe, understand, and compare various types and levels of work skills and activities. You will be able to (1) use methods and tools to assess your current abilities, skills, and knowledge, or special talents; (2) develop goals and plans of action to use on the job; (3) share this newly acquired knowledge with others in order to streamline jobs and increase job satisfaction, motivation, *and* productivity; (4) determine what really adds value to your job; and (5) implement plans, monitor achievements, and document and illustrate your accomplishments in a format that others can readily understand, or a "career passport."

There are many ways to enhance personal and organizational productivity. When people are empowered to help themselves, they help others along the way. These people-centered change efforts break down the organization's structural barriers and reduce resistance to change.

Our first step begins as a vision of what we want ourselves and the organization to become. Through hard work and dedication, we gradually transform our visions into actions that produce results. We need to resist the tide of complacency and overcome barriers such as fear of failure. We must also integrate work and workplace changes into our daily plan of action. Then we *can* make a difference. Gains in productivity are made just as they are made in many other areas of human endeavor—one small step at a time.

ACKNOWLEDGMENTS

A special thank you goes to my two daughters, Karen Anne Smith and Julie Martinez Smith, who greatly contributed to the various drafts of the manuscript. Ms. Terry Wykowski, Oxford Consulting Group, and B. Ray Helton, Peachtree City, Georgia, provided a valuable overall perspective on the manuscript. The diligence and enthusiasm of Ms. Sandy Pearlman, editor at St. Lucie Press, were greatly appreciated.

THE AUTHOR

Elizabeth A. Smith, Ph.D., is Vice President of Summit Resources. She attended the University of Alberta and graduated with a B.A. in psychology in 1956. She received her M.A. (1963) and Ph.D. (1968) in psychology from the University of Wyoming.

Dr. Smith has taught courses in psychology and management at the University of Texas at Austin; Air Force Institute of Technology, F.E. Warren Air Force Base; Houston Baptist University; and Rice University. She was Assistant Professor of Psychology at the University of Texas Health Science Center, Division of Continuing Education and evaluator for National Cancer Institute training contracts awarded to the M.D. Anderson Cancer Center. She received grant funds from the Regional Medical Program of Texas to write *Psychosocial Aspects of Cancer Patient Care* and *A Comprehensive Approach to Rehabilitation of the Cancer Patient* (both published by McGraw-Hill in 1976).

Dr. Smith conducts research and presents industry seminars on motivation, productivity, and quality. She has authored five books in medicine, psychology, and business, in addition to twenty-five articles. Her book entitled *The Productivity Manual* (Gulf Publishing, 1990) has been translated into Portuguese and Spanish. The second edition of this manual was published in 1995.

Papers were recently presented by Dr. Smith at the Fourth International Conference on Productivity and Quality Research in Miami, Florida and at the 1993 World Quality Conference in Helsinki, Finland. She has developed and published various instruments to assess managerial behavior and experiential learning exercises in the area of productivity and quality. Recent publications are *The Management Behavior Assessment Test* (Talico, 1994) and "Operational Definitions: Studying Productivity" (*The 1995 Annual,* Volume 2: Consulting, Pfeiffer & Company).

Honors include Outstanding Young Women in America, Who's Who of American Women, Notable Women of Texas, Psi Chi, and Sigma Xi. Dr. Smith has been a member of the Texas Medical Center-Rice University Chapter of Sigma Xi since 1970 and has been an officer and served on its board of directors. She joined the Gulf Coast Chapter of the Association for Women in Science in 1985 and is currently a Delegate to the Federation of Houston Professional Women. In 1993, the Federation named Dr. Smith "Woman of Excellence."

Dr. Smith is a member of various societies and organizations, among which are the American Management Association, Institute of Industrial Engineers, American Society for Quality Control, Association for Quality and Participation, and the Southwest Academy of Management.

INTRODUCTION

PURPOSE

- Introduce basic concepts of human and organizational productivity that will be used throughout the manual

- Summarize the main practical applications of the information on people, processes, and organizations

- Encourage open-minded divergent, creative thinking

- Provide ideas that can be evaluated and considered for possible implementation

INTRODUCTION

This manual contains basic, common-sense information about people, jobs, and the workplace. Simple descriptions and methods and contemporary examples and illustrations are used. The focus is partly on organizations, but mainly on how people think, learn, and perform.

Productivity can be defined in many ways. Also, productivity means different things to different people. In reality, productivity is how well we all work together. To work cooperatively, we must be able to discuss our jobs in terms that others understand, as well as perform our jobs at an acceptable level. Before we can do these two things, we must understand ourselves and our talents, Only then can we describe and represent what we do in ways that those who work with us can comprehend.

Performing at an acceptable level is something nearly everyone wants to do, but many may not be able to do. Reasons for failure could fill this manual. Rather, the positives are emphasized here. People who really want to do something can hardly be kept from doing it. They will find a way.

A sprinkling of fads and trends is balanced by current literature, opinions of "experts," and predictions for the future. A major concern is the changing expectations of workers based on the realism accompanied by reduced numbers of promotions. Changes in jobs and in the workplace occur daily. Positive and negative reactions to quality initiatives are announced orally and in print. New Age concepts, steadily growing competition in the marketplace, and a turbulent economic environment place the burden on the individual to figure out not only what to do, but how and when to do it.

PURPOSE

It is impossible to reveal what will work for you, or even what will necessarily work best in a given situation. The emphasis is on providing a way for you to:

1. Develop a personal system of information and use your mental "tools," or insightful, proven ways to assess and perform your job.   Factors such as individual differences, frame of reference, biases, and many other personal and organizational variables impact how people think and perform their jobs.

The best and most robust set of tools are never seen. Some are rarely used. Where are they? They are the tools everyone carries around in their head. Typical general-purpose tools are thinking, reasoning, evaluating, and using common sense. Each person has his or her own special set of professional tools, used, for instance, in accounting, engineering, sales, and marketing. The totally unique tools are the ones this manual is designed to bring to your attention and then help you sharpen and fine tune. It is then your responsibility to keep them sharp.

2. Identify, describe, understand, and compare various types and levels of the broad range of work skills and work activities.   Specifically, you will be able to:

- Assess your current abilities, skills, and knowledge or special talents using the author's conceptual model or one you create yourself

- Develop goals and plans of action to use on the job

- Implement plans, monitor achievements, and record accomplishments in a portfolio of skills, or a "career passport"

3. After completing this manual, you should be able to:

- Develop a vision, mission, and goals to meet your particular current and future needs. Study your vision, mission, and goals to determine whether they will take you where you want to go (Chapters 1 and 2).

- Gradually create your own system of knowledge, beliefs, and behavior based on a combination of demonstrated "facts" and what you believe to be standard operating procedures (Chapters 3 and 4).

- Evaluate the world around you, including the organization and how it works. Learn about dramatically new shapes and purposes of organizations, namely the learning organization. Consider the positive and negative forces that impinge on your feelings and accomplishments (Chapter 5).

- Separate the fact from the fiction associated with the many faces of productivity and with a never-ending sequence of change and improvement efforts. Use descriptive and numeric measures to develop a meaningful way to assess personal and organizational productivity. Current examples from various organizations will help you prioritize important factors, such as quality, value, and profit, among others (Chapter 6).

- View numerous types and descriptions of work activities and obtain a better understanding of your own job. This increased understanding will also carry over to those with whom you work—supervisors, team members, peers, and subordinates.

- Consider the role of internal and external customers and how their work efforts and needs affect you personally. Contrast work in service and product-based and crossover industries. View quality and value added from the customer's perspective (Chapter 7).

- Evaluate the relative merits of using tools—*operational definitions* that describe concepts in terms of how they are used, *systems approaches* to trace the logic and flow of work processes, and *building a model* to assess important concepts such as quality and productivity (Chapter 8).

- Consider uniqueness, or individual differences associated with abilities, skills, and knowledge. Select from among the methods and tools presented those which are most useful in examining your unique talents and the demands of your job. People express their uniqueness and apply their talents in a variety of ways. Develop a set of beliefs or assumptions about yourself and how work is to be accomplished (Chapter 9).

■ Use the author's Core-Unique-Expanding (C-U-E) conceptual model to assess your job along ten work-related dimensions. The model uses specific job factors and experience levels to group jobs or tasks into a unified whole.

You are encouraged to develop your own special ways to view and improve your job in order to streamline your efforts and increase productivity, motivation, and job satisfaction. A prime use of the C-U-E model is in developing a list or portfolio of skills, or a career passport, to document accomplishment in work to plan for today as well as the future. The model you build grows and changes according to your job, where you work, and what you do. It becomes your ballast in the growing "sea of change" (read *uncertainty*) that surrounds us.

The model is flexible and simple enough that many "competitive advantage concepts," such as value added, can be incorporated. The model can also be used to recognize and/or develop special talents or skills needed to perform the growing number of jobs requiring computer literacy and information processing expertise. For example, jobs could be custom designed to fit specific work-related needs or training needs in a new field or in areas where job standards are unclear, e.g., create a user-friendly information superhighway (Chapter 10).

CHALLENGES

Challenges to be considered are meant to inform and motivate rather than discourage. People, not organizations, are the only ones who can change and improve things. The following list covers major challenges faced on a daily basis:

1. Managers are gradually being transformed into leaders and may be further transformed into team members, facilitators, or mentors.

2. Cost-cutting efforts are often based on short-term thinking to achieve bottom-line, immediate results. Frequently, it appears that people are seldom considered an asset. These valuable "expendable" resources carry in their heads the history, culture, and knowledge of the organization which is vital to continued success.

3. Organizations will always be searching for something they do not have which other organizations do. For the last five years, it has been quality. The quest for quality will remain constant until someone realizes that the closer you get to quality, the further away it gets. One reason is that standards for quality are raised continuously. New nouns, verbs, and a

few adjectives will be added to the quest list. Upcoming names could include value and value added, better customer service, information as a strategic resource, etc. The constant amid all the uproar and confusion is you and how you perform.

4. Are we getting all the technology we are paying for? Technology often brings an infrastructure of support people and systems with it. Some technologies are expanding so rapidly that we cannot keep up.

5. The growing demands from customers challenge yet frighten many. What will the customer want next? Is the customer king? Mass specialization appears to be the order of the day. Does customization come at a price? Yes. Are most willing to pay for the wide selection of cars, cereals, clothes, etc.? Yes—so far. We will know for sure when customers quit buying.

6. Growing competition is not just local; it comes from half-way around the world. Working "smarter" and "better" is just a beginning point. The marketplace is where decisions are made. You and your organization are always in the marketplace.

WHAT CAN WE DO?

We have lots of options. Most of all, we can rely on our knowledge and follow our common sense. First, we can learn more about ourselves, our jobs, and those around us at work. This is not an easy job, but it will give us a vision and a purpose. Second, we must be proactive and plan ahead. We must decide where we want to go and how we are going to get there. Third, and most important of all, we need to be confident in our ability to learn, grow, and acquire new skills and talents for daily use in our work and personal lives.

This manual provides basic information. You can select what to apply, modify it, and make it better. Methods that are successful can be used again and become part of your current and future action plans. You can develop your skills in the area of greatest need. By considering what makes you more productive, you can concentrate on those areas. Your road map, or vision and goals, provides countless ways to take you where you want to go. But you must plan your trip carefully. Despite a few detours, persistence will get you there.

1

GETTING STARTED

PURPOSE

- Develop a clear vision of yourself, of your areas of competence, and of your job

- Begin the process of creating a mental model of your skills, abilities, and knowledge, or talents

- Consider ways to gradually accumulate knowledge and apply your talents through networking, developing shared visions, and other individual and group activities

INTRODUCTION

This manual is about you. You will write the most important parts. Information on your abilities, beliefs, values, work methods, knowledge, and many other areas of strength will be reflected in the picture or mental model you create. The process of building a model or representation of your talents will take time and patience. This learning experience will lead you in new directions at work. The model you create will increase your understanding of your current work and open the door to challenging opportunities.

People are the most valuable resource in any organization. They carry out the daily work of the organization. They also make discoveries and create new, innovative products and processes.

If organizations are to become and remain successful in today's turbulent times, they must encourage and support their work forces. In turn, people throughout the organization should work toward achieving the organization's mission and goals. People are more productive when their jobs closely match their areas of competence and interest. Motivation increases when people know how their jobs and what they do fit into the overall vision, plans, and goals of the organization.

PURPOSES AND CONTENT OF THIS MANUAL

This manual will guide you through the various steps needed to develop a realistic, detailed representation or model of your skills, abilities, knowledge, and numerous other talents and areas of interest. These steps will prepare you to get a better feel for what you do at work and how you do it. Then, it will be possible to learn more about what other people do and how they affect you and your job.

Basic information about people's talents, jobs, and the workplace is presented. Simple descriptions and methods and current examples and illustrations will help you focus on your unique abilities, or special talents.

The major purposes of this manual are to encourage you to do the following:

1. Take a closer look at the basics of behavior and business and "get a better handle on things."   Doing the main part of your job just a little bit better will increase your productivity. Increased productivity rarely occurs in sudden leaps. These "leaps" are really made up of many small steps. Over time, many small steps, when added together, do make a difference.

2. Assess the steadily growing stream of new ideas, concepts, and methods in areas such as quality, measurement, and management.   Separating fiction from fact requires intuition and effort. Isolating symptoms and real problems is seldom difficult. Symptoms, like headaches, are the obvious signs that something is wrong. To illustrate, a symptom, for example absenteeism, is treated as though it were the problem.

3. Share information, or network.   These processes open up many useful doors. Most of us are good judges of our abilities and know what we can and cannot do. We also know how to improve our own job and do it better. Do we tell this to anyone? Probably not. Does anyone ask? Rarely. Would anyone listen if we told them? Some might. Therefore, it is time for a change.

4. Consider a wide range of information and assess how it can be applied on the job.   By broadening your horizons, you can test ideas that you feel have a good chance of succeeding in the work setting. In other words, take action.

The major content of this manual:

1. Covers a range of current business-related issues, yet keeps the traditional issues in clear view. Ideas, examples, and illustrations enable you to place yourself and your job in perspective, or get a better focus on where you are and where you want to be.

2. Encourages you to look inside yourself and to explore ways to learn more about yourself. Only then can you start on the road of self discovery leading to "personal mastery." Discovering some hidden talents and acquiring new skills will increase your confidence.

3. Provides guidance and examples for you to:

   ■ Develop a clear vision of yourself and your job. Understand yourself. Accept yourself. Take responsibility for your feelings.

   ■ Create a mental model based on your areas of strength, interest, and excitement.

   ■ Use your mental model as a guide to assess yourself and others.

   ■ Apply your areas of competence or talents in ways which enable you to learn and to grow on the job.

   ■ Gradually build a concept of yourself that reflects confidence and determination. Confident, competent people have already taken a major step toward personal mastery. This last and most exciting step enables you to successfully weather the storm and challenges of the sea of change.

WHERE WE'VE BEEN

Cutbacks, reengineering, resizing, reorganization, downsizing, relocations, and all other forms of management and financial juggling often have negative emotional and monetary impacts on workers.

In some organizations, job loyalty, commitment, lifetime employment, job security, and possibly even the prospect of promotion and retirement benefits are gradually disappearing. Organizations hire and plan for the short term.

Some organizations outsource work they either do not want to do or feel others can do better. Outsourcing is growing, particularly during cyclic or seasonal overloads.

Here to stay are ever-advancing technologies, telecommuting, the latest quality improvement program—and fear of the future. Headlines in most daily newspapers feature downsizing, sharing services, and numerous cost-cutting and effort-saving programs.

Having a job with a strong, progressive company probably guarantees lifetime employment or long-term financial security. Job security decreases when organizational structures and systems to support the work force are in a constant stae of flux. The growth of autonomous work groups, cross-functional teams, and job enrichment and the increasing impact of technology isolate people from a core work team and possibly from a familiar work location.

The number of middle managers who coordinated efforts, served as conduits for information, and functioned as buffers steadily decreases. Support staffs are also slowly disappearing. Many of us are working harder but getting less meaningful work done. We now perform some of the functions middle managers and support staffs used to perform. This obviously lowers our productivity.

Work overloads make us wonder whether we can ever catch up. Support and direction from those around us—leaders, mentors, peers, team members, and numerous other resources—will strengthen our belief in ourselves, in our own abilities, and in our innate ability to achieve. Our ultimate goal is to have a challenging job with a future.

We are all responsible for paddling our own canoe. Experienced people will have built their canoes, shaped their paddles, and be ready to start. Others must build their canoes, then shape their paddles, learn to paddle, and start. As in most endeavors, the experienced group will have completed the trip and begun another one before the last group starts building their canoes.

WHERE WE'RE GOING

The prime focus of the rest of this chapter is on developing a personal vision that can be blended into your mental model. This model can be used as a guide to learning or to personal mastery that leads to action.

Developing Personal and Organizational Visions

Today's crises in meaning are not just in words, but extend to organizations as we know them. Levels of crises range from basic survival to the need to expand in order to meet the demands of customers. Organizations of all shapes and sizes and their CEOs are wrestling with the broad concepts of "vision," "mission," and "direction." Some organizations are like an ocean liner without a captain. The captains of many organizations have to figure out what their mission is before they can define it in terms people will understand.

Unfortunately, many employees do not know what business their company is in. This lack of definition and direction is a problem not only at work, but may carry over to their personal lives.

Leaders must help those around them understand and commit to the vision and encourage people to learn what they must do to change their vision into a reality. The hardest part is creating and maintaining the organizational environment where vision can be transformed into reality. These insightful leaders must not only be able to plan for the future, but must anticipate the future as well.

The need to create and implement vision appears increasingly in the literature. For example, in *The Age of Paradox,* Handy points out that we must look for pathways through turbulence and what appear to be contradicting beliefs, or paradoxes.[6] A paradox is an opinion or statement contrary to common or accepted opinion. Paradoxes are again discussed in Chapter 3.

When visions are shared, a basis for candid communication and creative risk taking is created. This creative risk taking can apply at any state of a person's life and in any organization. Also, shared visions based on shared values can become strong ties that bind people together. Methods to create a shared vision are given by Berg and Schmitz.[3]

1. Develop a Clear Personal Vision

Personal vision is the ability to focus on ultimate intrinsic, innate, or natural desires. It is a picture of a desired future. Vision is something concrete or a specific destination, like landing a man on the moon. A vision that lacks purpose is just a good idea. No one can create a vision for us. The actual words in a vision are not as important as the thoughts, feelings, and attitudes that emerge.

Facets and Descriptions of Visions

The following statements describe the various facets of visions.[10,11]

1. A vision is the vehicle for advancing to a larger story. Stories evolve as they are being told. A vision is a way to move ourselves forward to a place where we may be able to go in the physical sense. To illustrate, we may envision the type of organization we want to work for, the kind of job we want to do, and the talents needed to perform at the high level we anticipate. Ask yourself, "What do I want to create?"

2. A vision is a continuously evolving process as opposed to an attainable end state.   As you think about your vision, it begins to change. Some parts are clear. Other parts are in the shadows. At times, your vision will be alive with brightness, activity, and sound. Occasionally, your vision will be tranquil.

A vision is not planable, but it can be programmed. It cannot be made to order or rushed. The subconscious mind, which operates below the level of conscious awareness, plays a major role in learning. It functions on "automatic," similar to driving a car or performing a repetitive task.

3. Visions can appear in a "burst from the blue" or as a creative insight.   However, visions are often the result of methodical thinking, careful planning, and a fairly long incubation period. Visions are not linear, as in a linear progression of words or thoughts. Rather, visions are three-dimensional holograms that change and evolve before our eyes. They are exhilarating. Visions create sparks that lift people out of the mundane.

4. Visions exist in the relationship between conscious and unconscious thought.   They gradually take form and float around in our conscious and unconscious thoughts. Visions need to be viewed from the outside looking in and from the inside looking out. Although this may be confusing at first, it is necessary to look at your vision objectively, as in examining it for the first time. Then, reverse roles and view it from the inside looking out.

5. Aspiration and fear play major positive and negative roles in visions.   Fear may motivate, but also causes anxiety or tension. Aspirations can be positive motivators, provided they can be achieved. A vision that is unattainable is only a dream and nothing more. Both the negative and positive visions need to coexist. However, it is important that the person who is visioning be able to tell the difference between positive and negative visions.

6. Vision and mission statements can take the form of superordinate goals.   Some forty years after the concept of superordinate goals was introduced by social psychologists Sherif and Sherif,[13] it is being used in business literature.

The standard dictionary definition of superordinate goal is "...a universal proposition, or something of a higher degree or rank." "Higher rank" could be the lofty image or noble goals described in vision statements that allow for a broad, even universal proposition by any number of organizations throughout the world.

However, as originally defined, achieving a superordinate, or common, goal requires two or more conflicting parties to cooperate. In other words, two or more people or groups, often in conflict or at odds with each other, cooperate or pool resources to achieve a common, highly desired goal.

7. Vision grows in the feedback–feedforward relationship between the world in the mind and the present potential.[10] It thrives on the tension or difference between these two relationships. Visions are dynamic and are not necessarily exactly the same at two different points in time. Visioning and developing visions are continual processes.

8. Good leaders are visionaries. They are able to plan for, and in some cases anticipate, the future. These leaders are designers, teachers, and stewards. They encourage people to build visions, to learn, to grow, and to continuously expand their capabilities. No manager can dictate a vision. However, managers can create a conducive, supportive organizational environment that evokes enthusiastic commitment to visions, namely learning organizations. Learning organizations are introduced in Chapter 2 and further discussed in Chapter 5.

Characteristics of Vision Statements

Albrecht[1] provides insights into vision statements:

1. A focused concept that goes beyond platitudes. It is a value creation premise that people can actually picture as existing.

2. A sense of noble purpose that is really worth doing and that creates value. It makes a contribution, as in making the world a better place, and wins people's commitment.

3. A plausible chance of success that is believed to be realistic and possible. It may not be perfectly attainable, but is plausible to strive for.

Examples of Organizational Vision Statements

The following examples come from a wide range of organizations.

Example 1. The vision of Bill Gates, founder and chairman of Microsoft, is "...a computer on every desk and in every home, running Microsoft software."[1]

Example 2. The vision of the British Royal Mail is "...to be recognized as the best organization in the World delivering text and packages."[1]

Example 3. In 1960, John F. Kennedy stated his vision of a man on the moon before the end of the decade. His statement was, "I believe that this nation should commit itself to achieving the goal, before this decade is out, of landing a man on the moon and returning him safely to Earth."[8]

This vision, which was accomplished in July 1969, is an example of a superordinate goal. The whole nation, and much of the then free world, shared America's vision of a man on the moon.

Example 4. The corporate vision of GTE Directories Corporation, one of the 1994 Malcolm Baldrige National Quality Award winners for excellence in the service area, is "100% Customer Satisfaction Through Quality." [9]

Where Are Visions Leading Us?

Feelings of concern, perhaps even anxiety, often cloud our vision of where we want to be and where we currently are. Senge[11] uses "creative tension" to represent the gap between what we want our vision to be and telling the truth about where we are, or our "current reality." This creative tension can be reduced by (1) raising the current reality or (2) lowering the vision toward existing reality. However, without vision, there is no creative tension.

In *The Northbound Train,* Albrecht[1] uses the metaphor of riding a train as one way to create a vision and provide direction and energy or meaning. The "train" gives an organization the energy to propel it to success. Albrecht encourages leaders to think carefully and form their strategies before choosing their train. This type of thinking and action will require organizations to become more open and flexible. These innovative structures are discussed in Chapter 5.

2. Create a Mental Model

A mental model is used to determine how we make sense of the world and how we take action. Mental models are made up of stories, images, assumptions, and a good deal of information gathered throughout our lifetimes of school, business, reading, trial-and-error learning, etc.

Mental models range from simple generalizations about almost anything to complex theory. Although people may say and believe a wide range of things, their behavior supports their theories-in-use, or their mental models.[2]

Royal Dutch/Shell was one of the first large organizations to discover the pervasive influence of hidden mental models.[4] Shell's success in managing the unpredictability of the world oil business in the 1970s and 1980s came primarily from learning how to bring managers' mental models to the surface and challenge their mental models.[10]

Two key statements by Senge[10] set the tone and provide encouragement for the self-study that creating a model requires: (1) "...human beings are designed for learning" and (2) "Through learning, we re-create our selves." Senge believes that the impulse to learn is an impulse to expand our capacity.

W. Edwards Deming, well known for his longstanding efforts in total quality management, believed that people are born with self-esteem, intrinsic motivation, and dignity. Most of all, they have a curiosity about learning and experience joy in learning.

Just getting started takes effort. Our first step is to develop a vision. Our second step is to get you to think about your job. Our third step introduces you to a three-part model that is based on answers to the following three questions.

1. Is most of my job routine?

2. Am I really using my experience and training?

3. Am I challenged by my work and excited about doing it?

Think about where you are in your job—just starting, employed for a long time, etc. Then think about where you want to be. Is there a big difference between where you are and where you want to be?

We often spend a great deal of time and energy doing routine things, or working on the basics. We may even feel that these efforts waste our time and could be delegated. Naturally, we prefer to spend as much time as possible working in areas in which we are trained or are competent. It is normal to want to function at as high a level as we possibly can for as long as we can.

Although we may perform basic activities in a creative manner, we are much more likely to apply our creative potential when we work in our areas of competence or specialization. When we are challenged and motivated, we may develop new ideas for products, do forefront research, or work in areas that allow us to maximize our creative talents. As a result, our motivation, productivity, and job satisfaction increase. These three levels—routine, areas of competence, and areas of challenge—form the basic structure of the model we will create, beginning in Chapter 2 and ending in Chapter 10.

Finding ourselves has been a universal quest since the beginning of recorded history. Some "find" themselves in a sudden burst of insight that appears suddenly. Others struggle for years, often in some sort of tension, until they eventually come to grips with themselves and their needs, visions, beliefs, and values. Suddenly, things fit together. One, new insights are gained. Two, paths are found. Three, visions become clear.

Nearly everyone has to be prodded into thinking about themselves, their jobs, improving their skills, or doing a better job at work. Like exercising or dieting, you have to want to do it. Having a goal, a focus, or a vision provides feedback on where you are and how well you are doing. Feedback is a critical element in any learning process.

Once you begin to think about your special talents, and start to understand them, you get a better feel for what you do at work and how you do it. When you assess and mentally assemble the many facets of your job, you can develop in your mind a picture of your own skills, ability, and knowledge, or talents. Then, you can see how you and your job fit into the overall scheme of things. You will also learn more about what other people do and how they affect you and your job.

People "buy in" to something they build themselves. Buying in produces a sense of ownership in what is created. You are much more likely to use the model you build yourself than a model another person constructs for you.

3. Use Your Mental Model as Guide

As you grow personally and professionally, your model will also grow. A clear picture and understanding of yourself is one of the major keys to opening the ever-widening doors of opportunity. Rapidly advancing technology, the increasing number of new and challenging jobs, and global competition provide new avenues to apply what we know.

You can also use your own model as a way to assess the talents of others. Your model will provide guidelines or standards to assess the level of your own skills, abilities, and knowledge. In school, we compared ourselves with our classmates, both inside and outside the classroom. We make comparisons at work all the time and in our personal lives as well.

For instance, people who work in non-traditional settings (e.g., at home, late evening hours) or share a job will need to rely more on their own resources. They will have to follow a path they chart mainly by themselves.

Only when you can recognize your own inner strength, talents, and creativity can you begin to recognize these same attributes in others.

4. Apply Your Talents on the Job

Many people like to "learn by doing." Trial-and-error approaches are part of the growing and learning process. In order to grow, it is important to build knowledge and confidence by solving the common problems that occur daily. Experience in general and feedback from results of your efforts provide you with information to do your job better.

The best and most useful set of tools is unseen. The tools needed to meet the numerous challenges around you are in your head. Some are afraid to use them.

Individuals who keep adding tools and refining existing tools are very valuable. Tools become even more valuable when linked with personal vision.

You will need to fine-tune your tools to fit the demands of your job. Tools will help you achieve your goals and accomplish your mission in life. Your personal vision is the ability to focus on ultimate intrinsic desires. Vision is a specific destination, or a picture of a desired future.

When you know your talents, you can take on new activities or jobs with enthusiasm. Building confidence one step at a time leads to personal mastery. It will show in your personal and work life. Knowledge of self increases the probability of success. As the saying goes, "nothing succeeds like success."

5. Attain Personal Mastery

Personal mastery means having and maintaining a certain level of performance. When personal mastery become a discipline, we can clarify what is important to us. This clarification process prevents us from becoming or staying confused. When we learn on a consistent basis, we see the current reality more clearly.

Inner strength that comes from the discipline of personal mastery, as in knowing one's strengths and limitations, forms a solid, stable core within the person. People who know their own mental and physical systems have a better grasp of the inner strengths of others.

Organizations that mobilize the collective talents of their employees can literally blow their competition away. The synergistic effect of gradually adding talents together ultimately improves the entire value chain. People and their unique talents are our most valuable resource. When individuals are allowed, even empowered, to function at their highest level, their potential is greatly expanded. Their knowledge and expertise add value to the organizational endeavor.

GET PREPARED FOR ACTION

The next competitive advantage could be people. This means having a highly motivated, trained, creative, loyal work force. It also means motivating people and recognizing and rewarding their accomplishments. To develop this, we need to ask:

1. Who are they? (*Answer*: They are us.)

2. Where are they? (*Answer*: They are all around us. They work with us. They are our family, friends, and neighbors.)

3. What can we do? (*Answer*: We can do three things, as indicated below.)

Our actions include the following three steps.

1. Look inside yourself to find out what your "pluses," not your "minuses," are.   It is vital to build on strengths rather than weaknesses. Special talents are based on your major abilities, skills, knowledge, beliefs, values, integrity, or whatever makes you tick. Values, or deep-seated standards, shape your personality and literally affect everything you think and do.

We all have special abilities and talents that may not be fully used on the job. We need to believe that it is okay to let people know what we do well.

2. Talk to people at work.   Ask them questions. Listen intently to what they say. Remember what they say. Then get them to tell you what they do best. Don't forget to ask them what they like doing best. Then, you can discuss what you can do and what they can do, or compare notes.

To illustrate, Jack Welch, CEO of General Electric Corporation, often shares ideas with CEOs from other companies. Welch believes that executives need to get outside their organizations to see what works best and then borrow these ideas or techniques. This type of networking is a form of mentoring.[12]

One reason for failure to communicate openly and honestly could be lack of communication skills, namely "listening" skills. When you are talking, do you ever have the feeling that the person listening to you is thinking about what he or she is going to say next? How many people really listen to what you say? When someone is talking to you, are you thinking about what you are going to say next? One reason why dedicated listeners are hard to find is that we have so little training in developing and using listening skills.

3. Network your abilities.   Few people have problems networking their skills when it comes to sports. People eagerly look for tennis or racquetball partners of about equal ability or someone on an equal "par" to golf with. Why, then, are we so reluctant to discuss what we can do and what we like to do when it comes to work?

Networking takes time, effort, and persistence. When you network with peers in the same or similar jobs, you obtain valuable information about job content, contacts in other parts of the organization, and perhaps even job openings. When you network outside your organization, even outside your profession, you learn a great deal about other people's jobs, opportunities, and technology. Through sharing information on talents and interests, you can begin to understand the immense amount of underutilized, even unused, talent that exists in the workplace.

Informal contacts lead to jobs. When there is a job opening in an organization, the people who work there know about it long before it becomes official or an ad appears in the local newspaper. Results of studies show that jobs referred by word-of-mouth information and personal referral are more highly paid and more often newly created jobs than those found by other means.

In a study involving 5000 American families, about half of the young adults indicated that they heard about their current jobs through friends or relatives. Similarly, about half knew someone who worked for their current employer before they accepted the job.

Undoubtedly, personal exchanges of information are at the heart of the employment process. Paper, in the form of advertisements, resumes, application forms, etc., really is an "insulating material" that keeps people apart.

Networking turns an otherwise spontaneous, unplanned series of chance meetings into a deliberate process. Skilled networkers can build up corps of people who are watching for suitable jobs for them. They describe the kind of job they are looking for, and their network literally does the screening for them. Frequently, it is only a matter of time before information flows back and forth between people looking for jobs and those doing the hiring.

People who belong to professional societies and interest groups are a repository of technical information. Professional associates can access their own specialized network of people with expertise in engineering, marketing...computer programming and refer you on to someone who can help you. A good number of professional societies routinely receive information about job openings.

Networking takes practice. The more you do it, the better you get at it. Also, the more you network, the larger your network becomes. Networks are great professional and personal information resources.

A personal system of knowledge lets you become an expert in your own profession or field of interest. You have power when you have facts to support what you say. Facts are rarely disputed. Senge[10] believes that it is extremely important to be able to carry on "learningful" conversations that balance inquiry with advocacy. Through these conversations, people expose their own thinking and influence others in meaningful ways. Conveying information to others using words and methods they understand is a real talent. It is also a first step in creating value and putting your own professional imprint on it.

There is no time to sit around and wait to be discovered, much less promoted! It is your responsibility to network your skills. A supportive, stimulating work environment that allows and supports the two-way communication that networking requires is a great asset.

Develop Your Own Personal Vision

Before you write down your vision, think of where you want to be. You are going to a certain destination. Stretch your mind as far into the future as you possibly can. Think of yourself as being in motion, as in a car, in an airplane, on a train, skiing, running, or walking. This mental energy will propel you forward.

Is there a purpose to your vision? A vision is like a dream home, dream car...dream job. Think about your dream job. What types of work do you do? Is the work difficult? Do you enjoy doing the work? Are you interested in what you are doing? Is your work fulfilling? Can you describe your job to others?

1.1

Draw a vertical line down the middle of a blank sheet of paper. Write your thoughts on the left-hand side. Write the tangible ideas that can produce a vision on the right-hand side. Look back and forth between the thoughts on the left and the ideas or actions on the right before writing down the main parts of your vision.

Ask yourself the following questions:

1. Are most of the activities or events written down achievable within a reasonable time frame?

2. How much effort is required?

3. Can I achieve my vision?

If you have absolutely no hope of ever achieving your vision, it will always remain a dream. If you want to revise your vision so that it is achievable, make it more realistic.

Vision and Mission Statements for the Organization

Developing a vision precedes the development of a mission. Vision and mission can be combined and conveyed in the same statement. However, the author feels that the vision must come first and stand alone. The vision is the *what*. The mission is the *how* and becomes a way to achieve the vision.

Albrecht[1] also separates vision statements and mission statements. Vision and mission statements are a part of his strategic success model.

Vision statement. This statement is a shared image of what we want the enterprise to become, as expressed in terms of success in the eyes of its customers or others whose approval can affect its destiny. Leaders make this determination by looking to the future. Vision statements often imply some noble purpose and high values and point to something particularly worthwhile. Vision statements provide a guiding light. Mission statements point the way.

Mission statement.   This is a simple, compelling statement about how the enterprise must do business. It describes the critical values to which people in the enterprise commit their energies. These values are basic to the accomplishment of the mission and the fulfillment of the vision. It defines the customers and what the customers are to receive. It specifies value to the customers, including any special means needed to create value for them in order to keep their business. Mission statements establish a firm foundation that provides clear guidance for all major decisions.

Review Chapter 2 if you want to develop your vision and mission statements at the same time. Vision and mission statements may be considered the same or similar ways of stating nearly identical concepts. Having a vision and a way (mission) to achieve it is what is important.

SUMMARY AND CONCLUSIONS

1. When people learn more about themselves and their jobs, they can begin to perform in a more effective and efficient manner. As a result, they will be more productive employees. They will also be able to discover and nurture the abilities of others with whom they work.[7]

2. People who take the initiative to learn more about their jobs and the people around them gain control over their lives. In uncertain economic times, we may have to change jobs or careers more often than we plan.

3. Peer group networking is a good way to gather and transfer all kinds of valuable information within and beyond the organization. Peer groups play an array of support roles, including mentoring their own members.

4. By refreshing or retraining people in their individual areas of expertise, the organization gains the essential capabilities to stay ahead of the competition. Competitive advantage includes a highly trained work force.

5. Encourage and enable the changing mix of disciplines, such as cross-functional teams, to work together efficiently and effectively in an ever-changing, increasingly competitive environment.

6. When people create a vision, they are encouraged to think in broad terms. When a vision motivates people to pursue it, great things can happen.

PRACTICAL APPLICATIONS

1. The real key to performing at an average to above-average level is being familiar with your upper and lower limits. Then, it is easier to arrange your work in a logical manner and even ask for help when needed or delegate. It also means knowing about your personal areas of excellence or competence and where improvement or training may be needed.

   It is vital to be clear about what you can and cannot do. Concentrating on areas of known high leverage, like a special talent, will enable you to achieve maximum results with minimum effort.

2. Being clear about who you are and what your capabilities are makes it easier to network. You can gradually add to your story of information in numerous areas and apply what you know. Networks supply and convey a wide range of information in most areas.

3. The mental tools we develop when we think about our talents provide a standard-length yardstick for making comparisons. We compare ourselves on many dimensions—intelligence, abilities, interpersonal skills, and computer literacy, among others. These comparisons may provide us with the professional and personal feedback lacking at work.

4. The "me too" strategy of being a follower will no longer work. Unless people have their own ideas, visions, even dreams to lead them, they will not know how to achieve and maintain a successful path through the unpredictable world of full-time employment.

5. Sharing the ups and downs of the business world brings people closer together in many respects. People pull together more often when times are adverse than when times are good. Common interests, compassion, and a belief that good things will happen bind or connect people together. Binding together can be accomplished through the words of Ghandi: "become the change you wish to see in the world."

6. People who self-observe and communicate these observations become more aware of how they see themselves and how others see them. Vision, communication, and personal performance interlock and interact, as each is one of the many dimensions of leadership.

7. Leaders in learning organizations will focus on roles, skills, and tools for leadership. Leaders will be designers, teachers, and stewards who will have built and implemented their own mental models.

REFERENCES

1. Albrecht, Karl. *The Northbound Train,* New York: AMACOM, 1994.

2. Argyris, Chris. *Reasoning, Learning, and Action: Individual and Organizational,* San Francisco: Jossey-Bass, 1982.

3. Berg, Deanna H. and Schmitz, Steven A. "I Can See Clearly Now, How About You?" *Journal for Quality and Participation,* September 1994, pp. 54–57.

4. deGeus, Arie P. "Planning as Learning," *Harvard Business Review,* March–April 1988, pp. 70–74.

5. Gardner, H. *The Mind's New Science,* New York: Basic Books, 1985.

6. Handy, Charles. *The Age of Paradox,* Boston: Harvard Business School Press, 1994.

7. Kushel, Gerald. *Reaching the Peak Performance Zone,* New York: American Management Association, 1994.

8. Mills, Judie. *John F. Kennedy.* New York: Franklin Watts, 1988, p. 210.

9. *On Q.* "Three Companies Win 1994 Baldrige Award," December 1994, pp. 3–5.

10. Senge, Peter M. *The Fifth Discipline.,* New York: Doubleday, 1990.

11. Senge, Peter M. "The Leader's New Work: Building Learning Organizations," in *New Traditions in Business,* John Renesch (Ed.), San Francisco: Berrett-Koehler, 1992, pp. 80–93.

12. Shea, Gordon F. *Mentoring,* New York: AMACOM, 1994.

2

THE CONSTANTS
IN OUR LIVES

PURPOSE

- Consider the role of managers, the changing nature of the workplace, the role of productivity, and the need to redesign the organization

- Use vision statements as the building blocks for creating personal mission statements

INTRODUCTION

One of the few constants at work is the person doing the job. Almost everything related to the workplace is changing. For example, flexible working hours, telecommuting, and work sharing enable people to work when, how, and where they want. Technology, competition, and the environment are in continual flux.

Change is a mixed blessing—good when we want it and bad when we don't. The real challenge is to adapt to change successfully. Let's look at where we have been and then take a look at where we want to go.

With few exceptions, cradle-to-grave companies are gone. No single job, set of job skills, or college degree lasts forever. Some "excellent organizations" described in Peters and Waterman's 1984 book *In Search of Excellence* are, for any number of reasons, no longer excellent. Everything has a life span and a life cycle. This includes both people *and* organizations.

Technology and the continual search for the "best" methods to manage or lead directly affect job content, training, employee loyalty, and job security. Technology is expanding so fast that most of us can't keep up. Selecting the "best" technology at a price we can afford is a constant, unresolved dilemma.

To manage or to lead? Managing usually means directing, controlling, monitoring, and evaluating. Leading often implies being a role model, mentor, encourager, or even a cheerleader. Are people at work underled and overmanaged? Perhaps. If they work in teams, they may not need much direction.

Most current change efforts, such as total quality management and business process analysis, are often Born of production delay and quality assessment and improvement program designed to streamline efforts and reduce costs. When change efforts are first introduced, productivity often decreases. Enthusiasm wanes, and trust along with it, when new programs fail to live up to expectations. Implementing these programs requires an investment of time, effort, and money.

Change programs have pluses and minuses. When they don't work, they are criticized. When they work for others, they are good. When they work for you, they are excellent.

Perception plays a major role in our personal and work lives. Often, attitudes and what is perceived and believed outweigh what really happens. Even the constants in our lives are perceived in numerous unexpected ways.

CONSTANTS

Four major constants, or "givens," appear throughout this manual. The focus is on people, the workplace, the overall concept of productivity, and the organization.

THE CHANGING ROLE OF THE MANAGER

Empowerment, or passing down authority and responsibility, or power, to "subordinates," has greatly altered the role managers play. Empowerment gives people more freedom in how they do their work. Empowered employees who work with customers have less need to consult or communicate with their supervisors.

The gradual shift to participation has refocused the manager's attention on an array of team efforts. The growing use of work teams has increased the need for leadership and support. Managers must learn to balance the often conflicting needs of people, the workplace, and the organization and still please customers.

Downsizing and restructuring the organization have further eroded the need for managers. In 1987, one person in twenty was promoted into top management. In 2001, that ratio is expected to be one in fifty.[2]

Managers' functions change as the organization grows and changes. Like the cocoon that eventually becomes a butterfly, successful managers must gradually transform themselves into leaders, good role models, and mentors. Since managers do not have Mother Nature on their side, they must take most of the steps themselves. Fortunately, such changes are now occurring in some progressive, flexible organizations.

Newly transformed, committed leaders encourage and support processes of self-discovery and self-assessment in those around them. To understand others, they first study and understand themselves. Next, they look at the range of talents or potential of people at work and determine how everyone in the supplier–customer chain will benefit. Then, they work hard to get the desired results.

Managers must manage the dynamics of change, not the bits and pieces of change. The issue is how people deal with feelings as opposed to whether feelings are negative or positive. The most direct contact an organization can make is through the values of people. Values are really about beliefs and feelings.[3]

Managers and leaders must understand that the beliefs, attitudes, values, and needs of the work force are changing. People want more opportunity to use their skills, learn more, and do more. They want job security, equitable treatment, and flexibility in their work assignments. Most of all, they want to be told the truth. Without truth, there is little trust. Without trust, there can be no loyalty. Levels of trust and loyalty are low in many organizations. Can managers restore trust and loyalty? Yes. They must try. Trust demands learning.

THE NEED TO REINTERPRET AND REINVENT HOW, WHERE, AND WHEN WE WORK

Today, we can be recycled (retrained), replaced (outsourced), or terminated (made expendable). People as well as computers and robots anywhere in the world may compete for our job—and possibly get it. On the other hand, we can telecommute and work at home for a company thousands of miles away.

The concept of the "any place/any time" office allows people to conduct business from multiple locations at any and all times. In the next five to ten years, the workplace may be transformed into a cybernetic space with physical and visual dimensions. It will consist of a basic electronic environment with portals into the "real" world. The new generation of ultra-portable, extremely powerful computing devices will be defined more by what they connect us to than by what they process for us.[9]

Forces such as global competition, rapidly expanding technologies, and pressure to maximize profits currently appear more important than people within the organization.

Changes in jobs and the workplace do not take place in static situations. Think of how your job has changed. Change is a dynamic force. It also sets many other planned and unplanned changes in motion. Think about what happened the last time you tried to change just one thing at work or at home. We often end up changing many things we did not plan to change. And changing things always takes longer than we think it will.

Dramatic changes in the workplace may take their toll. Most people need support and reinforcement from those around them, or a feeling of belonging. They like familiar things around them—a work space or office to call their own, meeting rooms, or a lunchroom. Everyone wants to belong to or be affiliated with a viable entity, like an organization or work group. Maslow's need for belonging and for affiliation is best met by traditional work settings.

HOW TO ACHIEVE, SUSTAIN, AND IMPROVE PRODUCTIVITY IN THE LONG RUN

Both people and organizations have trouble with the "short runs" at productivity. A host of quick fixes, such as reducing staff to improve quarterly profits, turn out to be expensive and counterproductive. Paths to productivity must be carefully laid out. These various paths must support and enhance the vision, mission, goals, and strategic plans of the organization. Senior management commitment, particularly from the CEO, is imperative if change efforts are to be taken seriously, much less implemented.

Maintaining productivity is a painstaking, continuous effort. The process of assessing, maintaining, and improving personal productivity requires a blend of good interpersonal skills and knowledge of work processes and outcomes.

Basically, improving productivity is often a matter of finding out what people do best. The environment and flow of work can be set up to maximize their talents. Once people know you are interested in helping them do what they normally do "just a little bit better," they will cooperate and provide their own unique input. While this is obviously a long-term effort, it must be a joint endeavor involving leaders and those whom they are leading.

Unless people are involved from start to finish in designing and implementing productivity improvement processes, most will resist having productivity poured on them from above. Involvement results in "buy in," or having ownership in the process. Ownership builds acceptance and understanding.

Meeting the needs of internal customers (inside the organization) and external customers (outside the organization) should be a top priority. An increasing number of organizations direct the majority of their efforts toward satisfying, even delighting, external customers. Feelings are mixed about the need to satisfy internal customers you work with on a regular basis. Some feel that all customers should be treated alike. Others feel that there is no need to worry about internal customers; they will take care of themselves. Nevertheless, the overall shift is toward satisfying customers in general (discussed further in Chapter 7).

HOW TO *RE*-DESIGN THE WHOLE ORGANIZATION

Organizations differ in shape, structure, and function (see Chapter 5). Many organizations are highly structured bureaucracies. The book title *The End of Bureaucracy and the Rise of the Intelligent Organization* may predict the future.[10] The bureaucratic structure of many organizations resembles the Industrial Age more than the Information Age.

The following statement by Warren Bennis begins Part I of Pinchot and Pinchot's book:[10]

> *[The bureaucratic] organization is becoming less and less effective...it is hopelessly out of joint with contemporary realities, and...new shapes, patterns, and models are emerging which promise drastic changes in the conduct of the corporation and in managerial practices in general. So within the next twenty-five to fifty years, we should all be witness to, and participate in, the end of bureaucracy and the rise of new social systems better able to cope with 20th [and 21st] century demands.*

The learning organization could be one of the replacements for the bureaucratic organization. *Re*-design processes may help change the current shape of the organization. Motorola is a prime example of successful self-imposed upheaval.[5]

LEARNING ORGANIZATION

A learning organization "...is an organization skilled at creating, acquiring, and transferring knowledge, and at modifying its behavior to reflect new knowledge and insights."[4] When we create an organization that can learn better, we get a higher return on expertise.

Learning organizations are skilled at:

1. Systematic problem solving

2. Experimenting with new approaches

3. Learning from their own experiences and past history

4   Learning from experiences and best practices of others

5. Transferring knowledge quickly and efficiently throughout the organization in order to improve performance

Learning organizations focus on double-loop learning. Single-loop learning looks at ways to improve processes or methods. Double-loop examines the second loop of learning and answers the question, *"What* am I learning about *what* I am learning?"

In these dynamic organizations, people have opportunities to create, acquire, transfer, and transform knowledge in order to improve performance. This type of organization supports and recognizes individual efforts.

People are able to use their special talents to:

1. Learn and grow personally and professionally. People take ownership for their own development. They learn on a self-directed basis.[6]

2. Use information to create new knowledge or add value to something that already exists, like improving the scope of a literature survey or research paper.

3. Transform existing knowledge into a marketable form of value-adding knowledge which brings something special or unique and unexpected to the customer. Learning, an individual phenomenon, occurs only in people's heads.

Continuous learning is the heart of the learning organization. Organizations that stop learning stop growing. Organizations that stop applying what they have learned have a hard time competing. They may even fail to survive.

Learning organizations are not necessarily new. They have always been around, but they are few in number. A learning organization is an organization in transition. Senge[11] and Garvin[4] are excellent resources. The learning organization is discussed in detail in Chapter 5.

RE-DESIGN PROCESSES

Re-engineering, *re*-organizing, and other "*re*-efforts" imply that things may not have been done right the first time. Redesign is just one step in a continual process of change, or a continuous journey. "Redesigns" are often done to reduce costs, streamline operations, or achieve a competitive advantage.

Desired end results must be kept uppermost when redesign processes are being developed. When progress toward goals is monitored on a continuous basis, determining what is required and what is wanted is easier. The redesign process should keep intact relationships between people inside the organization and suppliers, customers, and all end users. This means having as few "disconnects," such as communication breakdowns, as possible.

Not all redesign processes focus on interpersonal skills and input from workers. Few redesign efforts consider how important beliefs, values, and behavior really are. The human element is the most critical aspect in all change efforts, but its importance in redesign efforts is usually downplayed.

Wanting to redesign and needing to redesign are two different things. If people are satisfied, motivated, and productive, there may be no reason to change anything. If the needs of customers and numerous end users are being met and the organization is operating effectively and efficiently, change may not be advisable. Redesign may be one answer, but it is not the only answer.

A typical mindset of many Americans is the lack of concern about perfection, or "nobody's perfect." Experimentation, or trial-and-error learning, is a great way to learn and also be creative, but may be costly in terms of time, effort, and money. Such efforts give rise to the redoing syndrome.

Over the years, the series of competitive advantages was capital, strategic planning, productivity, cycle time, quality, value, and information. Could people be the next, even the last, real competitive advantage any organization needs? The answer is yes. Many people are beginning to believe that human resources are our most valuable resource. In reality, those with proven work skills and good interpersonal skills have been our competitive advantage all along. Only when people are allowed or encouraged to work to their fullest capacity can they make good use of their talents and experience.

How and where will the "rediscovery" of people power occur? Organizations that encourage and support intelligent risk taking leading to creativity and innovation are likely candidates. Learning organizations are our best bet.

People's unique talents are also beginning to be discovered and rediscovered. This discovery could start with you as gradually you transform your vision into your mission statement.

MISSION STATEMENTS

One way to examine your goals is to consider personal mission statements. Mission statements lead to goals. Some people use the mission statements from their organization. Others may have their own or choose to develop new mission statements. As mentioned in Chapter 1, vision and mission statements are considered by some to be the same or similar.

Missions statements are dynamic, living documents. They provide a clear focus on where energies should be directed. The main purpose of a mission statement is to enable the person or organization to focus time and effort in the most critical areas and eliminate or reduce the number of inconsistent activities. Overall, mission statements:

1. Specify the nature of the business in which you should be involved, including your role within that business

2. Describe the life in which you expect to be involved

3. Clarify conditions under which decisions are made regarding: (a) whom you will serve, (b) products and services provided, (c) fundamental philosophy under which you will operate, and (d) personal values guiding your business or professional life

4. Outline basic philosophy and personal values with respect to whom you serve, namely customers, partners, vendors, and others

5. Function as a device for effectively communicating to others who can help you do what you are doing or intend to do[7]

Albrecht[1] provides the following examples of mission statements:

Example 1.   "The mission of Levi Strauss & Co. is to sustain profitable and responsible commercial success by marketing jeans and selected casual apparel under the Levi's brand."

Albrecht contends that this statement does not dramatize a customer need premise. It neither conveys the value premise of the product nor gives any clue about how the company sustains the hundred-year relationships it has had with its customers. In fact, the word customer does not appear in the statement. Essentially, all it says is "We sell clothes with the Levi's brand label."

Example 2.   The mission statement of Cathay Pacific Airlines is "To achieve consistent upward growth in the total quality of inflight service and in the support we give to each other."

Albrecht agrees with the strong customer focus in the value premise and accepts the meaning of service quality and on the teamwork involved. It highlights the inflight experience. However, Albrecht indicates that the statement has been shortened so that six "mission goals" can be printed on the back of wallet-size cards. These mission goals supply very well-phrased criteria to evaluate the way the cabin crew fulfills its mission.

Mission statements may follow Albrecht's[1] proposed format:

1. *Customers* should be defined in terms of the basic *need premise* that leads them to consider doing business with your enterprise. Customers should not be defined in terms of some market segment or statistical category.

2. *The value premise* should be defined in terms of the fundamental value it represents in matching the customer's need premise. The value premise should not be defined in terms of what your organization does, makes, sells, or delivers.

3. *What makes you special* should be your focus in creating value in order to win and keep the customer's business.

A prime use of mission statements is in communicating philosophy and values to employees or other significant persons. When a clear position is taken on specific issues, further misunderstandings can be avoided. Mission statements also create a personal image. Your mission statement will be useful, perhaps even necessary, in dealing with work associates and current and potential clients, vendors, partners, suppliers, and others in the value chain.

The process (read trial and error, frustration, thinking, discussion, evaluation, modification, excitement, and modification) of developing a mission statement is just as important as the end result. It is through processes that are in the formative stage, where nothing seems clear, that the major thinking takes place. It is during the process stage that the true mission statement gradually takes shape. Writing down the mission statement is the final act. Morrisey[8] indicates that the actual statement is merely a codification of the effort gone through. However, keeping the mission statement current will require spending some time back in the process stage just described.

Morrisey[8] believes that a personal mission statement is probably the most important strategic document you can have, regardless of whether you are functioning as a Fortune 500 corporation, as a small to medium-size business, or as an individual professional. Mission statements establish a firm foundation that provides clear guidance for all significant decisions. They provide a foundation for your future.

The following fourteen questions will help you develop your mission statement. About two hours is required to answer them in detail.[7]

1. What business or profession am I in personally?

2. What business or profession would I like to be in? What do I really enjoy?

3. What business or profession should I be in?

4. What is my basic purpose in business and in life?

5. What are or should be my principal business functions and roles, present and future?

6. What is unique or distinctive about what I can bring to my business or profession?

7. Who are or should be my principal customers, clients, or users?

8. What are the principal market segments, present and future, in which I am most effective?

9. What is different about my personal business position from what is was three to five years ago?

10. What is likely to be different about my personal business position three to five years in the future?

11. What are my principal economic concerns?

12. What are or should be my principal sources of income?

13. What philosophic issues, personal values, and priorities are important to my professional future?

14. What special considerations do I have in regard to a board of directors or other outside groups; employers; partners or associates; staff; customers, clients, or users; vendors or suppliers; professional colleagues; professional associations; family; church or community; myself; or others?

Mission statements can keep you from investing time, energy, and other resources in activities inconsistent with where you want to go, or your vision. Mission statements become living documents. Communicating your own philosophy and values to people at work, including associates, potential clients, vendors, and colleagues, is easier when you have mission statements.[8]

If your organization has mission statements, or you have your own mission statement(s), it is a good idea to answer the preceding or similar questions once every year or so. Mission statements clarify, for yourself and others, your career direction and your commitment to the business in which you are or expect to be involved. Mission statements will also reflect personal philosophy and values that influence how you function. Once you build a firm foundation of mission statements, it will be easier to develop realistic strategic plans.

What mental tools do you have with you at all times? What tools are available in your organization? When you use your computer and software, are you using tools? Do you use tools to gather information in order to improve the accuracy of your decisions? You will need tools to achieve your vision and your mission.

SUMMARY AND CONCLUSIONS

1. Four major areas appear at the top of most people's list of concerns. All emphasize change. If people and organizations are going to survive to the year 2000:

   ■ The future of "managers" will continue to dim until they transform themselves into true leaders and mentors. The new focus on leading is about nurturing and mentoring. The process of mentoring offers a wealth of management opportunities for organizational rejuvenation, competitive adaptation, and employee development.[12]

   ■ How, when, and where work is done must be studied and reevaluated. Flexibility seems to be the key.

   ■ The purpose of productivity improvement programs and quality initiatives should be clearly established. Input and commitment should come from everyone in the organization. Only then can efforts be made to design the best possible program.

   ■ Organizations need to be redesigned. Redesign efforts must be chosen carefully. These efforts must consider people, as well as the state, structure, vision, mission, and goals of the organization.

2. People play a pivotal role in all organizational efforts. For instance, keeping updated mission statements helps them stay current in their fields of expertise and interest. They can discuss their beliefs and current and proposed accomplishments with those around them. Much of getting work done relates to sharing belief and value systems with regard to what is central to the workplace. Shared beliefs and values are gradually transformed into organizational culture.

3. People want more opportunity to use their skills, learn more, do more, have job security, and be treated fairly and equitably. They want the

opportunity and authority to take more initiative and responsibility at work and be appropriately rewarded and recognized. Most of all, they want an opportunity to have input regarding their future. This means being associated with and part of a mission or vision.

PRACTICAL APPLICATIONS

1. When people learn more about themselves *and* their jobs, they will be more productive employees. They will be able to discover and nurture abilities of others with whom they work. "Peer group" networking is one way to gather and transfer vital technical and non-technical information throughout the organization. Peer groups play many support roles, including mentoring others in addition to their own work groups.

2. When people take the initiative, they begin to take control over their lives. In today's turbulent times, each person may have to become the captain of his or her own ship. You must never forget where port is and how to get there safely.

3. People form the dynamic working core of the organization. Organizations, as we will see in Chapter 3, must be competitive and do the "right" things if they are to survive. Specifically, organizations must:

   ■ Build and refresh or retrain people in their individual areas of expertise. Only then will the organization have the essential capabilities to compete successfully.

   ■ Encourage and enable the changing mix of disciplines in the organization to work together efficiently and effectively in a changing, increasingly competitive environment.

4. Future "winning" organizations must ensure that they have the critical capabilities needed to stay ahead. This is done by constantly building and updating their individual areas of expertise. The "mix" of people and disciplines must be encouraged to work together in an ever-changing, market-driven environment.

5. Future managers in these "winning" organizations will devote most of their energy to managing feelings, beliefs, and values. Managers must look ahead and plan for the future and convey this enthusiasm to those around them. Positive attitudes are contagious. These managers will need to operate in a new context, perhaps even one they did not design themselves. New contexts set the stage for change.[5] Change must be managed.

REFERENCES

1. Albrecht, Karl. *The Northbound Train,* New York: AMACOM, 1994.

2. Arnett, E. C. "Futurists Gaze into Business's Crystal Ball," *Washington Post,* July 20, 1989, pp. F1–F2.

3. Duck, Jeanie Daniel. "Managing Change: The Art of Balancing," *Harvard Business Review,* November–December 1993, pp. 109–118.

4. Garvin, David A. "Building a Learning Organization," *Harvard Business Review,* July–August 1993, pp. 78–91.

5. Goss, Tracy, Pascale, Richard, and Athos, Anthony. "The Reinvention Roller Coaster: Risking the Present for a Powerful Future," *Harvard Business Review,* November–December 1993, pp. 97–108.

6. Greenwood, Tracy, Wasson, Avtar, and Giles, Robbie. "The Learning Organization: Concepts, Processes, and Questions," *Performance & Instruction,* April 1993, pp. 7–11.

7. Morrisey, George L. *Creating Your Future: Personal Strategic Planning for Professionals,* San Francisco: Berrett-Koehler, 1992.

8. Morrisey, George L. "Your Personal Mission Statement: Foundation for Your Future," *Training & Development,* November 1992, pp. 71–74.

9. O'Hara-Devereaux, Mary and Johansen, Robert. *Globalwork,* San Francisco: Jossey-Bass, 1994.

10. Pinchot, Gifford and Pinchot, Elizabeth. *The End of Bureaucracy and the Rise of the Intelligent Organization,* San Francisco: Berrett-Koehler, 1993.

11. Senge, Peter M. *The Fifth Discipline,* New York: Doubleday, 1990.

12. Shea, Gordon F. *Mentoring,* New York: American Management Association, 1994.

BUILDING A BASE FOR YOUR PERSONAL EQUATION

PURPOSE

- Consider concepts basic to your personal equation, including biases
- Evaluate the influence of variables affecting your personal equation
- Examine the uses of operational definitions as ways to reduce bias and increase the precision of thought and expression

INTRODUCTION

You have created your vision (Chapter 1) and developed your mission statement (Chapter 2). Your vision and mission statements can be extended to include your specific career and personal goals. If you feel comfortable with both statements, you may want to fine-tune them in order to be better prepared for the future.

We all wonder about our futures? We have already noted that steady, full-time employment and lifelong careers are a remnant of the past. Job stability is decreasing. Growing organizational and environmental turbulence is attributed to activities ranging from poor planning to global competition. We all want a carefully charted career course. However, even with careful charting, such a course will have its ups and downs. The good news is that we have identified major problems, and we are well along the road to knowing what to do next.

Your unique talents, experience, and personality affect what you know and what you can do at a specific point in time. Ways to access your personal system of knowledge will gradually evolve. You can call the concept of learning more about yourself and writing it down whatever you want. I refer to this process as building a "personal equation."

Mental pictures of ourselves and of others revolve around special talents, including the skills, abilities, knowledge, and numerous attributes that add to our current status, future potential, and personality in general.

Over the last ten years, I have developed a basic model that describes, illustrates, and groups three separate, overlapping types and levels of abilities, knowledge, and work activities. This model is flexible enough to fit any person and any job. The model that you have been working on will be fully developed when you reach Chapter 9. However, you have already created your vision and mission statements, which underlie all conceptual and representational models.

Your personal equation will form the heart of this model. You will have a personal equation for knowledge, a slightly different one for learning, and a unique one for doing work. In fact, you will have many slightly different personal equations that will help you develop a good understanding of yourself and of your many talents.

As you read this material, you will begin to select and further develop ideas and useful methods for your own mental model. Your model should reflect some of the basics of behavior and incorporate the role of perception and biases. Biases influence what we see, what we say, and how we act in our personal and work lives.

BASICS OF BEHAVIOR

The following basics of behavior range from general to specific. Seeing the whole picture first lets us fit the small pieces into a meaningful whole. Our personal equations consists of many small pieces that become a whole. It is from Gestalt psychology that we learned that the whole is greater than the sum of the separate parts.

Unless we know something about people and where they work, we may make incorrect assumptions about any or all of the variables in an individual's personal equation. Three broad areas affect behavior at work: (1) rationality of people, (2) type of organization in which people work and what it allows them to do, and (3) the relationship between pay and performance.

Rationality

There are no guarantees that people behave in a logical, rational way. Most people are "intendedly rational," or they work at trying to be "normal." What is rational and logical to one person is not necessarily rational and logical to another. Rationality stems from thought processes as well as from values, beliefs, and numerous personality and environmental factors.

"Intendedly rational" usually evokes both concern and frustration. Many things people do make perfect sense to them but not necessarily to others.

Most people try to be logical and sensible. If they are not, they try to explain away their differences. People differ in degree of rationality. Is rationality normally distributed? A few people are at the "irrational" end, and a good number are at or above average in rationality, as opposed to below the average.

Some people have an inner sense of logic or balance. They always appear to know exactly where they are going and what they are doing. Do they have a clear vision and set of goals that keep them on track? Yes, they do.

Type of Organization

The type, size, structure, and age of organizations affect how people think and what they do. Factors such as socialization, culture, and communication networks are very important. Even with capable leadership, organizations, because of their size, structure, and age, have great difficulty changing. Organizations are discussed in greater detail in Chapter 5.

No two people are exactly alike. Diversity may bring in a "breath of fresh air," stimulate creativity, stir up opinions, and produce innovative ideas and solutions. However, when high-level teamwork is required, as when a project can be finished more quickly, perhaps even better, when the team thinks as "one," diversity may be inadvised.

No two organizations are exactly alike either. Organizations are dynamic and grow and change constantly. Like people, organizations are always in transition. Organizations become progressively flatter when the number of layers of middle management is reduced. Reductions may be based on economic concerns or may be due to the gradual shift to work teams and empowerment.

Organizations are locations where people work or, more recently, work out of, as in sales and telecommuting. Organizations provide an array of support systems and services (an infrastructure) for the person doing the job.

Of the many ways to view organizations, the following six cover broad but representative areas.

1. **What:** The vision statement, or ultimate goals and purpose of the organization, division, section...unit. This includes products and services that are produced for internal customers within the organization, external customers outside the organization, suppliers, and numerous end users, including specialty items for partners.

2. **Where:** The location may be literally anywhere in the world. Geographic area and regional differences should be identified.

3. **Who:** Everyone in the organization, including employees, associates, partners, and "owners" (share holders and stockholders). Customers and all types of end users may also make up the organization.

4. **How:** Processes, or the ways business is to be done, are often included in mission statements. Goals, objectives, strategic plans, and focus give the organization direction. Organizational form and structure (bureaucratic, learning organization), leadership, age, etc. have a major bearing on how work is accomplished.

5. **Why:** There must be a reason for doing something. Why am I in this job? Why don't more customers buy our products?

6. **When:** Market strategies for promoting, targeting, moving, and selling products. Cycle time and turnaround time are very important.

Handy[5] and Offerman and Gowing[12] suggest that there will be radical changes in organizational structure before the end of the century. Customers and clients at the top of the organization are the ultimate judges of success. Successful organizations of the future will have outstanding human relations.[8,17]

Although some organizations put customers at the top, most are a long way from doing so. Few employees know the goals and mission statements of their organizations. Worse yet, many do not ask. Few traditional managers pass on this valuable information to those working with them. A saving grace is the current interest in "quality," which often requires identifying the organization's mission and goals.

Pay and Performance

Reward systems play a major role in behavior by providing both incentives (want to do it) *and* sanctions (do not want to do it). Generally, what is rewarded gets done. One of the greatest longstanding mismatches is the discrepancy between what people do and how they are paid.

Differences between how people are paid and what they do are a major concern throughout the world—in every job and to every person. Bases for computing pay range from minimum hourly wage to complex clauses and bonus payments for top executives. Some organization are beginning to base the pay of their top managers on results (usually net profit or sales).

Extrinsic motivators, or salary and status symbols (such as expense accounts and reserved parking spaces), are nice, but they are not real motivators. They are bribes for doing work.

Profit-sharing and gainsharing plans are increasing in number. Both have guidelines and often formulas to compute how much monetary reward each person receives, depending on personal and organizational performance.

Intrinsic motivators, like recognition and having an interesting, challenging job, are what really motivate people. Use of non-monetary rewards is growing. Positive responses to peer recognition, as the result of a suggestion that is implemented at work, for instance, are high on everyone's list of motivators.

PERCEPTION = REALITY?: THE ROLE OF BIASES

Perception and biases have affected man's judgment and behavior from the beginning of time. Biases affect how we view, describe, and evaluate our world. Perception and biases influence everything we believe, see, say, and do at work.

Perceptions (what we think) and biases (what we believe) have a major impact on our on-the-job and personal behavior. Biases range from blinding us to reality to overestimating talents of an associate because "they are just like us."

Your mental picture or personal equation will be based on your perceptions, beliefs, and even biases about people and what happens around you. How you define or describe yourself and what you want to achieve will be tempered by the words and concepts you use.

One broad area in the study of individual differences is perception, or how the world is seen and interpreted. Perception affects everyone on the input or assimilation side. Essentially, input from our various senses colors all of our perceptions and what we do.

Perception

Input from our senses can block the natural flow of important information. Although it is normal to block out or try to forget some unpleasant parts of our lives, it should not happen often. Blocking out or distorting reality not only has a negative impact on our perceptions, but also substantially affects our ability, skills, knowledge, and attitudes. All in all, effectiveness is reduced and our credibility lowered.

Perceptions, biases, and attitudes often color what is both said and heard. The following quote sums this up nicely: "It is not what you show, but what is seen...Not what you say, but what is heard....Not what you mean, but what is understood."[22]

The game of baseball provides a good example of perception. Umpire A says, "I call balls and strikes as I see 'em. Umpire B says, "I call balls and strikes as they are." Umpire C says, "They aren't nothin' until I call 'em."

Biases

It is difficult to be sure that we see things and describe them as they really are. Knowing that biases exist, and that we are all slightly biased, is a good beginning point. When we accept and recognize our biases, we take them into account when we make decisions. Also, we can recognize them in others.

Biases are influenced by factors like personality, experience, culture, even one's job and profession. Accountants, for example, are more likely to see things in terms of cash flow and payout than are scientists doing research. The old saying about behavior, "it depends where you're coming from," enables us to get a feel for how another person understands reality.

Examples of common social biases and personal biases include the "halo" effect[10] and the reverse, or "horns," effect.[11]

Social Biases.   Our social biases are often based on politics, religion, or ethnic background or are affected by the people and events around us as we were growing up. Other biases are based on demographics, experience, education, and peer groups, among other influences.

Personal Biases.   Our personal biases are affected by human factors, or individual differences, such as knowledge, ability, skills, attitude, age, sex, and many others.

Only when we recognize our own biases can we realize how they have previously clouded our ability to see other people's biases in any systematic manner. If a person *thinks* something happened, in his or her mind it *did* happen! People seldom compare what really happens with what they believe happens. They make decisions without using input from others. Their strong beliefs or biases are barriers or filters that keep them from seeing things as they really are. Biases can and do overpower many other important factors.

The "halo effect" and its counterpart, the "horns" effect, are described and illustrated by Odiorne.[10,11]

Halo Effect. In general, when people are evaluated at work, managers may rate them in terms of an overall impression, or halo of goodness or badness. People who do one thing well do not necessarily do everything well. This tendency to make broad assumptions or generalizations occurs quite often. The following biases are relatively common:

- **Compatibility,** or the tendency to rate people higher than they should be rated because they think and act like you. Managers may select team members or subordinates in their own image, as they believe that people who think and act like they do will be easier to get along with. In this sense, they are right, but there is the danger of sameness, or lack of fresh or opposing ideas or input.

- **Effect of past record** may outweigh what has happened recently. Whether your performance is good or bad, your past record outweighs recent accomplishments. Because you performed well in the past, it is assumed you will always perform well. Or the exact opposite may be assumed— you performed poorly in the past and will continue to do so.

- **Recency effect** shows that people who did good work yesterday or last week can offset longstanding mediocre or poor performance. This strong bias has a negative effect on performance. It often creeps in because many of us have short memories.

- **High potential effect** is illustrated by looking good on paper, but not performing well on the job. This bias often appears at performance appraisal time. Also, people can (and do) make their job descriptions and resumes look better than they really are.

- **No-complaints bias,** or "no news is good news." Often, those who never complain, despite how bad things may get, are rated as highly productive.

- **One-asset person** is the glib talker, the "peacemaker," or the eternal optimist. Judgments are made on the basis of their one major, outstanding attribute. All other abilities and attributes are ignored.

- **Blind-spot effect** means that deficiencies or limitations are overlooked. First, people may find it easier to not see what is going on than to say something that might cause trouble. Second, the overlooked deficiencies are just like ours. This is one of the most common biases and one we should make every effort to avoid.

Horns Effect. The "horns" effect emphasizes the negative aspects of behavior. To illustrate, a recent failure may make more of a lasting impression than a whole year of very major, positive achievements.

For instance, undesirable personality traits may "turn off" customers and greatly reduce sales. Also, peers may try to avoid working with someone who is unpleasant or hard to get along with. Uncooperative behavior can disrupt nearly every aspect of work.

The negative influence of biases can be reduced by admitting that they exist. It is also very important to use a wide range of reliable sources of information, allowing you to check your beliefs and verify results.

Your own biases will affect the way you think and act. Biases also make a difference in the way people relate to you and interpret your behavior.

Ignoring reality is easy. When we see and believe only what fits our frame of reference or system of beliefs, our stability is not disrupted. We can strike a compromise between what we want to believe and what we must believe.

Perceptual biases affect people everywhere in the world, both at work and in their personal lives. Discussions of perceptual bias in this chapter focus on: (1) the content of your personal equation, (2) how you interpret the content of your equation, and (3) how you use your own standards or constant-length ruler to assess yourself and others.

3.1

List your work-related biases in the left-hand column. Then, list your personal biases in the right-hand column. Compare both sets of biases.

Work-Related Biases   *Personal Biases*

1. _____   1. _____

2. _____   2. _____

3. _____   3. _____

4. _____   4. _____

5. _____   5. _____

3.2

How do you plan to reduce both the number and strength of your biases?

1. _____

2. _____

3. _____

4. _____

5. _____

3.3

Think of the times you were a victim of biases. Was it at school, at work, or in a social setting? What can you personally do to prevent a repeat situation from happening again?

Simple mistakes are made because few people have systematic training in evaluation. Sometimes people who have been unfairly judged go out of their way to become fair judges themselves. However, the opposite also occurs.

Reducing the Number of Biases.   Biases often arise from errors in perception, as we have discussed. Another source of biases is failure to communicate accurately. People may say they know what we are saying because they are familiar with the words we use. Do they **really** understand? Should they have used clear, precise definitions and insisted on open, two-way communication?

Peers or close associated may be willing to discuss your biases with you. Biases are often a personal issue. Being aware of the full range of biases is a good first step. Having an open mind, or reserving judgment until more clear or accurate information is available, is another possibility. The point is to be aware of situations in which biases may occur. Try to reduce how often biases occur.

PERSONAL EQUATION

Your personal equation is the entire essence of who you are. It encompasses your whole being. Personal equations range from dreams and thoughts to actions. How you are the same as and how you differ from those around you at work is reflected in your personal equation. What makes you unique, or special, is really what's important. You *are* your equation, complete with pluses and minuses, although you should emphasize the pluses. You personal equation is what makes you stand out from your peers or your competition.

A definition of personal equation from the *Random House Dictionary* is "...the tendency to personal bias which accounts for the variation in interpretation or approach, and for which allowance must be made."

Most of us know what equations are and what they are supposed to do. We have used them successfully to pass exams. We may use them at work.

Our personal equations for knowledge, action, and many other endeavors are based on an array of personal factors and variables in our various work and social environments. These illusive, unpredictable personal elements are always the biggest unknown in any situation.

Equations contain any number of variables. The weight or relative value assigned to each is available will differ. We will not be able to assign a weight to each variable, but we will soon know what the variables in our personal equations are. This means that if three main factors or variables are important (for example, experience, negotiating skills, and knowledge of computer languages), each will contribute a different amount to the level at which a person performs. When written as equation, which is seldom done, variables can be expressed as decimal fractions. Ways to set up and use such equations are beyond the scope of this manual. Possibilities include correlation, linear regression, and matrices.

My personal equation appears in the words, examples, and illustrations in this manual. My equation is the sum of my beliefs, values, experience, talents, and biases. How I view and interpret my world, as reflected in the content of this manual, *is* my personal equation.

Some obvious elements in my equation relate to being proactive, putting priorities on things I have to do, focusing on people first and then on the problem, soliciting input from others, using a systems approach, and trying to be creative. You will discover more as we go along.

The following sections on personal equations cover (1) history, (2) variables affecting personal equations, (3) developing a personal equation, and (4) uses of a personal equation.

History

Astronomy may have come to mind when you first read the words *personal equation*. In astronomy, personal equation refers to reaction times of each observer who watches the same event in the sky (eclipse, rising of the moon, or stars passing a specific point in the heavens).

The first documented incident that gave rise to the possibility that people's reaction times differ occurred at the Greenwich Astronomical Observatory in 1796. In 1816, Bessell examined data from observations and discovered that a young assistant consistently recorded the time at which stars crossed a hair line in the telescope fully one second later than his master. The assistant was dismissed.

Bessell reportedly described these variations among individuals in the speed with which they react to a visual stimulus as the personal equation.[24] Some of the first accounts of human factors affecting the results of observations of astronomical events were documented by Hirsch of Switzerland in the 1860s.

In general, personal equations of all observers (not just those observing astronomical events) take into account differences in observers' visual acuity and reaction times. If there are five observers, for instance, there will be five slightly different times to record.

No matter how often observations are made, there will always be very small differences in the reaction times of the same (untrained) person.

As a simple illustration, if the timers at community swim meets are inexperienced, results may vary. Training and practice reduce the variability of results, as individual differences are reduced but not eliminated.

Variables Affecting Your Personal Equation

Literally thousands of variables and forces could affect you and your personal equation. However, at work, most things are relatively stable and predictable. Some major sources of influence are learning, the uniqueness factor (or individual differences), and the need for clear, precise communication using concepts that people understand. Of the problems experienced at work, reportedly 95 percent relate to some form of verbal or written miscommunication. This estimate was made before computers were used as extensively as they are today. The figure can be adjusted up or down, depending upon your recent experience.

1. Learning.   Most people want to learn, provided they are interested in the topic. Learning expands our capacity and increases our level of skill in critical areas. Most people learn by doing, as in using trial-and-error methods to master something challenging, like a new software program.

Much learning is job-related. For example, if productivity and quality are major concerns at work, you can build these two concepts into your own standards for your personal equation. Quality can be a particular standard of excellence. Achieving and maintaining personal standards is a way of life for some. For others, reaching their desired standard is only a dream. Standards play a vital role in any learning process

As standards and guidelines for your goals increase, you can change or adjust your equation as needed. This is like wearing stretch clothes that conform to your body shape. The type of information you put in your personal equation or model must not only fit, but grow and change as you update your equation or model.

2. Uniqueness Factor.   Think about the factors that make people unique or make them special. Variables or factors that affect behavior come from every influence—home, work, peers, colleagues, friends...the media. From a practical standpoint, knowing more about which variables have the greatest impact on human behavior will help predict on-the-job performance in specific work settings. Then, managers or team leaders can make better use of the unique talents of the work force in general.

3. Clear Communication.   Misinterpreting what people say, blocking out certain unpleasant or unfamiliar information, or liking people better who are just like us gets in the way of making good decisions. Being objective and using precise terms that people understand are two among many ways to reduce misperceptions and biases. The section on operational definitions at the end of this chapter further explores the issue of communication.

Getting Started on a Personal Equation

Can you build your personal equation in one giant step? The answer is no, but the small, gradual steps you take while reading this manual will enable you to develop a solid base of information. Athletes acquire new skills in small, gradual steps. You improve your golf, tennis, or racquetball game in small steps. Why not apply these same principles on the job?

Keep thinking about your personal equation as you read. Jot down a few ideas or underline some key thoughts. As the strengths of your beliefs and base of information change and evolve, you will think of factors to put in your personal equation. If you want to plan ahead, turn to the end of Chapter 4 and write down some relevant ideas or factors that will become the first major recorded elements in your personal equation.

As you read along, you will begin to see how your abilities add up to form a whole. You will gradually learn not to underestimate yourself, but rather to speak up for yourself. Supervisors and peers are reluctant to play Sherlock Holmes to solve the mystery of our talents. As more time is spent working in teams, our peers and others around us will get to know quite a bit about our real talents. Also, once we feel comfortable with people at work, we may be more inclined to discuss our talents (read *network*) with them.

We often use certain parts of our equations in the same way. Once we get to know people, either at work or socially, we can begin to figure out how they will think and act in certain situations. Many times, our relatives and friends can predict what we will do. These same people may understand our personal equations better than we do!

When we use our personal equations at work, we will find out how exciting the *process* of creation and discovery can be. Ironically, we seldom apply at work what we know and accept in our personal lives. If we did, we would know more about why people think and behave the way they do. This would help us figure out how to gradually modify or change behavior in a positive direction and increase efficiency, or at the very least reduce frustration. Once you have developed your personal equation, you can compare it with the personal equations of other people at work or in your network.

When we make suggestions for change or improvement in such a way that people think the idea was theirs, they may say, "I thought of that myself." They may not even recognize that someone else suggested the idea. They will gradually incorporate these ideas into their own personal equations. However, putting a new concept in our own personal equations, or seeing someone else do so, takes time and effort. But this is what change and improvement are all about.

As mentioned in Chapter 1, people develop ownership in something they create themselves. When they are involved in developing something, they are also committed to support and use what they create. People also need to know the possible uses or practical applications of something they create before they start working on it.

Example.   Major elements in the personal equation of a woman actively involved in the financial world of investing might include: (1) do solid literature review of current financial information and make lots of phone calls to find out the information needed, (2) review three- to five-year performance, (3) consider the experience level of the fund manager, (4) low expense ratio, (5) no load funds, and (6) no sales charges or transaction fees. She writes detailed notes to document and support her choice, including the underlying logic. The same thorough method is used over and over again. No speculation. No sudden changes. And it works.

Uses of a Personal Equation

Ways to use your personal equation are discussed here. Your personal equation is guided by your vision. This means that your personal equation, like your personal vision statement, is a continuously evolving process. Again, your personal equation will change and grow before your eyes.

1. Provides an island of stability in a sea of change.   Reportedly, people change jobs every four to five years and make career changes every six to seven years. Because the probability of making job and/or career changes is high, it is vital to have an up-to-date list or inventory of your full range of talents, achievements, and future plans (read *vision and mission statements*).

As technology advances and jobs become more complex, it is up to each of us to develop and maintain a negotiable type of record, which can become our "career passport." This valuable, do-it-yourself document contains talents, achievements, and dreams. The confidence you show based on increased knowledge of yourself, for instance, improves your chances of: (1) being promoted or assigned to a desirable, high-profile job; (2) keeping your job despite downsizing, outsourcing, or reassignment; (3) getting a new job that will better suit your talents and areas of expertise; (4) moving ahead of the competition when you apply for a new job; and (5) enriching or expanding your present job to provide more opportunity and satisfaction.

2. Enhance people's mental image of themselves.   How we feel about ourselves shows at work and in our personal lives. Self-esteem and belief in oneself are essential elements in motivation. Both are a positive influence on our ability to perform. Also, appropriately recognizing and rewarding performance are strong positive incentives.

3. Provide a way to determine a constant core of resources.   These resources are based on our education and on our learning experiences. Much is observed and learned on the job. Peers, associates, supervisors, mentors, and other contacts in our world of work influence us in both direct and subtle ways.

You can use your own guidelines or standards to assess people around you. At school, in sports, and even in ethical matters, we use our personal guidelines or rulers to see how well others measure up to our standards.

4. Share information.   When information on talents is shared openly and willingly, these talents will be recognized, used, and rewarded. Individuals who network their talents experience a new sense of accomplishment as they learn about new opportunities. Networking with business contacts is the best way to get current information on available jobs and possible future job openings.

5. Information base.   This provides a base of information that can be modified or updated as jobs, processes, and demands change. Knowledge gained through training programs, independent study, or learning on the job, as in leading a team, can be documented. Information that is accumulated gradually and written down becomes a job history. This written record could provide valuable information at performance appraisal time or when special projects are being assigned. If people working for you had similar up-to-date records, the expertise of your whole work team could be shared and used in making work assignments.

Example 1. Motorola, Inc. screens up to fifteen job applicants for every person hired, even though only seventh grade reading and ninth grade math skills may be required. After hiring, Motorola must then spend an average of $250 per employee to train U.S. workers in quality control techniques.

Example 2. IBM spends approximately 17 percent of its $60 billion in total revenues each year on education and training. This includes funds for 7000 teachers' salaries, classrooms, and textbooks.[23]

6. Support of the "enterprise ethic." This new, paradoxical view of work is based on a belief in one's own abilities, a pessimism about steadily decreasing job opportunities, and the need to connect with other people.[8]

Paradoxes are seemingly self-contradictory statements that express a possible truth. Paradoxes abound in today's world—individual, intelligence, aging, productivity, work, organization, time, riches, and justice.[6] It is not necessary to resolve paradoxes; it is just necessary to recognize and manage them.

Handy presents two opposing views about the individual: (1) we need to plan our own path through life, respect the rights of others, yet to hold fast to the right to be ourselves and (2) we are recognized not for ourselves but only by the organization we represent or the university from which we graduated, among other affiliations. There are many acceptable opportunities for us to be recognized for both our individuality and for our membership in an accepted, recognized group.

This next section on operational definitions (1) introduces basic concepts and examples, (2) provides guidelines, (3) outlines major information sources, and (4) discusses uses and practical applications.

OPERATIONAL DEFINITIONS

These definitions reduce the number of problem caused by basic misunderstanding and lack of precision in expression. Operational definitions are used to define major concepts that are often misinterpreted or taken for granted. Adequately defining commonly used words and concepts allows us to explain and illustrate terms based on how they are used. We can think about certain concepts and write down *exactly* what we mean. When others also do this, it is easier to reach agreement on real meaning.

Basic Concepts

To describe things as they really are, we need to be precise in how we select and define the words we use. We also need to verify whether our information is reliable. Once operational definitions are developed, there is no further reason to confuse meanings. Precise descriptions of major concepts and processes are used in benchmarking, in evaluation, and in measurement. The overused statement, "we have to define something before we can measure it," applies.

Example 1.   Concepts to describe human abilities, like "excellent" or "average," may need to be defined using a rating scale, such as a seven-point scale. Verbally defining each of the seven points on the rating scale with words raters agree on increases the consistency or reliability of ratings. Agreement can be reached by discussing and modifying definitions until all raters agree on exactly what "4," a central point, means. Then, other points or units could be defined in a systematic manner (for instance define "3" and "5," then "2" and "6," and finally the extremes, "1" and "7").

Precise rating scale definitions are a tremendous asset in benchmarking. Clearly defined rating scales used in personal assessments are outlined   by Shippman, Hughes, and Prien.[18]

Example 2.   The demand for "zero defects" for products, processes, customer satisfaction, etc. began with the Martin Company, developers of the Pershing Missile for the U.S. Army. After a lengthy process of testing and steadily reducing defects or errors, the missile was delivered to Cape Canaveral ahead of schedule. When the final testing was done in December 1961, there were zero defects. Phil Crosby[2,3] was instrumental in this achievement.

The goal of zero defections is carrying over into customer services. Consider that companies can boost profits by almost 100 percent by retaining just 5 percent more of their customers.[16]

Example 3.   The level of customer satisfaction at Federal Express is 100 percent and nothing less.

Guidelines

Major guidelines outlining a framework for developing operational definitions are presented below.

Before developing definitions for any concept, determine if new definitions should be created or existing ones expanded. Don't reinvent the wheel. If there are no definitions, develop consistent procedures and stick to them. This ensures uniformity in (1) scope or content, (2) methods of obtaining information, and (3) constructing the definition.

1. Arrange for experienced and less experienced people to work together.   If people in the design unit, for instance, developed definitions for specific quality standards and the production unit has not, both units could work together and share information. Both units would have built-in "ownership" of the definitions developed jointly.

This cross-functional association benefits learning and communication. Value-added effects may result from the synergy of combining efforts. Broader, more complete definitions result when groups with a wide focus and broad experience base work together cooperatively. This will be discussed further in Chapter 6.

2. Build definitions using representative samples of activities and outcomes in both service *and* product areas. Theoretically, input should be obtained from everyone who will eventually use the definition. From the practical standpoint, a representative sample of service-based and product-based input could work well. Your sample should cover a normal distribution of those involved in the develop–use–evaluate chain. Suppliers, partners, end users, and regulators will each define quality in different ways.

Broadly focused groups have a wide range of orientations, experience levels, and needs. Some groups will come from very different organizational cultures. Resulting definitions may be ranked according to importance by applying criteria related to completeness, relevance, or other mutually agreed upon factors. Standing in the other person's shoes helps achieve understanding.

When the gamut of customers and suppliers agrees on exactly what each other means and on what they expect, the number of misunderstandings and expensive surprises is reduced. Processes used to obtain this information can range from a simple, home-grown questionnaire to the sophisticated Delphi technique,[4] which requires a series of written responses over a period of time.

3. Encourage those doing the job to provide input about themselves and the nature of their work. When people make contributions, they experience a sense of pride and ownership, as they are directly involved with and committed to the process. They "buy in" to the process *and* to the result, like the design and production units did in #1 above. Since they believe in definitions they help create, they are much more likely to use the definitions than those who were not similarly involved and committed. They also know when and how definitions and standards can best be used.

4. Where possible, ensure that definitions reflect the culture, attitudes, and typical behaviors occurring within the organization. In organizations where total quality management or other quality improvement efforts exist, major work-related factors may already be documented in guidelines or in a manual on quality. Definitions in organizations with a strong culture will be more uniform than, for instance, definitions in start-up companies, where people are new to the job and know very little about each other and the organization.

5. Select specific key results or end-result areas described above.   Key
result areas should be readily understood and acceptable to all parties.[1] However, suppliers, partners, all types of end users, and regulators, including various
levels of government, will each define key result areas in different ways. Their
definitions may cover the input side or the output side. For example, if you are
defining quality, it may be necessary to develop a separate definition for each
type of customer or end user. Suppliers, manufacturers, and a host of others, like
the marketing department, may also be involved.

Then, choose the most useful, practical definitions coming from end result
or output areas. Verify with various work groups and all others involved in this
lengthy, complex processes that definitions are practical and acceptable. It may
be possible to rank order the definitions starting with the "best." Don't expect
complete agreement. Eventually two or more diverse definitions may blend into
one broad yet completely adequate definition.

**6. Once a definition has been developed, get feedback on the "fit" of the
definition.**   One method is to encourage open communication between everyone in as much of the entire work cycle as possible. Include customers, clients,
partners, and numerous end users. Feedback does not end with the customer or
client, but rather is recycled throughout the system. This continuous recycling
process generates ideas for new services and products and for enhancing customer and client satisfaction. This can be done slowly by using surveys or more
quickly by asking people directly (face to face or by phone or fax). Most people
will be so surprised you asked their opinion, they will answer right away.

**7. Develop flexible definitions that can be broadened to reflect the chang-
ing nature of work and the workplace.**   Although anyone from within or
outside the organization may develop definitions of key concepts, all definitions
should have a customer orientation. Everyone has some type of internal customer in the organization and external customer outside the organization.

8. Improve definitions as needed.   Expenditures of time, effort, and money
to create these definitions ought to be minimized. Improvement that is an end
unto itself destroys any possible benefits. Results, as opposed to busy work or
unnecessary activities, are the main goal. Slight changes or updates should not
be expensive or time consuming.

Whether we know it or not, we are alternately customers and suppliers. We
are customers when we buy a book, for example. We are suppliers of information when we tell someone what is in that book.

**9. Check the validity of the operational definition to determine if you are
finding out exactly what you are supposed to find out.**   Use follow-up
surveys, questionnaires, or direct telephone contact to assess the satisfaction

level of developers, manufacturers, customers, end users, suppliers, and partners. This time-consuming process helps determine if you did what was wanted.

When asked, customers will tell you how well you are meeting their needs or honoring contracts for services or products. They can also provide excellent ideas on how to improve products and services and how to set standards.

Follow-up activities serve no purpose unless customers' suggestions are evaluated, cycled back, and used to improve products or services. How well you treat your customers depends on how long you want to stay in business.

Information Sources

Information for operational definitions can literally come from anywhere. However, two broad categories are "hard" (or quantitative) data and "soft" (or qualitative) information.[14]

Hard Data

Most data in this category are based on rational, undisputed facts. Data are usually reported only in numerical terms and almost always represent output. Four numeric categories are *output* (units produced), *costs* (unit costs), *time* (on time shipments), and *quality* (failures).

For example, quality could be measured in number of defects per thousand or million produced. Output represents the hard, countable facts of production or the number of customers served in a specific time period.

If hard data are not available, it is possible to convert soft data to one of the four basic measurements of hard data (number of units produced, time, cost, and quality). This is not an ideal method, however, as soft data will lose some of their meaning. However, soft data are gaining recognition as a major source of valuable information.[19]

Soft Data

Data in this category are subjective and often difficult to define, collect, and analyze. Much data represent throughput, or the "in between" processes, like thinking, evaluating, and creating. Soft data also come from observations, discussions, interviews, and various types of job-related documents or records, such as job descriptions and performance appraisals.[7,13]

Specific examples include work habits (on time), new skills (conflicts avoided), work climate (job satisfaction), feelings/attitudes (loyalty), development/advancement (promotions), and initiative (new ideas).

Another comparison method is the quantitative-qualitative dimensions.[15] Quantitative information is primarily "hard" data. Qualitative information is considered "soft" data.

Smith[19] contrasts quantitative and qualitative information according to focus, setting, sources of data, role of evaluator, method, data analysis, statistics used, reliability and validity, and reporting of results.

Additional sources of information are an organization's key end result areas: sales, financial return, service, efficiency, quality, and effectiveness.[1] Additional key result areas include human resources, growth, operating efficiency and productivity, competitive advantage, and loss control. These areas apply equally to service-based and product-based industries.

A person may describe his or her work and accomplishments in terms of key result areas. The listed are projects completed, applications filled, customers served, or number of people supervised.

When quantitative and qualitative data obtained from the same or very similar sources are compared, each one supports or supplements the other. This way, reliability and validity can be checked. Reliability is a measure of consistency throughout a series of measurements, observations, or repeated activities. Validity represents how closely a measuring instrument indicates what it is supposed to measure.

The same or similar information from two different sources can be compared. One-the-job performance represented by measured output (quantitative) could be compared with peers' descriptions of performance (qualitative).

If the type of data you use comes from someone else, it is still your responsibility to ensure the data are meaningful, representative, and serve the purpose intended. Use existing records or available information only if you believe they are reliable and valid. Easy paths to information seldom lead in the right direction.

Uses of Operational Definitions

The most common application is (read *should be*) in benchmarking. Other uses of operational definitions include developing a common language and clarifying and standardizing procedures and methods, among many others. Operational definitions are used in the service sector and in product-based and materials-processing industries.

Benchmarking

Benchmarking is a continuous, systematic process used to evaluate products, services, and work processes of organizations recognized as industry or world leaders. Of the three types of benchmarking, most definitions are of competitive benchmarking. Operational definitions form the core of benchmarking.

Carla O'Dell,[9] Director of the International Benchmarking Clearinghouse, a service of the American Productivity & Quality Center in Houston, Texas, defines benchmarking as "…the process of identifying, understanding and adapting outstanding practices and processes from organizations anywhere in the world to help your organization improve its performance."

Common Language

It is essential to have a common language that everyone throughout the organization understands. It provides a standard set of base terms that unify concepts and reduce disagreement. The only universal language of business is financial accounting.[17] Using a language that is primarily numeric is not an effective way to communicate complex issues related to people. Globalization of business requires customers and suppliers around the world to communicate quickly, accurately, and effectively. This necessitates a language that may start with financial data but must go beyond it.

Clarify Start-Up Procedures

Setting ground rules and clarifying what needs to be done is best accomplished when work teams from various disciplines (cross-functional teams) first meet. After a short period of working together, they will develop a common framework to examine concepts unfamiliar to their own discipline or experience level.

Operational definitions help describe the fine points related to products, processes, and services. When common terms emerge, all parties experience a feeling of unity. This process works well when creating ground rules for a new project, when current projects become bogged down, or when it is necessary to clarify meanings of concepts and processes used to reach consensus.

In a start-up business in particular, suppliers and customers need time to get acquainted. They bring their unique backgrounds, interests, knowledge, needs, etc. to the discussion table. In the early stages of working together, they start to share ideas about what is needed and what is possible. "Fuzzy" concepts that would not ordinarily be addressed are discussed in an open, friendly atmosphere. Concepts that were initially difficult to understand can be clarified.

Operationalizing major concepts provides a common framework and facilitates two-way communication. Those working together will select critical variables and standards for performance and quality and create definitions and standards that are common to their business relationships. The continuous process of defining and redefining concepts and processes builds continuity and predictability. The ultimate goal is to create a set of definitions that enhance understanding and communication and streamline business interactions, yet provide a strong base for quality and productivity.

When processes used to define, assess, implement, and monitor quality are understood, the quality of all levels and types of work efforts and relationships can be gradually improved.

Standardization

Ways to operationalize concepts in a given area, unit, or industry can be standardized to ensure uniformity of scope, content, or level of complexity. These procedures provide a unified framework to examine factors that affect the design, development, and provision of products and services. Such standardization is extremely beneficial, whether working with suppliers and partners who are next door or on the other side of the world.

When operational definitions are used as a basis for benchmarking, results are communicated to a "clearinghouse" of "best" or most frequently used definitions and specifications. Definitions of important activities are used to make between- and within-industry comparisons. Resulting information is used to develop more reliable and valid assessments of bottom-line benefits, such as customer satisfaction, competitive position, and, last but not least, profit.

Uniqueness

Clients, customers, end users, partners, suppliers, and others have their own ideas or company-based standards for "service" and "quality." Workplace diversity is growing daily. It is imperative to recognize and appreciate other people's special talents, professions, experience, and points of view. Users often create a number of definitions from which they select the "best" or most appropriate, a definition they understand best or one in which they have a vested interest. Differences are based on personal preference, type of organization, culture, and nationality, among other factors.

Fine Tuning

If definitions of key factors and major end result areas already exist or have been benchmarked, further refinement may be required. In organizations where various types of quality improvement efforts are either being explored or are in place, expanding or refining definitions is an ongoing process. This type of improvement and fine tuning increases the precision and scope of definitions of an array of products and services to enhance end user and/or customer satisfaction and ultimately increase quality and productivity.

Job Analysis

Work done on the job can be grouped into areas that describe various types and levels of work activities (e.g., clerical, support, professional, specialist, knowledge workers). Separate operational definitions could be used for each category. This process could be applied to analyzing jobs, developing job assignments, doing performance appraisals, and even cross-training.

Value Added

Operational definitions with important innovative dimensions have the potential of adding value. Adding value simply means increasing the desirability or worth to the customer, like a bonus gift, some extra service not expected, or additional features the customer did not pay for. These value-added definitions often stimulate new ventures and provide ideas on increasing market share.

Some of your best customers will know how value can be added to existing products or services—but you must ask them. When you know what customers want, you can communicate these ideas and methods to the people who develop and deliver the products or services. This adds a new value-added dimension to customer satisfaction and can take the form of tailor-made products.

Good products with value added are very likely to propel a company ahead of its competitors. All things being equal, commodities and services with value added will outpace their competition.[20] Value added, introduced in Chapter 6, is discussed in detail in Chapter 9. Because value added is one of the major concepts in productivity, it plays a major role in people's personal equations.

Ownership Increases Involvement, Commitment, and Cooperation

People who work together "buy in" or have ownership in concepts they develop, as discussed earlier. Work groups or teams, and their leaders or supervisors, that jointly develop operational definitions for major concepts increase their understanding of the entire work process, and not just concept development. Group synergy produces a product greater than the sum of its separate parts.

Staying Current

Revising and updating operational definitions to reflect new ideas and job and workplace changes keeps definitions current. Benchmarking and using operational definitions can become a way of life. It is possible for an organization to develop its own definitions of various key concepts which gradually work their way into the organization's culture, mission statements, and even strategic plans and goals. When people throughout the organization tune in to what basic elements are important, what key results are, and use a common terminology to describe what they are doing, they will have traveled a long way on the unmapped, endless road to quality.

Shared Expectations and Knowledge
Build Long-Term Relationships

Over time, important operational definitions of key concepts will specify what customers want yet reflect what suppliers can provide. Resulting definitions of appropriate services are built on shared expectations and knowledge of suppliers and customers. This joint endeavor solidifies interests and efforts as each party buys into the other's concepts and standards. These steps provide the foundation for developing contracts or building partnerships.

Stepping Stones to a New Direction

Once operational definitions are jointly developed, acceptable standards that take quality, cost, cycle time, and other critical variables into consideration can serve as a basis for benchmarking or developing standards in other areas. It may be possible to anticipate cost overruns or customer complaints. These new efforts may form a core of concepts on which to base customer forums. Forums that foster free and open communication between customers and suppliers produce innovative ideas and relationships and encourage the formation of partnerships for mutual gain.

SUMMARY AND CONCLUSIONS

1. The constantly changing job market, continuous need for training, and rapidly expanding technologies make it virtually impossible for most people to feel secure in their jobs. Having an up-to-date, renewable

career passport or document, perhaps in the form of a complete personal equation, is one answer. A portfolio of skills is needed to negotiate the evolving information economy.

2. Our eyes and ears let us see and hear what we want to, which is not always what we should see and hear. Everyone's system of beliefs and values and the way they do things is affected by their own frame of reference. Our personalities and the world around us also play major roles. Precise definitions in the form of operational definitions help clarify problems of meaning and reduce misunderstanding which result from biases. Open, two-way communication can also minimize the negative role biases play in our everyday lives. Being a keen or trained observer, which is seldom easy, can reduce the frequency and intensity of both misperception and biases.

3. People can build factors into their personal equations that are most likely to influence how they do their jobs. This valuable information helps them do their jobs better and can also improve all forms of interpersonal relationships.

4. Operational definitions describe and illustrate concepts according to how they are used. These precise, carefully developed definitions clarify meanings of words and events people often take for granted. Operational definitions enable people in different departments, in different organizations, or around the world to use a common language to describe and assess standard concepts, such as quality, productivity, and even performance level.

PRACTICAL APPLICATIONS

1. Reducing the influence of biases increases a person's ability to see clearly and make good judgments. Perceptions that cloud reality reduce the effectiveness and efficiency of performance.

2. A major reason for learning more about behavior is to be able to make better predictions about how people react at work. Being proactive and anticipating what may happen are very valuable personal characteristics. The type, size, structure, culture, and age of organizations also have a major impact on how people think and react.

3. When you start to build a model car or airplane or use a pattern to make something, you study the pieces, lay them out, and figure out how they

Creating Productive Organizations: Manual

all fit together. This takes time and patience. It usually means following directions or guidelines. However, few people have built a model of their talents. If you have a model in your mind or, better yet, written down, you are one of the foresightful few.

From the practical, business standpoint, a model of your talents is more useful than many of the models you have built in the past. Admittedly, the model of your talents would be less fun to build, but it might serve you better over your lifetime.

4. Major applications of operational definitions:

- Create awareness of the need to develop flexible, practical, comprehensive definitions when dealing with complex issues, such as quality, productivity, competence, etc. In quality and productivity change and improvement programs, benchmarking is becoming an increasingly standard tool. It is vital that concepts and processes benchmarked be defined accurately and completely using terms that all benchmarking parties understand. Otherwise, results will not be reliable, consistent, or valid and measure what they are supposed to measure. Operational definitions of your abilities, knowledge, skills, interests, motivation, and many other factors will become key elements in you personal equation.

- Broaden, clarify, and improve the precision and scope of concepts commonly taken for granted or misunderstood. Examples are preparing quality manuals, doing performance appraisals, and all types of oral and written communication.

- Take the "hidden meaning" out of biases in order to provide a common base line to make judgments and convey results to those who do not share your frame of reference, work background, culture, or even language. Shared understanding leads to shared values. Managing shared value systems is what business is all about.

REFERENCES

1. Bain, David. *The Productivity Prescription*, New York: McGraw-Hill, 1982.

2. Crosby, Philip B. *Quality Is Free*, New York: New American Library, 1979.

3. Crosby, Philip B. *Quality without Tears,* New York: McGraw-Hill, 1984.

4. Dalkey, N. C. *The Delphi Method: An Experimental Study of Group Opinions*, Santa Monica, Calif.: Rand Corporation, 1969.

5. Handy, Charles. *The Age of Unreason*, Boston: Harvard Business School Press, 1989.

6. Handy, Charles. *The Age of Paradox*, Boston: Harvard Business School Press, 1994.

7. Marshall, Catherine and Rossman, Gretchen B. *Designing Qualitative Research*, Newberry Park, Calif.: Sage Publications, 1989.

8. Nichols, Martha. "Does New Age Business Have a Message for Managers?" *Harvard Business Review*, March–April 1994, pp. 52–60.

9. O'Dell, Carla. "Out-of-the-Box Benchmarking," *Management Review*, January 1994, p. 63.

10. Odiorne, George S. *MBO II: A System of Managerial Leadership*, Belmont, Calif.: Fearon Pitman, 1979, pp. 235–250.

11. Odiorne, George S. *Strategic Management of Human Resources*, San Francisco: Jossey-Bass, 1984.

12. Offerman, Lynn R. and Gowing, Marilyn K. "Organizations of the Future," *American Psychologist*, February 1990, pp. 95–108.

13. Patton, Michael Quinn. *Qualitative Evaluation Methods*, Newberry Park, Calif.: Sage Publications, 1990.

14. Phillips, Jack J. *Handbook of Training Evaluation and Measurement Methods*, Houston: Gulf Publishing, 1983.

15. Ranftl, Robert M. *R&D Productivity* (2nd ed.), Los Angeles: Hughes Aircraft, 1978.

16. Reichheld, Frederick F. and Sasser, W. Earl Jr. "Zero Defections: Quality Comes to Services," *Harvard Business Review*, September–October 1990, pp. 105–111.

17. Senge, Peter M. *The Fifth Discipline*, New York: Doubleday, 1990

18. Shippmann, Jeffrey S., Hughes, Gary L., and Prien, Erich P. "The Use of Structured Multi-Domain Job Analysis for the Construction of Assessment Center Methods and Procedures, *Journal of Business and Psychology*, Summer 1987, pp. 353–366.

19. Smith, Elizabeth A. "The Role of Qualitative Information in Productivity Measurement," *Industrial Management*, March/April 1991, pp. 19–22, 24.

20. Smith, Elizabeth A. "Value Added: Perception vs. Expectation vs. Reality," *The Quality Observer*, in press (predicted publication date July 1995).

21. Smith, Elizabeth A. *The Productivity Manual* (2nd ed.), Houston: Gulf Publishing, 1995.

22. *The Better Work Supervisor*, Concordville, Pa.: Clement Communications, March 19, 1984, p. 1.

23. Tucker, Allyson. "Educating the Workforce of the Future," *Harvard Business Review*, March–April 1994, pp. 47, 50–51.

24. Tyler, Leona E. *The Psychology of Human Differences* (2nd ed.), New York: Appleton-Century-Crofts, 1956.

SETTING UP VARIABLES FOR YOUR PERSONAL EQUATION

PURPOSE

- Consider the influence of beliefs about people, the nature of work, and change on the personal equation
- Write the first elements of your personal equation

INTRODUCTION

Everyone has talents they recognize and talents they do not recognize. These skills, abilities, knowledge, insights, experience, and other unnamed or undiscovered areas make people what they are, both on and off the job.

Fads, following the leader, and fear of being left out are but a few of the things that keep us from discovering and applying our talents to the fullest. Fear of what other people think and fear of not performing are only two examples.

At work, we are often so busy doing our jobs that we rarely take time to think about what we know. Training programs and time away from the office break our routine temporarily and expand our minds. Have you ever come back from a seminar with an exciting idea or a new slate of things to do only to find your co-workers unreceptive or even negative to your efforts when you tried to apply what you learned? You may have changed, but probably nothing else has.

Few organizations have the means to absorb what the work force learns in seminars or in training programs. It seems there is no good way to measure whether what was learned was later applied on the job. The follow-up on learning effectiveness is minimal.

Much newly acquired information can be reinforced and retained longer when organizations are supportive and work groups are receptive. Moreover, when seminars are closely related to the actual jobs performed, newly acquired information can be applied immediately.

Many work settings are not set up for one-on-one learning or mentoring. Fending for ourselves is both time consuming and inefficient. When we do this, we don't even know if we have learned what we need to do our jobs better.

We all have strengths. Sometimes we let negatives overpower positives. We tend to think more about our weaknesses than about our strengths. We think of uncompleted tasks, things we don't know, and our areas of deficiency. Rather, we should be thinking about how to better apply what we know. We could do just this by helping or teaching someone else what we know, or we could learn from someone else.

Ten beliefs used in my personal equation are presented next. Many are standard ways of thinking. You can select any you like for your own personal equation, but it is better to develop your own. Your beliefs should fit in with your background, way of thinking, and your job-related needs and expectations.

1. People Are a Valuable Resource

We want to believe that we are the most valuable resource in any organization. Are organizations changing their attitudes about people? Yes—but slowly. There is growing recognition that human resource excellence is a major element of total quality.

People are changing their attitudes about organizations as well. It is an understatement to say that loyalty, consideration, support, and lifelong commitment to an employer are not as strong as they used to be. Some insightful organizations have redesigned themselves to attract a high-quality work force.

The real emphasis at work should be on ability, knowledge, and skills; how people feel about themselves and the organization; and how they can streamline and improve their jobs and accomplishments. All this can be done within acceptable guidelines that support mission statements, goals, plans, etc.

Many efforts to focus primarily on numeric bottom-line results, like profit and cost savings, erode the role of people. Everyone has a good feel for how best to add value[12] and when to apply extra effort to get a bonus if there is a gainsharing or profit-sharing program.

New and prospective employees want to believe the company really wants them and will value their talents, and they will flock to those organizations that do. A large number of the "new breed" of young college graduates seriously study many organization to see how well each fits into *their* scheme of things.

Are people tired of fighting for a "secure" place in the working world? Are they tired of trying to do a good job despite being overmanaged and underled? Are they frustrated when a stifling organizational culture limits their ability to think, grow and learn? The answer to all three questions is yes.

People, not organizations, can make things happen. People originally developed and accepted the bottom-line measures of profit, cost savings, and other numeric factors, often with dollar signs attached. Nevertheless, *people* are also responsible for creating the organizational structures, rules, and processes that govern behavior. Therefore, people are the only ones who can shine the spotlight back on themselves. They may end up questioning the almost exclusive use of numeric measures that do not truly represent their unique output.

2. People Are Hungry For Feedback

People have always been hungry for feedback on how they are doing. We all like immediately knowledge of results on our own performance. We also like to know how we compare with others performing similar jobs.

People in learning modes openly accept feedback in the form of constructive suggestions for improvement. Ongoing or timely feedback on performance helps people learn more about themselves and about their jobs. This information is used in career planning and in mastering new, demanding skills. The desire to know more about oneself is referred to as "enlightened self-interest."

Accurate, timely feedback is what competitive racing, card games, and interactive video are all about. In these instances, feedback is ongoing.

In sports, we compete against others or against our own record. Imagine competing in a sports event and not knowing the outcome for six months or even longer. Even worse, what if your results were written up by someone who never saw you compete? Does this remind you of performance appraisals?

Despite all the change and reorganization efforts imposed from above and the groundswells from the lower ranks, feedback per se and feedback mechanisms resemble those that existed at the beginning of recorded history.

We all want to be appropriately rewarded for doing our jobs well. Rewards are effective in getting temporary compliance but not lasting commitment to any value or action. The concept of economic value added is not new, but it is being restated in today's terms. Economic value added provides employees with incentives to (1) improve profitability, (2) grow profitability, and (3) withdraw resources from uneconomic activities. Quaker Oats uses this system.

Even in self-directed work teams, there still is not enough meaningful, timely feedback on performance. Despite changes in roles and responsibilities, internal feedback mechanisms seldom change. Ideally, feedback should come from numerous sources and from all possible directions in order to counteract the information vacuum in which many people appear to operate.

Learning organizations are able to provide immediate, timely feedback on performance. Information critical to improve performance is readily available from peers, supervisors, managers, and leaders. "Full-circle" or 360° feedback is available on all facets of performance and on guidelines or standards for achieving and maintaining quality and specifically productivity. "Full circle" reaches people at all levels in the organization, as they get feedback on performance from their supervisors, peers, and subordinates.

The concept of feedforward implies that what is learned is moved forward a step at a time and is used to solve the next problem. This allows you to develop the solution-after-next. A common problem is failure to look beyond the immediate issue to future needs. A long-term solution also gives direction to the near-term solution. Having several alternative solutions-after-next stimulates creativity. This process supports continual change and improvement efforts.

3. Normal Distribution

This function can be derived mathematically.* The normal distribution function is based on the assumption that most things and events (height, weight, even opinions) are normally distributed. This means, for example, there are a small number of very short and very tall people. There is a larger number of moderately tall and moderately short people. The middle group is "average" in height.

Descriptive statistics are based on normal distributions. Distributions are considered normal when the data used represent the shape of the standard bell-shaped curve. Major variables used to describe normal distributions are average

---

* From the academic standpoint, this function, also known as the Gaussian curve, predates Gauss. Abraham De Moivre (1667–1754), a refugee mathematician living in London, derived the equation for this curve in 1733. Laplace (1749–1827) and Gauss (1777–1855) each derived the law independently, presumably without knowing about De Moivre's original derivation.[15]

(or mean) and standard deviation (or measure of "scatter" or "cluster"). All basic statistics books describe normal distributions in detail.

To return to personal equations, opinions and beliefs about certain issues and events differ in strength. Our beliefs about equal pay for equal work can be very strong. On the other hand, we may be neutral about empowerment and negative about upgrading our current word-processing software.

When we make up our minds, our decisions can range from strong to weak. We may not even know our position on a hypothetical rating scale unless someone asks us or we are called upon to defend our decision. A person playing "devil's advocate" may cause us to change the strength of our beliefs by challenging our opinions. Challenges usually firm up or weaken our positions.

We seldom take time to think about, much less clarify, just how strong another person's statement is or consider how strongly we express ourselves. Many people who think and act in terms of black or white, or *it is* or *it isn't*, are often misinterpreted. Statements must be evaluated on the basis of how strongly people believe them and then verified by reaching consensus on exactly what was meant. This can be a long and involved process. You may need to achieve consensus with yourself when you develop your personal equation. You may have changed—happily for the better!

Chaos theory is just the opposite of the predictable, traditionally bell-shaped normal distribution. When polar opposites are studied separately, a better understanding of each of the opposing factors often results.

Many of us learn faster when we think in terms of opposites, like black and white. Then, when we have two firm "end" anchors, we can begin to fill in the space between these two opposite end points. When we mentally develop a middle ground, we have one point in the middle. The rest is easy to fit in. After we reach a level of understanding that requires few additional thoughts, we are satisfied.

Chaos theory is based on mechanical principles developed by Sir Isaac Newton (1642–1727). Chaotic systems are characterized by a sensitivity to initial conditions that result in unpredictable but orderly final conditions.[5]

Chaos and order are mirror images, as each contains the other. Wheatley's[16] interpretation of chaos theory is that disorder, as represented by change emerging from chaos, gives birth to newer, high forms of order.

A bit of history on the recognition, descriptions, and applications of chaos theory is called for at this point. Edward Lorenz, a research meteorologist from Massachusetts Institute of Technology, had studied weather patterns for some time. He wanted to develop a system to improve the accuracy of weather forecasting. In the early 1960s, Lorenz demonstrated the first concrete example of a system exhibiting the "wild" or exponential growth of uncertainties. And so "modern" chaos theory was born.

The book and movie of *Jurassic Park* illustrate chaos theory. Dinosaur DNA was cloned, and genetically engineered dinosaurs were hatched in incubators. These purportedly same-sex dinosaurs unexpectedly reproduced. Offspring were falsely assumed to be controllable, but went wild.

This fascinating theory based on non-normal or non-linear distributions is making its way into the business literature. High-speed computers are used to solve equations associated with dynamic, non-linear systems. Solutions to these equations are used to increase the power of lasers and encode electronic messages for secure communications, among other uses.[17]

Example 1. If a random or non-biased sample of people expressed opinions about an important issue, there would be a wide range of differences. People's opinions would range from absolutely against something to strongly for something. When someone says "I don't think so," do they mean "never," "sometimes," "it depends," or "always?" (This is one of the reasons some people have difficulty figuring out the "best" answers on multiple choice tests.)

A clearly defined rating scale will help you achieve consensus. It is also possible to define points on a rating scale so that people understand them.

Example 2. Do people working in the area of quality improvement know how strongly team members believe in the whole quality concept? It is likely that no one really knows the strengths of beliefs of even their team members. If people rated the strength of their beliefs about quality using a seven-point scale, ratings would range from 1 to 7. Those reporting 7 are either strongly dedicated to quality or wish they were. The majority of ratings will probably be in the middle range (or 3, 4, and 5).

4. If Something Exists, It Can Be Described and Measured

If something can be described and defined, it can be measured. If it can be measured once, it can be measured again. If it can be measured over weeks, months, or even years, the data that are obtained can be compared. Then, standards, or baselines or yardsticks of measurement, can be created using appropriate statistical procedures.

Benchmarking and self-assessment are the core of the quality movement. Managers know that if you can't measure it, you can't manage it. The specific attributes measured must be clearly identified and described. Only when what is being measured is clearly defined, such as specific job skills, can measurement take place.[12] Once something has been measured, it can be benchmarked.

Although Deming indicated that there are no absolute values of anything, it is still possible to get approximate values that are perfectly adequate. Such values can be used to detect or demonstrate trends or deviations from what is "normal," the norm, or average. We all have our own mental guidelines that help us decide whether something is as it should be. After making our evaluation, we form our opinion about describing or measuring something. Then, we use our decision as a baseline or standard for making comparisons.

5. Nothing Lasts Forever

College students are being trained in areas that did not exist even five years ago. In ten years, when today's crop of new graduates look back to the year 2000, they will be amazed by all the new things around them.

No industry lasts forever. Two longstanding examples are pony express and buggy whips. Both were replaced. We could add others, like radios, televisions, and computers requiring tubes. The list grows daily.

No technology stays the same for long. One mind-boggling illustration is the steadily increasing power and speed of computers and the progressive reduction in size, or miniaturization, of component parts.

Organizations that are static seldom survive. Organizations must always be in the process of learning, changing, and evolving in order to meet the demands of customers who are also learning, changing, and evolving.

People don't stay the same, either. People pass through stages. Shakespeare said seven. Some say more and some say less. The number of stages is not the issue here; the issue is that as people grow older, they change in many ways.

Learning changes people and organizations. Most learning should relate directly to an organization's vision and mission. What is learned must be directly applied to business outcomes, as at AT&T Capital Corporation, where businesses are designed around customer needs rather than around products or functions.[14] However, there is room for learning that expands the mind and stimulates creative thought (more about that later).

At AT&T, future learning efforts are built on competencies that are key to its mission (e.g., increase revenues and market share). Information is obtained from "learning audits" which are conducted within selected business units. It is in these units that information is obtained and used later to develop future goals. This information is also used to modify vision statements and stay current with technological developments. Audits show that finding out what was learned in one year can be applied to achieving future missions. AT&T is a good example of a learning organization.

AT&T's Consumer Communications Services in Basking Ridge, New Jersey won one of the two 1994 Malcolm Baldrige National Quality Awards for excellence in quality management in the service area. This unit, the largest of 20 AT&T business units, has 44,000 employees and serve mores than 80 million customers. The unit provides domestic and international long-distance communications services primarily to residential customers.

6. Change Is Inevitable

Nothing is so constant as change.[6] Since the beginning of time, philosophers have written about the inevitability of change. Most change is slow and gradual. However, sudden changes probably disrupt us most.

You could group "nothing lasts forever" with "nothing is so constant as change" if you want to. Depending on your age, you may be happier thinking about *change* rather than *nothing lasts forever*.

Roger Mack's famous written in 1790 provides a perspective on change.[7]

> *Changes never answer the end. One reason is that when men propose changes they always think of them as taking place in a static situation, whereas the making of the change of necessity alters the situation so that the change really takes place in another situation. And then many changes are dynamic and set in motion many other changes.*

Do you look for constancy in your daily life? Change disrupts balance and upsets routine, even psychological balance. Resistance to change is natural. Change occurs when resistance is reduced, as in altering opinions.

Some things never change, like common problems associated with communicating and getting reports done on time. Do things generally stay the same no matter what they are called? Yes. For example, productivity, quality, and even bottom-line costs, despite what they were called thousands of years ago, have been, and will continue to be, the major forces driving constant change.

Making the unknown known and then getting people to accept the change is not easy. People may accept change only if they helped design and/or introduced it. They will have "bought in" to it. Some put their unique stamp on change by rewriting or rewording concepts in their own special terms. Unless people are ardent supporters of change, they will not support or believe in anything related to change.

Perhaps you are thinking that some people simply do not ever change. The unofficial statistics are that at least two to five percent of the population will *never* change. They are hard core non-changers!

An older, established organization with an inflexible structure will have trouble changing its old, established, tried-and-true ways. Older organizations are faced with the need to reengineer, redesign, reinvent, and do many of the *re-* activities previously mentioned. If the organization can change, why can't people change? It is easier to change the organization than to change people. In changing people, it is often necessary to change attitudes, beliefs, and values, essentially core values.

Despite all the problems associated with change, it is important to set the tone for change. Change should be managed as a whole. It should not be broken into smaller pieces so that each piece can be managed separately. The main job is to manage the dynamic, or moving, parts, instead of the visible pieces.

Organizations are webs of well-connected units. A change in one unit may throw another part off balance. This is discussed in Chapter 8.

People fear the unknown aspects of change—growing older or learning a new job skill. Good communication and openness are antidotes to the fear that usually accompanies change. Being prepared to change means being open-minded about ourselves, our work, and how we do our work. The nature, direction, speed, and cost of change are unknown variables along the road to change.

The logical, high-energy solution to change is to introduce it. If you wait until someone else introduces it, you must react to it. Better to introduce it. Jobs are not fixed; they can be changed. People are treated as variables that can do the job. In organizations it's the person, not the job, that is most important.

The new management paradigm discussed in Chapter 2 suggests that managing people is managing feelings. Values, beliefs, and attitudes are really part of feelings. One way to effectively deal with change is to incorporate it into people's systems of beliefs.[1] Be sure to get the people you are hoping to change involved in all phases of change efforts, from start to finish.

Today, "transition management teams" are often delegated the responsibility for managing change. They build change into the organizational culture—its vision, mission, strategies, and goals and the values held by its employees. Ideally, these teams communicate with everyone in the organization involved in change efforts. These teams get the views of everyone in the organization and remain in close contact with them throughout the entire process of change.[9,10]

7. Everything Grows and Matures at Its Own Rate

People and organizations have life cycles. People of a certain age have some idea where they are in their life cycle. However, the life cycle of an organization is seldom mentioned, much less understood.

A young, start-up organization is much more flexible and moves faster than an older, mature, established organization. The young organization will have a flexible structure that can adapt to varying forces in the environment, like new international competition and continually changing demands of customers.

The new, fast-growing organizations have not had to reinvent themselves.

They "did it right the first time." One of the best examples is Mrs. Field's Cookies. This company is also an example of a learning organization.

Some people are pretty much satisfied with the way things are. So are mature organizations. These organizations also want a peaceful, stress-free existence and are essentially taking early retirement. They can no longer function with the "new rules" their young competitors follow. Some of these rules mean being lean, fast-moving, innovative, and flexible. Most of all, lean and flexible.

Don't despair—mature organizations can be perked up and rejuvenated. But it will take a very dedicated CEO with strong leadership capabilities and a clear vision of the future. The work force must be well trained and highly motivated. Many organizations are doing every form of "rightsizing" to stay afloat.

Unfortunately, some organizations are using after the fact, or reactive, methods. It is too late for these organizations to use proactive measures, like plan ahead or change their mission and goals, or focus. Their competition is simply moving too fast for them to keep up.

8. Jobs Differ in Level of Complexity

People, activities, processes, work, etc. differ in level of complexity and degree of difficulty. If people were to list ten or fifteen major tasks or activities performed each day, they could put them in order from most difficult to easiest. This order would change as they acquire new skills. What were once considered difficult tasks would become easier the more often they were performed. Newly learned "state-of-the-art" skills would then be assigned the highest level of difficulty. The point is that learning, practice, and getting better, or improving, alter or refocus how we judge the difficulty level of tasks. Essentially, the more we know about something, the "easier" it gets.

We all use our ideas, or frame of reference, to judge others. If we find one job to be easy, we tend to believe that everyone also finds it easy. In a similar vein, the level of complexity for the same job will differ between people. Depending on work experience, skills, and other human factors, what is easy for one person may be difficult for another.

9. Uniqueness Principle

Individuals should be recognized, even encouraged, to express their uniqueness—talents, ideas, even dreams. People are unique in their food preferences, the cars they drive, and their tastes in entertainment, so why not at work?

The uniqueness principle has already been introduced. It is really another way to emphasize individual differences or human factors. *Breakthrough Thinking,* by Nadler and Hibino,[8] is about the uniqueness of people.

Illustrations of breakthrough thinking are (1) the whole is greater than the sum of its parts (this concept was based on Gestalt psychology) and (2) there is no one best way to do anything.

Enthusiasm in the workplace and spinoffs from sharing unique knowledge and expertise will produce a positive work environment. Only then will positive changes and improvements abound in work groups and in the organization. By encouraging diversity, the immensely valued activities of creativity and innovation will flourish.[3,4]

10. All Activities Are Made Up of Smaller Units

It is often stated that the whole is greater than the sum of its parts. Smaller parts, whether information or feedback, build on each other. Small units gradually evolve into something better and more complex, flexible, or elegant.

The exact shape and configuration of smaller units may be repeated as larger units. Consider fractals. The book and movie of *Jurassic Park* describe and illustrate fractals. Fractals result when even a small amount of information is fed back on itself. This process of "evolving feedback" produces a new form similar to the original.

A business world application of fractals is what happens in meetings—a small bit of information, when fed back on itself or consistently repeated in a slightly different form, results in something new, and probably of a higher order than the original.

Another simple example of fractals is the predictable events which occur during the course of each work day—good news, a few complaints, telephone calls, and then off to a meeting. If the same person's work activities over the course of a week, month, or year were studied, each activity would be repeated in about the same form, with about the same relative frequency for the weeks, months, even years. There is some truth to the statement "history repeats itself."

A final illustration is business process reengineering, which is defined as "the rapid and radical redesign of strategic, value-added business processes— and the systems, policies, and organizational structures that support them—to optimize the work flows and productivity in an organization."[7] This process examines small units and the processes used to accomplish them. The goal is to improve how the various processes performed by units are fit together or sequenced in order to accomplish breakthrough or superb performance.

Klein[7] includes the technical aspects of the process (technology, standards, procedures, systems, and controls) and the social aspects (organization, staffing, policies, jobs, career paths, and incentives). However, the newly named "business process analysis" and business process reengineering are not really new. They are just being rediscovered. Henry Ford used these methods in 1910.

Whether business process reengineering or other methods are used to examine the separate pieces, it is *how* well the whole system functions once it is reassembled that is important. Systems theory is further discussed in Chapter 8.

When we deal with processes and products, there are points of contact, or "connects," like seams in a garment or welds on a pipeline. When contacts are weak, or broken, the whole unit can fail. "A chain is only as strong as its weakest link." Tangible items and concepts are only as strong as their weakest parts. When "connects" are strong, they are taken for granted. We often assume that points of contact are always strong, but this is not always so.

People, events, and processes also have contact points. When these points are weak or missing, "disconnects" occur. These breakdowns can occur at any point in the flow of events. Liaison people know how to deal with the "disconnects." They usually know why, when, and where disconnects occur. They also know how to make connections strong again. Having the information and the talent to prevent, even anticipate, disconnects is a highly desirable attribute.

FIRST ELEMENTS IN MY PERSONAL EQUATION

4.1

Use the space below to write down ideas or factors that you believe should go into your personal equation. Be sure and build a strong base. What you write here can be changed as you learn more about yourself and the tools and methods presented in later chapters. Think carefully, as this is your first step. We will return to this section later, as what you write here will be used in Chapters 7 to 10.

Relevant Ideas or Factors

1. _____

2. _____

3. _____

4. _____

5. _____

6. _____

7. _____

8. _____

You will use some of the ideas or factors listed above in the model to be developed as we go through the chapters. This model is completed in Chapter 10.

SUMMARY AND CONCLUSIONS

1. Knowing about the systems in which people function allows us to make reasonably informed predictions about their expected behavior.

2. The ten basic variables in the author's personal equation relate to people, the "facts of life," and assessment.

   - **People:** (1) are valuable resources, (2) are unique, (3) perform jobs that differ in level of complexity, and (4) want immediate feedback on performance.

   - **"Facts of life"** or the "way things happen": (5) nearly everything is normally distributed, (6) nothing lasts forever, and (7) change is inevitable.

   - **Assessment:** (8) everything grows and matures at its own rate; (9) if something exists, it can be measured; and (10) the whole contains many small parts and is often considered greater than the sum of its separate parts.

PRACTICAL APPLICATIONS

1. Knowing some of the predictable elements in people's work and personal lives helps improve the speed and accuracy of decisions. Anticipating problems minimizes wasted time and effort. The number of "disconnects" in a logical flow of events is also reduced.

2. Certain "givens" have historically stayed the same—like people's reluctance to change. There is no use trying to change people unless you have a carefully constructed plan that begins with increasing awareness of the need to change and directly involve them in the process.

3. Nothing is really as complex as it first appears. Everything is made up of smaller parts which can be selected and examined in a logical manner. Don't be overwhelmed by complexity, when simplicity surrounds you. Those who make things simple always have an easy-to-understand explanation for most things that happen. The world favors simplifiers. Anyone can make things complex.

REFERENCES

1. Duck, Jeanie Daniel. "Managing Change: The Art of Balancing," *Harvard Business Review*, November–December 1993, pp. 109–118.

2. Evans, Bergen. *Dictionary of Quotations.* New York: Avenel Books, 1978.

3. Handy, Charles. *The Age of Unreason*, Boston: Harvard Business School Press, 1989.

4. Handy, Charles. *The Age of Paradox*, Boston: Harvard Business School Press, 1994.

5. Hutchinson, Doug. "Chaos Theory, Complexity Theory, and Health Care Quality Management," *Quality Progress*, November 1994, pp. 69–72.

6. Kanter, Rosabeth Moss. *The Change Masters.* New York: Simon and Schuster, 1983.

7. Klein, Mark M. "IEs Fill Facilitator Role in Benchmarking Operations to Improve Performance," *Industrial Engineering*, September 1993, pp. 40–42.

8. Nadler, G. and Hibino, Shozo. *Breakthrough Thinking,* Rocklin, Calif.: Prima Publishing, 1990.

9. Nichols, Martha. "Does New Age Business Have Message for Managers?" *Harvard Business Review*, March–April 1994, pp. 52–60.

10. Offerman, Lynn R. and Gowing, Marilyn K. "Organizations of the Future," *American Psychologist*, February 1990, pp. 95–108.

11. Senge, Peter M. *The Fifth Discipline*, New York: Doubleday, 1990.

12. Smith, Elizabeth A. "A Conceptual Model for Introducing Quality into Measurements of White-Collar Productivity," in *Productivity & Quality Management Frontiers-IV*, Sumanth, Edosomwan, Poupart, and Sink (Eds.), Norcross, Ga.: Institute of Industrial Engineers, 1993, pp. 391–398.

13. Smith, Elizabeth A. "Value-Added: Perception vs. Expectations vs. Reality," *The Quality Observer,* in press (expected publication July 1995).

14. Wajnert, Thomas C. "Letters to the Editor," *Harvard Business Review*, September–October 1993, pp. 196–197.

15. Walker, Helen M. *Elementary Statistical Methods*, New York: Henry Holt, 1957.

16. Wheatley, Margaret J. *Leadership and the New Science,* San Francisco: Berrett-Koehler, 1992.

17. Williams, L. Ditto and Percora, Louis M. "Mastering Chaos," *Scientific American*, Vol. 269, No. 2, August 1993, pp. 78–85.

ENVIRONMENT, ORGANIZATIONS, AND TECHNOLOGY

PURPOSE

- Examine the positive and negative forces in the environment
- Consider the impact and uses of technology
- View organizations from the perspectives of type, divisions of work, culture, systems, structure, strategy, and control
- Evaluate the role of positive and negative forces in the organization

INTRODUCTION

This chapter looks at environment, technology, the organization, and what people do at work. Numerous forces or variables in each of these three areas affect people and their world of work.

To review, the first two chapters covered vision and mission. Chapter 3 examined biases and perception. Chapter 4 indicated that people (1) are very valuable resources, (2) are unique in many ways, (3) want and need feedback, and (4) may engage in lifelong learning vital to professional and personal satisfaction and to job security.

This chapter (1) takes a broad look at the major environmental forces affecting the organization; (2) critiques the purpose and virtues of technology; (3) examines the type, culture, and other facets of organizations; (4) focuses on various types and characteristics of workers and the kinds of work they do; and (5) asks you to look carefully at the major parts of your job.

Learning broadens an individual's base of knowledge. New knowledge can be used to make better decisions. For instance, you can't expect super performance from a bureaucratic structure that lacks mission statements, specific goals, or knowledge of its customer base.

The environment, organization, and technology play prime roles in our work and personal lives. Forces in the external environment, such as competition, have a major impact on the organization and the people in it. Technology, like computers and other electronic equipment, impacts more of our work and home life than ever before. Although a tool, technology can be a catalyst for creating a new direction and for increasing efficiency.

ENVIRONMENT

Environmental forces range from positive to negative. These forces affect the organization as a whole, but also affect how people think and act and how they do their work. Positive environmental forces, like a good geographic location or an excellent educational system, are major deciding factors in starting or relocating a business. Organizations mirror the constantly changing environment.

The organization itself and positive and negative external environmental factors affect how people think and perform. Biases *and* perception change how forces are interpreted and greatly affect personal and organizational reactions to these forces.

The internal environment includes strategic priorities, culture, knowledge base, and other factors. The external environment is affected by unpredictable factors, like competition, the economy, and availability of a work force.

Organizations are products of their dynamic, constantly changing environments. Not only does the outside environment affect what people do and how they react, but the environment within the organization also has a dramatic effect on people and the work process.

Work Environment

From the close-in view, the quality of the working environment has a profound impact on employee satisfaction. Feelings that people have about their jobs, colleagues, and where they work are indicators of internal quality. The study of how people perceive their work environment and how they are treated is referred to as quality of work life.

Environments differ along many other dimensions, including complexity, uncertainty, and presence of unpredictable elements. Emery and Trist describe four distinct types of environment that range from placid to turbulent.[7] In the last ten years in particular, external environments have been increasingly uncertain and unpredictable.

The continual need to adjust to a changing environment means that people, even CEOs, are replaced or move on. As markets change, new missions are created and goals expanded. Organizations, like people, grow and change. Organizations constantly strive to adjust to their environments in order to achieve and maintain a relatively steady state.

CEOs should understand and readily adapt to their organizations' constantly changing environment within a specific time frame. Otherwise, their organizations may not survive in their present form—or they may not survive at all. All change takes place at a price. In general, organizations need to be proactive and anticipate changes within themselves and in the environment.

It is often easier to change the organization than to change people. The rigid, established form and structure of organizations is evolving into a more flexible structure. This new structure supports creativity and innovation.

TECHNOLOGY

Technology is the science or study of the practical. Simply stated, technology refers to processes or methods that transform inputs into outputs. Technology is often viewed as a tool, one which possibly empowers people. Basically, technology covers an entire process, beginning with an idea and ending with a completed process or product. Processes, as part of a systems approach, are discussed in more detail in Chapter 8.

The concern over the impact of new technology dates back to the Scottish economist Adam Smith (1723–1790). Since the 1930s, technology has been the subject of empirical analysis or use of methods based on observation or experience alone. Starting in the early 1960s, a prime concern was the extent to which technology impacted organizational structure and patterns of work practices. When organizational structure changes, it changes the way people think and how they do their jobs.

Two of many interpretations of technology are as a change agent and as a competitive weapon. Even though computers have transformed the ways most work is done, whether resulting technologies have made work better or more enjoyable is strongly debated.

As a competitive weapon, literally, "he who has the best technology wins." "Winners" simply rotate positions with other "leaders," depending on their particular advantage at a specific time. To further complicate matters, perception and biases markedly affect choices of "winners."

The main uses of technology are.

1. Improve previous technologies, as in building on the cumulative ad-vances in the computer and biotechnology industries. This can be done by improving software.

2. As a source of new directions or uses growing out of technology itself, like spin-offs from space-age research. In this instance, technology is a guiding light.

3. Increase personal and organizational effectiveness and efficiency. Technology allows people to perform routine activities more quickly and should enable them to devote more time to important activities.

Technology fusion, or combining existing technologies in engineering and science disciplines, for example, creates new hybrids; these new technologies are greater than the sum of their separate parts.

Common ways to react to the impact of technology are to (1) accept the status quo or "anything goes," (2) reject without question, or (3) study the uses and misuses and accept what works best. The role technology plays is affected by numerous factors in the environment (e.g., availability of information, budgets, and competition from other technologies).

A prime issue in managing technology is making the best use of the rapidly expanding technologies in fields ranging from data processing to space exploration. Areas include (1) managing multimedia networking systems; (2) integrating computer networks; (3) capturing, adapting, and presenting information in usable, cost-effective formats; and (4) handling "information highways" which transmit information in education, health care, manufacturing, government, and other fields. These and similar superhighways may provide the foundation for the nation's transformation to an information- and knowledge-based society.

A vital issue is for managers to understand, appreciate, and become part of technological change. This change takes place slowly. Considerable money, effort, and (re)training are part of this long-term investment. Despite its size, shape, or cost, technology is mainly a tool. *People* are now the measure by which machines or tools are judged. During the Industrial Revolution, *machines* were the measure by which people were judged.

Effective use of technology is rapidly becoming the price of admission to modern business life. A valuable point to remember is that much of technology centers on systems, not people. The systems may even run the people!

Having a clear vision of cause and effect and of what is achievable and/or desirable enables companies to surge ahead and remain ahead of their competition. A company's capacity to absorb, adopt, and transfer technology is increasingly becoming the key to business strategy.[2]

ORGANIZATIONS

Organizations differ in origin, history, size, shape, purpose, ownership, and even age. Organizations are dynamic; they grow and change constantly. Processes, services, and products vary between organizations and within the same organization. Nevertheless, people still do about the same kinds of things at work the world over—plan, worry, compete, attend meetings, produce products or provide services…and usually get paid.

Usually is the correct term here. The number of tax-exempt organizations is growing. Their main mission and goals relate to philanthropy (community service, raising funds for any number of worthy endeavors). Their core employees are paid a salary. Volunteers who work just as hard (and in some cases harder than) the paid staff may not receive any pay.

An organization's core competencies do not last forever. Even highly successful and profitable organizations do not last indefinitely, unless they are in continuous learning, growing, change, and adapting modes.[31]

The organization is viewed as an open, sociotechnical system made up of a number of subsystems. Sociotechnical systems are a combination of people (socio) and technology (technical). Organizations transform inputs of energy, information, and materials from the environment into outputs, which are returned to the environment. The organization shapes and integrates human activities around various technologies. Typical subsystems of the organization include psychosocial, managerial, technical, structural, goals, and values.

People working in organizations anywhere in the world do about the same kinds of basic or "core" work (more about "core work" later). They process different raw materials or input and provide an array of services or products for their internal and external customers. All organizations run on people power.

The new organization may be a collection of project groups linked by video conference, voice mail, and E-mail. This new, gradually evolving form of organization, or "virtual" corporation, may not have a physical location. It may be easier to understand when displayed on a computer screen than in reality. In the future, organizations may have no boundaries, as barriers are removed from traditional functions like management and controlling.

Types of Organizations

The main types of organizations are (1) bureaucratic or classical, including the professional bureaucracy; (2) divisionalized or divided into smaller parts, (3) innovative, organic adhocracy, and matrix, M form, or network structures; and (4) the learning organization.

This section enables you to compare your organization with the type that you feel it should become. Knowing the facts is a form of power. When the "knowns" of any situation are clear, logical decisions be made about future actions.

An ingrained theme of this book is that large organizations must change their structure, focus, *and* the way they treat their work force if they are to survive into the next century. These "revolutionary" ideas are well documented in the literature.[20,23,26] Organizational design will be the basis of gaining competitive advantage in the global marketplace.[10]

Organizations are primarily service based or product based. These two types of bases are discussed in Chapters 7 and 8.

Bureaucratic or Classical

This form of organization has a hierarchy of authority, specific rules and regulations for work, standardized training, and division of work. An example is a mass-production organization with an operating core, highly specialized routine tasks, and very formal standardized procedures.

Typical professional bureaucracies are hospitals, universities, law firms, and the "Big Eight" accounting firms. Their environment is complex but relatively stable. These organizations have a large operating core of highly trained professionals and an extensive support staff. Professors, nurses, doctors, attorneys, engineers, and many others work in professional bureaucracies. Many bureaucratic structures are gradually being transformed into any number of different forms, some of which are discussed below.[23]

Divisionalized

Most of the largest, oldest corporations in the United States are in this group. Each division has its own structure. The relationship between headquarters and the divisions is close. Divisions may be created around customers (such as restaurant owners) or around product markets (like that for cellular phones). Market diversity is one of the main attributes of divisions within a larger organization. This form works best when the environment is not very complex and is relatively stable.

Innovative, Organic Adhocracy or Matrix, M-Form, and Learning Organizations

Although this open, dynamic form has many names, the basic structure and principles are similar. The structure and the environment are organic or dynamic. Communication channels are open. There is little standardization or formalization and few active management hierarchies. Team leaders coordinate line and staff relationships. Separate parts of the organization, or matrix groups, are loosely organized around high-risk, venture product teams. Team members are highly specialized professionals with specific knowledge and expertise, like scientists. Creativity and innovation are encouraged and supported.

An innovative organization is usually a totally new structure. It may also be one in which changes have been made in established methods or structure.

Adhocracies

Two major types of adhocracies are operating and administrative. The operating adhocracy consists of multi-disciplinary, innovative teams (like consulting firms), who solve clients' problems. The administrative adhocracy has a central operating core that is structured as a project-oriented group responsible for coordinating the activities of other groups.

Adhocracies have a bias for action, as they are hands-on, value-driven companies. Their simple form and lean staff foster autonomy and entrepreneurship. They focus on customers.

Matrix Groups

Matrix groups originated in the early 1960s. They met the unique needs of the aerospace program and related industries. There was growing pressure for these industries to share resources and to work together. There was an equal need for high information processing and communication capacities.

Matrix groups combine a group of product departments (e.g., combining departments manufacturing component parts for the space shuttle, and functional departments doing computer simulations). Each department has a manager, and each manager is a member of both a functional department and a project team. Each employee has two supervisors, a department manager and a project leader.

A production manager or project leader has the authority and responsibility to see that projects are completed. People from various departments are first assigned to a specific project for varying periods of time and then assigned on an as-needed basis. One or more representatives from each functional department may work together briefly on temporary assignments and then return to their own departments.

M-Form

This matrix structure is decentralized and has many divisions. Each business or business unit within the entire organization has its own operating division and is responsible for day-to-day operating decisions. The corporate office is responsible for financial control in all divisions and the overall strategic development of the organization. An analogy is that the organization is in a circular format rather than hierarchical. The circular format includes the corporate office in the core, with customers, suppliers, distributors, and franchisees in different, slightly large concentric circles.[20]

Learning Organization

This dynamic organization accepts and adjusts to constant change. The concept of systems theory is used in the learning organization. It has no particular form that can be drawn on an organizational chart. It many even be a state of mind. A learning organization achieves its goals through building problem-solving teams, empowering its staff to be innovative, counseling and coaching employees, and basing accomplishments on negotiating. The organization can capture learning in its different parts and transform this learning into the corporate knowledge base needed to create new capability.[11,26]

Basics of learning organizations include (1) the philosophy of continuous learning, (2) development of "teams at the top" that are in touch and in tune with everyone in the organization, and (3) senior management who exhibit leadership in the creation of an overall vision from which strategic plans can later be developed.

Organizations having many of the characteristics and attributes of learning organizations may be considered a form of learning organization. The focus must be on education, training, and development. In general, people in a learning organization share a common program and language or way of communicating.

To increase learning, it is necessary to shift to a systematic approach so that (1) the members work individually and as a team to expand their capacities to produce results and (2) the organization can transform itself to meet its strategic goals.

Learning organizations must also be teaching organizations. Those that are not a teaching organization cannot compete effectively.[1] Learning organizations modify their behavior and capabilities by acquiring and creating new knowledge and insight to achieve their purpose and increase the quality of relationships with customers, employees, stockholders, and others.

Building a learning organization takes considerable time and effort. Senge[26] and Garvin[11] describe and illustrate these processes. Briefly, focused efforts should include (1) business process analysis that defines how people interact and communicate; (2) standardization of processes associated with carrying out various functions, such as production and accounting, with the overall goal of identifying "best practices" that can be implemented in other parts of the organization (perhaps even in other organizations); and (3) continuous improvement through an array well-considered quality and productivity improvement efforts.

The main advantage of these innovative structures is that they can readily respond to internal and external pressures. There is no need to have duplicate functional departments. Communication is free and open. Solutions may emerge from any of the matrix-type groups due to the synergistic effect of working together. Synergy results from the diverse disciplines found in matrix groups, as well as from the energy each person brings to the job.

One possible disadvantage is that overhead increases as more managers and support personnel are needed during the start-up phase. Because of dual group membership, more time is spent coordinating, communicating, and simply meeting in groups. The same person may also work in more than one group. There may be power struggles and conflicts over leadership, as it is often difficult to trace accountability and authority.

Jack Welsh, General Electric's CEO, commented in GE's annual report, "Our dream for the 1990s is a boundaryless company...where we knock down the walls that separate us from each other on the inside and from our key constituencies on the outside." To do this, barriers would be removed from traditional functions, and labels like "management," "salaried," or "hourly," which normally get in the way, would be abolished.[14] As organizations become more flexible, the remaining boundaries are in the minds of managers and employees.

An organization's core capabilities do not last forever. Even a clearly defined set of goals, high profits, and a seemingly endless stream of customers are no guarantee that things will always be the same. To remain highly successful and profitable, organizations must be in continuous learning, growing, changing, and adapting modes. Pluses can turn into minuses and assets into liabilities unless an organization constantly tests and reshapes itself.

Divisions of Work

Within the organization, work is divided according to function, product division, customer, marketing channel, and territory.

1. **Functions** include business or related activities that are logically grouped together, like marketing and product development. Each division performs very specific types of activities. Managerial functions are based on activities commonly performed, namely supervise, plan, organize, mentor, direct, staff, lead, plan, and many others. Technological functions may be grouped together and include data processing, communication, and research and development.

   The major purposes of functions are to systematically summarize current knowledge, search for new knowledge, and teach this information to members of the organization. A second role is to develop guidelines, or best practices, for individual functions, like engineering or purchasing, and determine who their customers and partners should be. Ideally, when employees learn a given set of functions, like managing and leading, they carry these skills to other areas, such as quality assurance and customer service.[30]

2. Each **product division** has a manager, as in production divisions in automobile manufacturing. Although top management has less control over daily activities, performance of each division is easy to compare with other similar or parallel divisions.

3. Separate divisions may be designed around needs of **customer** (General Electric's appliance division, for example). Managers are responsible for working directly with customers' unique needs. Customer satisfaction is a prime concern.

4. Each department in a **market channel** advertises and sells the same product to many different types of customers. One example is selling the same computer to wholesalers, department stores, and mail-order houses.

5. The emphasis may be on a specific **territory** or in a certain part of the country. The focus may be at the point of sale in order to give customers special attention and speed up the transaction.

Organizational type and division of work have a strong impact on how work is done, how quickly it is done, and how well it is done.

WAYS TO COMPARE ORGANIZATIONS

The following six areas introduced in Chapter 3 are presented and discussed here in the same order.

1. The *what* can be the vision or the picture of the future we want to create. People and organizations alike must have a vision. Visioning is an ever-evolving process, a continual pursuit of the elusive ideal. *What* and *why* are closely related, as both are included in vision, mission, and goals statements.

Products or services provided to internal and external customers, partners, and suppliers are also the *what*. In reality, everyone in the organization both *supplies* something and *needs* something. Everyone in the organization is a customer of and a supplier to others in the organization.

2. The location, including geographic and regional differences, or the *where*. There are virtually no geographic boundaries in the workplace due to telecommuting, working at home, and rapid, accurate ways to electronically transfer all types of information from one location to another. Work can be done by a very diverse work force, anywhere at any time. Outsourcing as a growing trend further diminishes geographical boundaries.

3. The employees, or the *who*. In the year 2000, the labor market will have more two-career families, lower skill levels, more women, greater racial and ethnic mix, and a growing number of middle-aged individuals. Most will require some form of job training.

What makes or breaks an organization is not its technology or its environment, but its human resources. People of all disciplines, descriptions, capabilities, interests, and talents are the life blood of any organization. An increasing number of CEOs and chief financial officers are finding this out.

The number of associates, partners, and "owners" is growing rapidly. In 1974, Congress enacted the first of a series of tax measures designed to encourage employee stock ownership plans. The number of employees owning stock is now in the tens of millions. An increasing number of employees own part of the business, as at J.C. Penney's and United Airlines. In some instances, employees own more than half of the company.

Gainsharing, or group incentive plans which enable employees to share in the financial benefits that result from increased productivity, are also expanding. One example of an organization with a gainsharing plan is Northern Telecom.[3]

4. Processes, or the *how* of doing business, include the mechanics of getting work done and all support processes, such as communication and monitoring. More and more companies are developing partnerships with their suppliers. Another form of a working relationship is to combine work forces, often to reduce costs. Suppliers often provide ideas for new products or suggest ways to streamline effort and cut costs all the way around. Human creativity and technological innovations are major factors affecting how work is done.

5. The vision, mission statement, goals, objectives, and strategic plans, or the *why*.   Briefly, this is a statement of why the organization exists. Few employees know the mission statements of their organizations. This is partly because many organizations do not have mission statements that can be written down or communicated in simple terms. Most mission statements capture the essence of the organization's goals, objectives, and strategies by stating expectations for customer service. Other areas of concern cover growth, improvement, financial performance, communication, respect for people, teamwork, and environments that foster the growth of, development of, and harmony among employees.

6. Marketing strategies used for every phase of the flow of activities in the design...production cycle, or the *when*.   If sales and marketing people really knew the best answers to *when* and *how,* their organizations would be overwhelmingly successful. In any field, good timing is one of the major keys to success.

Organizations that survive and function effectively in competitive, often turbulent external environments have a built-in ability to make rapid changes and remain focused while reconfiguring to meet the change required by the external environment. Reducing and/or minimizing distress and disruption in the workplace is the main way some organizations survive.

Culture, Systems, Structure, Strategy, and Control

The concepts of culture, systems, structure, strategy, and control form the base of organizations and help define them. However, all five change and evolve just as people and organizations do.

Culture

The concept of organizational "culture" is of recent origin. This broad concept evolved mainly through the disciplines of social psychology, industrial psychology, organizational psychology, sociology, anthropology, and organizational development.

One definition of culture is "...what a group learns over a period of time as that group solves its problems of survival in an external environment and its problems of internal integration."[25] This learning combines behavioral, cognitive, and emotional processes.

Organizational culture consists of:

1. Observable artifacts, which run the gamut from physical layout to dress code, to symbols and slogans, to emotional intensity, to annual reports.

2. Values, norms, work atmosphere, and assumptions, or "the way work is done" or "how to treat customers." Although most values are acquired and reinforced in childhood, conforming to work norms often comes with experience and learning to work with people. The internal workings or the mechanics of the organization, as well as the type and structure of the organization, affect its culture.

   Some companies have problems translating cultural values at the organizational level into behavior at the individual level. Companies like AT&T, IBM, and Motorola have strong, established cultures that can respond quickly to both positive and negative environmental forces.

   General Electric, founded in 1892, is considered a teacher to companies around the world. 3M still sets the pace for business innovation and product development. Disney, Microsoft, Johnson & Johnson, and Nordstrom have strong values and are visionary in their practices.[28]

   In turbulent economic environments, companies use their shared values, experience, and firm, established leadership to make necessary adjustments in order to successfully weather the storm of uncertainty.

3. Take-it-for-granted unconscious assumptions determine perceptions, feelings, thought processes, and behavior. Assumptions can range from how expense accounts are handled to copying the leadership style of the CEO.

4. Coping with problems of adapting to the external environment and integrating the various systems within the organization is a balancing act. However, there are usually realistic compromises that can be used to produce a workable solution.[25]

The type of culture in an organization is like a person's special way of thinking and responding. Culture affects how information flows. To change an organization's information culture means altering basic behaviors, attitudes, values, management expectations, and incentives that relate to information. Attempts to change the technology that delivers the information only reinforces existing behaviors.

Companies with strong cultures, like those mentioned above, as opposed to companies with no definite culture, are better able to survive the storms encountered in a turbulent environment.

Systems

An organization is a system of inputs, throughputs or processes, and outputs. Systems are one way to represent a sequence of activities or develop a framework that ties separate parts of the organization together. When separate parts are combined, a comprehensive whole results. All systems require input from people in the form of effort, information, and material resources (capital, raw materials). All parts of the system are interdependent. Change in one area produces change in another. Systems approaches are discussed in Chapter 8.

The organization is influenced by informal and formal structure. Informal structure consists of unwritten, unspecified activities, like "how we do things." Formal structure is often represented by charts or diagrams which show how various parts of the organization relate to one another. For instance, communication channels are often set out by the formal structure or by rules.

Structure

Organizational structure can be compared with the beams and cross-members that support a building, the bare floors, and the walls. Everything is static. Structure gives strength, stability, and predictability to the organization. Until people move in, the organization is just a diagram or organizational chart on a piece of paper.

Formal structure sets out how the various parts of the organizational system communicate with and relate to one another. Formal structure spells out authority and responsibility relationships, as well as span of control, use of rules, control systems, and even the number of hierarchical levels in the organization.

Constraints inside the organization, such as policies and procedures set out in an organization's formal structure, provide stability and direction. When people enter the organization, the formal structure changes to an informal structure. Communication does not necessarily flow upward, and reporting relationships so carefully laid out on the organizational chart do not necessarily work.

External constraints that affect the structure can be positive (increased customer demand) or negative (more foreign competition).

Structure must be designed in a way that supports the company's central purpose, core values, vision, mission, and purpose. To illustrate, NovaCare, Inc., one of U.S.'s largest providers of rehabilitation services to nursing homes and hospitals, oriented its ethics efforts toward building a common core of shared aspirations to meet the rehabilitation needs of patients through clinical leadership. NovaCare's four key beliefs are respect for the individual, service to the customer, pursuit of excellence, and commitment to personal integrity.[21]

Radical changes in formal organizational structure are predicted to occur before the year 2000.[13,20] These new structures will have the customer at the top of the organization and management at the bottom. Customers and clients will be the ultimate judges of success. Organizations are moving toward the M-form, or decentralized, multi-divisional structures. These structures will have semi-autonomous operating divisions, each of which is responsible for day-to-day operations.[22] Organizations of the future will have an employee focus designed to recognize and meet the needs of the work force.

Strategy

Strategy is difficult at best to define. It is not a constant but rather evolves. Strategy takes the form of long-range planning, development, and setting priorities. Major variables affecting strategy are mission and goals, type of process, services, products, location, customers, and external environmental forces.

Unless everyone understands the direction in which the organization is going, it is impossible to manage anything, let alone productivity and quality in their broadest sense.[6] Some people are never told in what direction they are going; others never ask. This is where good two-day communication comes in.

Control

Restraining forces and positive forces need to be controlled. Conflict due to opposing forces often reduces the efficiency and effectiveness of people and the systems in which they operate.

However, no organization could exist without fiscal control. It is much easier to make financial comparisons between and within organizations than it is to assess the value of human resources or other intangible assets, like customer goodwill. Financial data are usually readily available in the form of assets, operating expenses, net sales, accounts receivable, inventories, earnings per share, long-term debt, and many other types of information.

Other forms of control are management, or activities related to monitoring and providing feedback on all phases of the activities and accomplishments related to performance appraisals.

There are numerous rules in organizations regarding relationships between employees, guidelines for safety, sick leave, etc. One caution is that getting too caught up with the rules, procedures, or other strategies can reduce effectiveness and certainly detract from achieving and maintaining a competitive advantage.

Pressure to adhere to ethical standards, like using personal and organizational integrity as governing ethics, is also a form of control. Areas contributing to integrity include company history, types of business units, industry regulations, and management personality in particular.[21]

A strong, well-established organizational culture is also a form of control, as employees know what is expected and accepted as standard behavior.

Examining Forces in the Organization

Our focus starts with broad areas, and then moves to you and your job. You will get a broad perspective of where your job and the jobs of your associates fit into the organizational scheme of things

The environment inside and outside the organization affects what people plan to do and what they actually get done. One way to view these forces is force field analysis.[15-18] Lewin, a psychologist and a pioneer in the area of group dynamics, used terms from physics and mathematics.

This field of forces is the foundation for what later became known as field theory. Lewin applied the concept of field of positive and negative forces to human behavior. He believed each person exists in a psychological field of forces, or life space, that determine and limit his or her behavior. A person's life space consists of conscious and unconscious goals, fears, dreams, hopes, past experience, and future expectations. Life space represents the world as a person sees it, which is not necessarily as it really is or as others see it. The physical world of work, social conditions at work and at home, and a person's current situation at work affect thought and behavior.

Dynamic equilibrium and reciprocality of movement form the major part of field theory. Reciprocality of movement means that any change in the psychology field produces some change in a person's behavior and vice versa.

Driving Forces, Restraining Forces, and Equilibrium

In general, people, organizations, and even nature seek a steady state, or equilibrium. Various parts of any system of any size are pretty much in balance most of the time. However, when one part changes, it causes another part to change, perhaps in an unpredictable way. Systems that get out of balance are not as strong or as predictable as they are when they are in balance.

Various forces from outside and from inside the organization affect people and organizations. Two opposing forces direct behavior away from the status quo: driving forces and restraining forces. All driving forces are not necessarily positive, just as all restraining forces are not exactly negative. Driving forces move things along in a direction. Restraining forces push against the driving forces and can hinder progress toward a stated or desired goal.

Driving forces direct behavior away from a steady state. A prime driving force is the need to get work done or being a good team leader. Cycle time (or how long it takes to do a specific task) is a driving force in many assembly-line operations. Subtle but very real driving forces are vision, mission, and goals statements. Attitudes, beliefs, and values also fuel driving forces and propel them forward.

Restraining forces hinder movement toward a desired goal or state of rest. These negative forces may keep the system out of balance by preventing it from reaching equilibrium or achieving a constant, steady state.

A major restraining force could be anything that keeps you from getting your job done properly. Poor scheduling makes people late; defective parts lower the quality of a product being assembled. Biases (discussed in Chapter 3) are but one of many variables affecting how people think, express themselves, and act.

The strength of driving and restraining forces changes constantly. Driving forces behind quality have increased dramatically in the past few years, but restraining forces due to downsizing have also increased.

Some questions arise:

1. What driving and restraining forces do you have at work?

2. Do either of these forces involve people, processes, or things like equipment or hardware?

3. What can you do?

The following steps can be taken to identify and reduce the disruptive influence of forces inside and outside the organization:

1. Decide what forces affect you and your job the most. There may be two different sets of factors, or some of the factors may be the same for both you and your job.

2. Decide what forces you can and cannot control. Consider forces both inside and outside the organization.

3. Ask others around you, perhaps those in your work group or team members, what forces they can and cannot control.

4. Compare notes. Exchanging information and discussing common problems and how to solve them often leads to new ideas and inventive, cost-effective ways to deal with problems.

5. Do something. Even the smallest step in the direction of solving a problem, or changing something that has been bothering you for a long time, does make a difference. It is often the small things at work that are most frustrating. Simply taking action conveys to others that you want to change things and make them better. Others will follow suit.

You really can do something. Nohria and Berkley's[19] article entitled "Whatever Happened to the Take-Charge Manager?" is refreshing. It looks at what can be done if people have confidence in themselves instead of following the fad bandwagon. "Flavor of the month" managing is gone. Being a pragmatist and making do with what you know is back in vogue.

5.1

In the space provided below, list the driving and restraining forces inside and outside the organization. Do not indicate how they affect you or your job. That will be covered in Question 5.2.

	Inside the Organization		Outside the Organization	
	Driving (+)	Restraining (−)	Driving (+)	Restraining (−)
Can do something about (Self)				
Can do something about (Job)				
Cannot do anything about (Self)				
Cannot do anything about (Job)				

You will now get a feel for the range and type of forces inside and outside your organization. When you have determined which ones you can do something about and which ones you can do little or nothing about, you can consider what your next steps will be. If you are one of those rare people who "take charge," you may not have written down anything in the lowest block.

Look carefully at what you can do something about. Most aspects probably relate to your own abilities and skills. Some areas, however, will relate to communication. Reportedly, 95 percent or more of our problems stem from poor communication, like misreading directions or not paying attention.

To maximize your efforts you can:

1. Reduce the restraining or negative forces. Typical negative forces may be restrictions, like deadlines, monetary limitations, or not having enough information to complete your report. Negative forces can also be imagined, like fear of failure. We can always think up reasons for not wanting to do something or for not doing something to the best of our ability.

Covey[5] suggests spending about two-thirds of our energy on reducing the restraining forces and one-third on increasing the driving forces. Because each situation is different, you will need to study the nature of the restraining forces and work on them. When external driving forces are synchronized with the internal motivation of people who work together, a synergistic problem-solving team results.

2. Increase the driving or positive forces. Most managers have direct control over the driving forces and know how to increase them, as in pushing for more sales or increasing marketing efforts. Increasing the driving forces can also increase restraining forces. This approach is used most often, even though it is the least effective.[5] For example, people who work overtime to meet a supervisor's imposed deadline may resist by working slower. Increased tension and frustration as the result of working longer hours can reduce morale and cost more money in the long run.

3. Increase the driving forces while reducing the restraining forces. This may be a compromise, but giving in a little on both sides of the issue provides leeway. However, if you remove or reduce the restraining or negative forces, such as those associated with meeting deadlines, the result may be substandard quality, in which case your customers will be upset.

Negotiating is a possibility. This means taking time to set out the positive and negative issues and learning more about each. Often, better solutions are reached through negotiating and sharing information than through a single-minded, inflexible approach. Ideally, win–win negotiations allow everyone to "win" in some area. The art and science of negotiating is used to resolve conflict not just in politics and in the legal system, but in the world of everyday business. The overall results are positive.[8]

If you feel you cannot do anything about some of the forces inside or outside the organization, discuss this with a peer, supervisor, or someone who may be able to see things differently. If you have problems in one area, chances are that someone else will have the same or similar problems. Together, you may be able to work out a solution. There is power in numbers.

The balance between increasing the driving forces and reducing the restraining forces is delicate. Alternating between the two methods to see what works best is a possibility. Because of wide individual differences in employees, what works one time may not work another time. The point is to examine driving and restraining forces critically and use a flexible approach based on individual and organizational needs.

Changing or even attempting to slightly modify behavior is a major challenge. The greatest gains and reward in our own personal accomplishments often come from our peers.

Increasing awareness of restraining and driving forces and how they affect you and your job enables you to have a fresh look at those around you and at your department...organization. At the organizational level, there are many restraining and driving forces, and each interacts with the others. Just determining some of the major driving and restraining forces will be helpful. For instance, the structure and communication channels in your department may inhibit the formation of teams. Supervisors may restrict or even resist new ideas. Don't bat your head against a brick wall. If you can't achieve something one way, perhaps you can another way. This is what creativity and innovation are all about.

If steps in the solution are not obvious, start with what you want to accept as the solution and work backwards until you have the second last step, the third last step...and then the first step. Coates[4] provides an example of a reverse scenario method for identifying problems and presents steps necessary to develop realistic solutions.

When you use reverse scenario building, you work backwards, one small step at a time, until you get to the beginning point. When you reverse the process and move forward, also one step at a time, you reach your goal. In this way, you will have gone full circuit through the entire process.

This mental exercise enables you to solve problems on paper and to do any number of trial runs or scenarios. Using this process several times will likely produce a better, more comprehensive answer than just thinking about the steps in the problem-solving process. Use of scenarios in setting up problems and in developing realistic alternatives is described in detail by Wack.[4,29,30]

The flexibility in thinking required by this backwards–forward approach increases the number of options considered and helps establish a thinking and leadership style that allows problems to be anticipated.

You may want to rethink this whole process by taking it one step closer to home and looking inside yourself. We all put some type of restraining forces on ourselves. Some forces limit what we think and what we do at home and at work.

5.2

Refer back to Question 5.1. Do any of the major restraining forces inside your organization affect your job? Do they affect you personally? If so, list the forces and what you plan to do to reduce the restraining forces or increase the driving forces.

The following are some guidelines for your answers. Some categories may overlap. What some consider to be restraining forces may be driving forces to others. It is often a matter of perception.

The personal restraining forces relate to job skills that can be remedied with training. Some forces may be due to interpersonal conflict or low self-confidence. We are our own best salespersons, but many of us sell ourselves short.

Shouldering the burden of added responsibility which accompanies a more demanding job does increase the number of driving and restraining forces.

FUTURE DIRECTIONS

Where are we going? How fast are we going? Do you want to go? Joint ventures, cross-functional alliances, and globalization necessitate knowing something about organizational culture, both locally and abroad. The growing number of joint ventures and cooperative efforts requires contracted relationships and strategic alliances.[9] We no longer need to conduct business face-to-face. Through electronic communication, we can buy, sell, order, even build products and provide services anywhere in the world.

One alliance which is larger than some of the largest countries is the (European) Economic Community. Originally designed to be functional by the end of 1992, a number of concerns have resulted in delays and changes in direction. In any event, this alliance consists of twelve nations and a population of over 320 million people. Effective January 1, 1995, Finland, Sweden, and Austria joined, bringing the total to fifteen nations. To function successfully as a person, group, or an organization, it is necessary to have an appreciation for cultural, ethnic, geographic, political, language, and economic differences.

For the past ten years, there have been rumblings that the traditional organization should be turned upside down. Customers would be at the top, and the CEO would be at the bottom. An increasing number of corporations and institutions are adopting mottoes and slogans about " putting customers first" or "customers are number one." Customers and front-line workers deserve their place at the top of the organization. Without them, everyone else would be looking for other employment.[24]

The purported growth of empowerment, or passing down of authority, responsibility, or power to subordinates, will further change the shape and structure of organizations. The concepts basic to empowerment are more readily accepted than the application. Empowerment is not easy to implement, as it takes a blend of risk, open-mindedness, and patience. People cannot be empowered quickly, as they must learn what they can and cannot do. Groups may have "team leaders" instead of managers. Cross functional groups in particular provide wide expertise and diverse experience.

The empowered work force uses a common set of principles to relate to customers. These principles include: (1) belief about the marketplace; (2) core competencies in general (their own, those of their peers...the organization); (3) measures of success, such as customer satisfaction and shareholder value; (4) operating the organization, specifically type of organization, theory of business, etc.; (5) thinking and acting with a sense of urgency; (5) deep-seated belief in people; and (6) sensitivity to the needs of employees and to those to whom they relate on a daily basis.[12]

The most difficult thing to change in organizations as we know them today is shared values, or the guiding content and fundamental ideas around which a company is built. Shared values are part of the organization's culture.

SUMMARY AND CONCLUSIONS

1. Bureaucracies may be unable to compete, as today's challenges are too great for such an inflexible structure. Pinchot and Pinchot[23] believe that only self-organizing systems, such as free markets, self-rule, and an effective community, will be able to successfully meet the challenges of today and tomorrow.

2. Thoughts and actions should not be limited to traditional roles people play in the organization. The boundaryless company will have leaders whose vision and goals are limitless.

3. Shared values are one of the strong driving forces in business.[12,28] When people share a vision, they share values. Organizations of the future will have to be sensitive to the diverse needs of their employees.

4. Our desire to achieve, to learn, and to grow must not be confined to the organization as we see it, but must fit in with what we want the organization to become.

5. Selection of technology must be based on (1) our own needs and competencies, (2) cost and availability, and (3) the job we are currently performing. It is our responsibility to get the best possible match of our abilities, our job, and accessible, affordable technology. We must be wary of the possibility that technology can do two things: (1) be coercive and (2) propel people to greater heights.

6. Bureaucratic structures may be on the decrease.[23] Bureaucracies are highly centralized. Nordstrom, the Seattle-based department store, is just the opposite of a centralized bureaucracy. At Nordstrom, the entire employee handbook is written on one five-by-eight in card.

7. There is a growing emphasis on the "bottom line," as organizations regroup, reorganize, and even downsize in order to successfully face competition. There needs to be a balance between excessive cost cutting, short-term thinking, and the ability to attract, train, and retain a loyal, dedicated work force. What really makes or breaks an organization is its human resources. A trained, motivated work force is the greatest asset an organization can possess.

PRACTICAL APPLICATIONS

1. Existing learning organizations, or those that are evolving, offer a great deal of promise. Their flexible structure allows people more freedom to do their work. Learning organizations will revolve around cooperation, collaboration, open communication, encouragement, and support of creativity and innovation.[3]

2. The overall role of managers must be redefined. They will need to shift their current efforts to control subordinates' behavior to facilitating and development-based activities. These same leaders must commit to and learn the skills required to facilitate problem solving, defuse defensive routines, and demonstrate good listening and speaking skills.

   The commitment to continuous learning should hone in on both processes *and* results. All learning should support the mission and goals of the organization.

   Garvin[11] suggests setting forth an organization's learning objectives for the year. Learning objectives would be based on strategic needs and would complement the business plan. Sample areas include target experiments to obtain specific information or results, alliances to gain information, and rotation of personnel to maximize learning.

3. The concept of equilibrium and of driving and restraining forces places a different perspective on how people view themselves, their jobs, and the world around them. Constantly changing forces, like competition and customer demand, surround us wherever we are and whatever we do. Forces can change unpredictably. Separating the constant forces from the cyclic or unpredictable forces makes it easier to anticipate, but not necessarily control, our immediate environment.

4. Although the size, culture, systems, structure, strategy, and control mechanisms may differ among organizations, people are bright and creative enough to develop innovative ways to do their jobs.

5. Employers have expectations about their employees. Similarly, employees have expectations about their company. From a mechanical standpoint, people want to be part of an efficient, well-oiled machine that has a destination in mind a good road map for how to get there.[27]

In general, those who work in organizations:

■ Want the opportunity and authority to take more initiative and responsibility at work. They also want to be appropriately rewarded and recognized.

■ Place a high priority on job content and activities that truly reflect their talents.

■ Want an opportunity for input regarding their future, which means being associated with and part of the organization's vision and mission.

■ Want to be given a chance to be loyal, to make a commitment, and simply believe in their organization and in themselves.

REFERENCES

1. Avishai, Bernard. "Educating the Workforce of the Future," *Harvard Business Review*, March–April 1994, pp. 50–51.

2. Branscomb, Lewis M. "Does America Need a Technology Policy?" *Harvard Business Review*, March–April 1992, pp. 24–28, 30–32.

3. Chew, W. Bruce. "No-Nonsense Guide to Measure Productivity," *Harvard Business Review*, January–February 1988, pp. 110–111, 114–116, 118.

4. Coates, E. James. "Productivity Managers: A Worst-Case Scenario," *Industrial Management*, May/June 1987, pp. 24–25.

5. Covey, Steven R. "Involving People in the Problem," *Journal of Quality and Participation*, September 1994, pp. 68–71.

6. Crosby, Philip B. "Getting from Here to There, 21st Century Leadership," *Quality and Participation*, July/August 1992, pp. 24–27.

7. Emery, Fred. "Participative Design: Effective, Flexible, and Successful, Now!" *Journal for Quality and Participation*, January/February 1995, pp. 6–9.

8. Fisher, Roger and Ury, William. *Getting to Yes* Boston: Houghton Mifflin, 1992.

9. Galbraith, J. R. and Kazanijian, R. K. "Strategy, Technology, and Emerging Organizations," in *Futures of Organizations*, J. Hage (Ed.), Lexington, Mass · Lexington Books, pp. 29–41, 1987.

10. Galbraith, J. R., Lawler, Edward E. III, and associates. *Organizing for the Future*, San Francisco, Jossey-Bass, 1993.

11. Garvin, David A. "Building a Learning Organization," *Harvard Business Review*, July–August 1993, pp. 78–91.

12. Gault, Robert F. "Large Companies, Are You Listening?" *Management Review*, September 1994, pp. 42–44.

13. Handy, Charles. *The Age of Unreason*, Boston, Harvard Business School Press, 1989.

14. Hirschorn, Larry and Gilmore, Thomas. "The New Boundaries of the 'Boundaryless' Company," *Harvard Business Review*, May–June 1992, pp. 104–115.

15. Lewin, K. *Principles of Topological Psychology,* trans. by F. Heider and G. M. Heider, New York: McGraw-Hill, 1936.

16. Lewin, K. "Defining the 'Field at a Given Time,'" *Psychological Review*, 1943, pp. 288–290, 292–310.

17. Lewin, K. "Frontiers in Group Dynamics," *Human Relations*, Vol. 1, 1947.

18. Lewin, K. in *Field Theory in Social Science: Selected Theoretical Papers,* D. Cartwright (Ed.), New York: Harper, 1951.

19. Nohria, N. and Berkley, J. D. "Whatever Happened to the Take-Charge Managers?" *Harvard Business Review*, January–February 1994, pp. 128–137.

20. Offerman, Lynn R. and Gowing, Marilyn K. "Organizations of the Future," *American Psychologist*, February 1990, pp. 95–108.

21. Paine, Lynn Sharp. "Managing for Organizational Integrity," *Harvard Business Review*, March–April 1994, pp. 106–117.

22. Peters, T. J. "Restoring American Competitiveness: Looking for New Models of Organizations," *Academy of Management Executive*, Vol. 2, 1988, pp. 103–109.

23. Pinchot, Gifford and Pinchot, Elizabeth. *The End of Bureaucracy & the Rise of the Intelligent Organization*, San Francisco: Berrett-Koehler, 1993.

24. Richards, Phillip. "Right-Side-Up Organization," *Quality Progress*, October 1991, pp. 95–96.

25. Schein, Edgar H."Organizational Culture," *American Psychologist*, February 1990, pp. 109–119.

26. Senge, Peter M. *The Fifth Discipline*, New York: Doubleday/Currency, 1990.

27. Senge, Peter M. "The Leader's New Work: Building Learning Organizations," in *New Traditions in Business*, John Renesch (Ed.), San Francisco: Berrett-Koehler, 1992, pp. 80–93.

28. Taylor, William C. "Control in an Age of Chaos," *Harvard Business Review*, November–December 1994, pp. 64–66, 68, 70–76.

29. Wack, Pierre. "Scenarios: Uncharted Waters Ahead," *Harvard Business Review*, September–October 1985, pp. 72–89.

30. Wack, Pierre. "Scenarios: Shooting the Rapids," *Harvard Business Review*, November–December 1985, pp. 139–150.

31. Womack, James P. and Jones, Daniel T. "From Lean Production to Lean Enterprise," *Harvard Business Review*, March–April 1994, pp. 93–103.

PERSONAL AND ORGANIZATIONAL PRODUCTIVITY

PURPOSE

- Compare similarities and differences of product-based and service-based industries

- Evaluate descriptions and definitions of work-related factors directly related to productivity

- Consider and evaluate definitions of productivity in product-based and service-based organizations

- Assess personal productivity

INTRODUCTION

"How well we all work together" is a simple, basic way to define productivity. Getting people to work together in the first place, and having them do it "well," is a universal, timeless problem. When people work well together, the assumption is that the match between what people do and their talents is close and the work environment supportive.

Despite the large number of rapidly changing variables within and outside the organization, several major concepts are critical to personal and organizational success. These basic concepts have been mentioned previously, but they set the tone for this chapter.

Chapter 5 considered the organization from many perspectives. The organizational culture includes the core values or the strong beliefs central to your organization.

These values relate to personal, professional, economic, even political beliefs. Values, like myths, legends, and stories, are often transmitted by company culture. Core values may differ between organizations. One organization's core values may relate to providing superior customer service. Another organization may emphasize maintaining high quality standards and putting people first.

If people are to be productive, there must be strong, goal-directed, visionary leadership that endorses and actively supports the daily efforts of its employees. Positive change efforts must also be supported.

Organizations that recognize and reward intelligent risk taking enable their workers to be creative and develop innovative new services and products.

A trained and properly empowered work force can "do the right thing" with little intervention from supervisors. When people know how their job fits into the overall scheme of organizational activities, they will know how to change their jobs, and make them better. This point echoes the theme of this manual.

In this chapter, (1) service-based and product-based organizations are compared along various dimensions and (2) numeric and descriptive terms and examples clarify meanings of concepts related to personal and organizational work activities and results, or productivity.

PRODUCT-BASED AND SERVICE-BASED ORGANIZATIONS

Over 70 percent of the U.S. gross national product is in the service sector. This percentage edges up a little each year. Increasingly, the United States is becoming a supplier and user of services. Growth of service industries currently exceeds that of product-based industries.

Criteria for service-based industries are difficult to develop, as they depend on people. People, as we know, are not necessarily rational or predictable. The amount of direct customer contact varies. It is high in fast food, but low in mail order. The following descriptions of each industry put things in perspective.

Some organizations provide services and/or products in the same physical unit, such as computers and software support services in the form of toll-free customer assistance. The health care industry is both product based (hospital beds...prescriptions) and people based (physicians...X-ray technicians).

The following section describes and illustrates major dimensions in product-based and service-based industries.

Work in Product-Based and Service-Based Industries

In general, most operations in product- or manufacturing-based industries are easier to observe, understand, document, and measure than those in service industries. Input and output are usually tangible, like food, chemicals, road equipment…buildings. In service areas, intangibles include illusive concepts like customer good will and "opportunity."

Your profession, experience, training, and current job have a bearing on what you do and how well you do it. Your job may be primarily in service-based or product-based areas, or in both. You will define your job according to what you do. If you are a financial analyst or accountant, you will emphasize profit. If you are a team leader of a research group, you will want a highly motivated, creative, efficient work teams. If you are an engineer, your concerns will be efficiency and cost. Happily, if you are an entrepreneur, your major focus could be anything, but you will thrive on innovation.

Customers may work in your office or around the world. A clear idea of who your customers are, what they expect, and what they need adds to a steadily increasing base of useful information. Our internal customers may share our office or be reached through satellite communication 10,000 miles away. Our external customers may stand in front of a cash register or help us design a new product they need.

Product-Based Industries

A product is a transformation of energy and matter into a presumably desirable form, at desirable locations, and at an appropriate time.[19] Products or goods are usually classed as tangible outputs, or results of some activity, as in manufacturing or materials processing. Products are tangible and can be readily observed, and their attributes and deficiencies measured and recorded.

Considerable effort goes into all forms of monitoring and quality control. For example, when sheet metal passes through various processes that change it into finished products, it is examined for possible flaws or defects, and deviations are noted. Measurements, quality standards, cycle time, and other precise, well-documented parameters are used to determine if the completed products meet the required standards for quality.

Those working in product-based industries concentrate on areas like number of units produced, cycle time, maintenance cost, process flow, error rate, and number of rejects.

Service-Based Industries

Services are all those economic activities in which the primary goal is neither a product nor a construction,[18] as in health care. In general, service businesses are equipment based and people based, although there are some crossover areas, like software packages when you buy a computer.

A service is an intangible performance that is interpreted in different ways by various customers. Quality of services is judged by speed, courtesy, and competence of service performance. When quality of service is judged, ratings of tangible aspects are less important than the intangible aspects.[27]

In the service-based areas, results can be more subjective than objective. Service industries are people intensive and have a strong customer orientation. Many factors affect how customers define "service" and whether they are pleased with services provided. L.L. Bean's customer service is often benchmarked.

Service frequently takes place while the customer is present. Services are very diverse, or heterogeneous. It is difficult to monitor or control consistency in performance. The unpredictable nature of many services is due to uncontrolled interactions between the provider and receiver of services. Examples are job interviews, eye examinations, or service in a restaurant.

Some businesses, like insurance, deal with third-party agents who are at least one step removed from the customer. Disconnects can and do occur in the provision of third-party and contract services.

Typical service-based industries are banking, legal, and travel, among others. There is a great deal of opportunity for companies that want to excel in what are often "customer-unfriendly" areas by making them "hassle free." Most problems relate to the provision of services, as in automotive repair and home maintenance.

Criteria for judging service-based industries are difficult to develop. Many services are still judged using basic standards developed for products. However, services are people intensive and are assessed with standards that define and measure people's numerous activities, often with the customer.

People in service-based areas concentrate on number of customer contacts, customer satisfaction, range of services provided, and introducing new customer services. Some may be preoccupied with quality in general.

Service areas employ the gamut of people, ranging from unskilled laborers to high-level professionals. Types of services range from heavily automated car washes with low labor content to service businesses with high professional labor content, like management consulting firms. The health care industry is both people centered and product based. Price, delivery, and quality considerations are weighed against pressures to provide better health service for less cost.

Major ways service and product industries differ are as follow:[23]

1. Service industries usually have a higher labor cost relative to total value of output than product-based businesses. These industries are people intensive and often provide perishable commodities, like food.

2. In the service areas, since output is basically intangible, measurement is difficult. In the health care industry, the quality of patient care is interpreted in various ways, depending on the customer's specific needs.

3. Service-based industries have no capacity to store their services. An airplane in flight cannot store or reuse vacant seats. Empty seats are a perishable commodity. Yesterday's empty airplane seats are financial losses. The airline industry may have to adjust to lower utilization until satisfactory ways can be found to influence customer demand patterns.

4. Services have to be provided where the customers will go, like restaurants. However, mail-order houses can locate almost anywhere.

5. To serve customers, workers become a major part of the entire service operation rather than merely an economic resource to be employed.

Product-Based vs. Service-Based Organizations

What is being done to improve the quality of service? Customer surveys, questionnaires, direct interviews, and numerous other efforts try to capture what the customer really thinks and wants. Successful companies have strong feelings about how to treat customers. Most agree that "the customer is king."

Table 6.1 compares major work activities performed in product-centered and production-based operations and customer-centered service operations. The five major dimensions are (1) type of product; (2) design, development, and delivery; (3) customer orientation; (4) logistics; and (5) measurement. These categories are not necessarily exclusive, as there will be overlap between the dimensions.[23]

DEFINITIONS USED TO DESCRIBE WORK

Typical input is grouped as capital, labor, energy, and materials. Input can be physical effort, a brilliant idea, money invested in education, or a special musical instrument to help further a concert career.

To create an idea, for instance, original input or thoughts are gradually transformed to throughput and then to output. In team efforts, ideas input at the start of a project are changed in numerous ways by the throughput processes, like critique, evaluate, modify, and improve. These same four sample through-

Table 6.1 Comparison of Typical Product-Based and Service-Based Organizations

Products-centered and production-centered operations	Customer-centered services and operations
Type of Products/Activities and Production/Creations	
■ Finished goods are tangible and may be an investment	■ Services are perishable and consumed when produced, like an airline ticket
■ Production at surtiile location	■ Site selection depends on where customers are
■ Output tangible and unique to manufacturer	■ Output intangible, as in coordinating activities
■ Production is independent of consumption	■ Production is often simultaneous with consumption
■ Product design is centered on the customer; process design is centered on the employee	■ Both product design and process design are centered on the customer
Design/Development/Delivery	
■ Developers seldom have contact with users	■ Direct contact with partner and end users
■ Technical skills dominate operations	■ Interpersonal skills dominate operations
Customer Orientation	
■ Customer loyalty builds over time	■ Very dependent on advertising and promotion
■ May have contact with end user	■ Has direct contact with end user
■ Customer is involved in very few production processes	■ Customer is involved in many production processes
■ Employee–customer relationships are seldom complex, as employees may seldom see customers	■ Employee–customer relationships are often very complex, such as terms and conditions of a sale
■ End users are gradually forming partnerships with suppliers	■ Often based on customers' perceptions
Logistics	
■ Capacity depends on inventory	■ Provided on customer demand
■ Work in progress	■ Queue, or waiting line
■ Supply usually exists	■ Provided on demand

Table 6.1   Comparison of Typical Product-Based and
Service-Based Organizations (continued)

Products-centered and production-centered operations	*Customer-centered services and operations*
Measurement	
■ Easy to use standards, measurements, inspection, and control of quality	■ Use flexible standards or guidelines often developed jointly with customers and providers
■ Output depends on individuals working cooperatively, as in assembly lines	■ Output depends on groups working together synergistically
■ Product or output is homogeneous, as in mass production	■ Heterogeneous, due to customer-provider interaction
■ Quality is determined by output alone	■ Often judged by speed, courtesy, completeness of services provided
■ Quality measurements built into contracts and agreements	■ Quality is judged during service delivery

put processes may be repeated or cycled several times before output of a plan of action is considered acceptable.

Definitions of concepts associated with various types of work change constantly. People's unique views of what they do at work carry over into their definitions. Accomplishments, end results, and outcomes, or overall productivity, reflect all the efforts used to do the job.

Definitions range from objective to subjective. They can be clear and precise, as in amount of data a trained clerical worker logs in one hour. Productivity can also be a matter of personal opinion or reflect project leaders' estimates of achievements of project groups. Although estimates of productivity can come from intuition, or wishful thinking, most people rely on some form of reliable or consistent information or specific data. In any field of human endeavor, a fine line separates personal opinion and objectivity.

Key definitions used to describe and represent productivity often identify how to get more output per unit of input within a specific time period. This is easier said than done, however. Definitions need to include descriptions of a broad array of talents people possess. A sound base of information can then be used to make job assignments or evaluate performance.

All overall definitions of work imply the need to recognize and foster continuous improvement and high involvement of people. Also, factors like time to complete projects and provide services and cost to meet specific standards (namely quality) are carefully balanced against outcomes.

Two major problems are associated with describing the full range of work activities: (1) work performance is hard to identify and (2) not all results have measurable output or practical bottom-line value. However, if something exists, it can be described and measured.

Some standard ways to define and describe work efforts and accomplishments are presented next. Definitions may apply equally to people and to organizations. Various types and levels of work from production operations and from service-based areas illustrate definitions of productivity.

Definitions cannot be diluted to suit our own needs. We can't write our own prescriptions for what we want to see and hear. Rather, work efforts should be described as clearly and objectively as possible. In benchmarking, for instance, clearly defined concepts are used to produce standards, which in turn become building blocks for creating inelastic yardsticks for measurement. We can't measure what we can't define.

Definitions are often associated with measurement. Measurements that are repeated at specific time intervals are used to make comparisons. These comparisons can then be used to show change. Measurement, like a snapshot taken at a specific point in time, shows only what is happening now. Measurement is static. It never shows the energy people use to do their jobs, nor does it reveal how to do them better. Only careful study of where we are and where we want to be will begin to open doors in what we hope is the "best" or "right" direction.

Broad definitions of personal and organizational productivity can be expressed in terms of ratio of (1) output/input, (2) quality, (3) effectiveness, (4) efficiency, (5) value and value added, (6) profit, (7) creativity and innovation, and (8) quality of work life.[21] Productivity is an umbrella word.[20]

1. Ratios of Output/Input

Simple ratios show the relationship between two similar numbers or amounts. Most output/input ratios used in business represent energy, labor, material, or capital. Results are meaningful only if each separate input and output makes a significant contribution to the whole.

Ratios serve little purpose unless data on output and input come from the same area, specifically, energy output/energy input, labor output/labor input, material output/material input, capital output/capital input. People's efforts can be grouped as "energy."

A major problem in using ratios is obtaining data that accurately represent work people perform. Ratios show accomplishments at a specific point in time. Time perspectives may range from short term (less than a day) to long term (twenty years or more). When data are gradually accumulated and analyzed over fairly long periods of time, standards can be developed. Later, new data can be compared with established standards and predictions made using appropriate, statistically sound methods.

Ratios are based on the assumption of equivalents. In all six of the following examples, results will be meaningless or misleading unless input and output data on equipment, raw materials, number of people in each unit, measurements of time, and other critical variables are as close to the same as possible. This means comparing similar things (i.e., compare apples with apples and oranges with oranges).

Acceptable, thoroughly researched criteria, standards, or base rates used in ratios greatly increase their value. Typical standards in service, manufacturing, and materials-processing industries could be identical—quality, on-time delivery, reduce cycle time, or meet user's criteria. Specifications for input and output should be consistent with the goals of employees and/or the organization.

In the service sector, countable units of work may be unrelated to the real purpose and goals of the company. To illustrate, the number of letters written in response to customer complaints can be counted. The goal, however, is resolution of the problem and not how many letters are written. A salesperson's demonstration of high motivation is a good measure of work performed, but number of sales is the goal. The number of sales is the measurable goal.[28]

Complex ratios, or ratios having two or more sources of input and output, provide a broader view of productivity. You will be reminded periodically that measurement should not be overdone, nor should it be excessively complicated. Numbers tell a story, but they do not tell the whole story, as you will see.

Any number of examples of output/input ratios could be presented for service-based and manufacturing industries. Data from ratios can readily be converted to percentages or decimal fractions.

First-pass yield, a simple measure of efficiency and quality, is the percentage of tasks or units completed right on the first try. First-pass yield is often miscalculated, as rework and on-line repair are often left out. In manufacturing industries, rework is easy to visualize. In service areas, rework can be all the retyping and word processing that goes into producing a completely error-free document. Unless readers know how long it took to produce the document, they will incorrectly assume that it was error free the first time it was typed.

Ratios for productivity in product-based and/or manufacturing-type industries are illustrated for simple overall productivity (Example 1), actual and scheduled output (Example 2), and output within a specific unit (Example 3). In service industries, ratios are presented for productivity of work teams (Example 4), cycle time in white-collar work (Example 5), and managerial performance (Example 6).

Product-Based and/or Manufacturing Industries

Three examples are presented.

Example 1.   A general ratio representing overall productivity, where output is a prime concern:

$$\text{Productivity} = \frac{\text{Output}}{\text{Total input}}$$

Example 2.   In production operations, energy or effort people expend, even movements robots make, is measured by:

$$\text{Productivity} = \frac{\text{Actual output in units}}{\text{Scheduled output in units}}$$

Comparisons of actual output with scheduled output show whether production is on time. Although input is not shown in the above ratio, type of input may range from raw materials to human effort. There can be no output without input. Stages of the sequential processes used to produce output can be documented, monitored, and measured, and specific ratios can be created for each step.

Example 3.   It is assumed that unit A and unit B are producing computer chips and that there is a logical reason for making comparisons. Comparisons may be based on cost per unit, time to produce each unit, or number of defective chips per million produced. Output in unit A is compared with output in unit B.

$$\text{Productivity} = \frac{\text{Output unit A}}{\text{Output unit B}}$$

Service-Based Industries

Ratios represent various forms of input and output data in each of the following examples. When input and output data are reliable and valid and data representative, or based on an adequate sample of work activities and results, ratios give meaningful results. However, information on various types of work performed is not easy to quantify, as in excellence in leadership, quality of mentoring, or value of sales presentations. Expressing descriptive information in numeric or ratio form is inappropriate, as it gives a false sense of accuracy.

Time required to complete specific projects or perform operations is very important in service-based operations.[26] Customers, clients, partners, suppliers, and others in the production and delivery chains play different but vital roles.

A major concern that is generally understood and acknowledged is the cost of time. Time has always been a major factor in manufacturing-based industries and is increasingly becoming a prime bone of contention in customer service. Time and quality go hand in hand. Can the time "not do to something well" be added to the cost of quality? Are customers willing to pay the price for well-finished products and polite, unrushed service? It depends. If there is no time to wait, less than first-class service may be acceptable.

Example 4. Because much white-collar work is done in multi-purpose groups or work teams, team productivity is represented by:

$$\text{Team productivity} = \frac{\text{Work output of engineers on team}}{\text{Work output of all team members}}$$

The real problem is how to identify and measure output of engineers and other team members. Every person on a team plays a unique role, as each thinks, acts, performs, and influences others in different ways. Ratios used to represent human factors reveal differences in skills, abilities, and knowledge.

Example 5. Cycle time, a classical measurement in manufacturing, is determined by dividing the number of units of work-in-process inventory by the number of units completed within a specific period of time.

Cycle time should be tracked in all businesses. Measures of time to complete specific projects or perform operations is vital in service-based operations.[26] Internal and external customers want the shortest possible cycle time consistent with good service.

Every operation of a business is a discrete cycle of activities made up of multiple sub-cycles, each with its own set of actions in process that affect all outcomes. Each cycle a person performs interfaces or overlaps with a cycle(s) another person performs. When each separate cycle is examined and accomplishments are added together, the resulting reports provide a complete picture of the work done.

Actions in process are similar to a work-in-progress inventory on an assembly line. In the white-collar area, examples of actions in process include number of orders being processed, number of ongoing quality improvement projects, number of new positions to be filled, or number of reports to be completed.

$$\text{White-collar cycle time} = \frac{\text{Number of actions in process}}{\text{Completion rate}}$$

Example 6. Productivity of managers could relate to creating value in excess of cost. This can be achieved through the concept of value added, an extremely important but somewhat illusive commodity. Added value, both in myth and reality, represents that extra touch or unexpected plus.

Knowledge workers add value to activities or processes performed and services provided in order to make an "average" process better. An example is a writer reviewing a manuscript one more time than planned to "fine-tune" it. Value is added when something is done a little "better." Value added can be unanticipated, like a lucky break. Managers who are excellent mentors or role models contribute something special that only those who are being mentored (mentees) can describe—understanding, faith, or encouragement beyond that experienced by other mentees.

An ideal ratio would be based on information showing that the highest level of quality of managerial performance was obtained with the lowest possible expenditure of resources:

$$\text{Managerial productivity} = \frac{\text{Management output (value added)}}{\text{Management cost}}$$

An Administrative Productivity Indicator (API) is a single overall measure quantifying how successfully a unit achieves it purpose. Work output is the physical, measurable, or countable things describing what administrative units do to achieve what they were organized to do.[2]

$$\text{API} = \frac{\text{Work output}}{\text{Labor hours input}}$$

In summary, ratios are one of the many way to describe and illustrate achievement. They are only a guide or beginning point. When additional information is known, more complete ratios can be developed using a larger number of factors. Although multi-factor ratios are beyond the scope of this manual, they are often used as a basis for profit-sharing, or determining an equitable proportion of the organization's profits to allocate to employees.

Data obtained from ratios are assumed to be reliable, or give the same or very similar results when measurements are repeated. Data are considered valid when they measure exactly what they are supposed to measure. Resulting ratios, like any other measuring device, are only as "accurate" or representative as the information used to create them. Many believe, perhaps erroneously, that numbers are more accurate than descriptive information.

Throughput

Throughput rarely appears in productivity ratios. It is taken for granted. An automobile's throughput is also taken for granted. The power of the motor and the way the transmission, brakes, and steering mechanisms work cannot be seen, but they respond when needed.

The importance of human throughput, such as loyalty, honesty, flexibility, and motivation, is unfortunately often taken for granted. Like throughput in the automobile, little attention is paid to human and organizational throughput until something breaks down. Throughput is discussed in greater detail in the following section and in Chapter 8.

Many change efforts focus primarily on process, for example business process analysis and total quality management, among others. Processes are not straightforward. Because some processes overlap, separating one process from another poses problems.

Chapters 8 and 9 deal with the many processes associated with looking at your own special talents and arranging them into a meaningful picture or description which others can both understand and use.

2. Quality

Exhibit 6.1 is a question-and-answer approach that basically represents the current status of quality in the United States.

Definitions of Quality

The following represent a broad spectrum of definitions of quality.

1. Degree to which a service or product conforms to a predetermined set of requirements or specifications.[3] This means meeting or exceeding standards created or designed by customers, partners, or any type of end user or stakeholder. It also means anticipating customers' needs and surprising, even delighting them with quality when they least expect it.

2. Motorola's Six Sigma, or approximately three errors per million, to simply "do it right." Motorola strives to further reduce this defect rate. At Motorola, quality is a company-wide process.

3. "A way of managing." "What the customer says it is." Quality is an ethic. Quality and innovation are mutually dependent, or you can't have one without the other. Quality is often the most cost-effective way to manage and the least capital-intensive route to productivity.

4. "Do it right the first time." This means planning ahead. Quality is often achieved in the product area by planning first (proactive) and/or by inspection (reactive). In the product area, many quality efforts are based on tangible products and measurable results. Minimizing repair, downtime, inspection costs, etc. reduces overall costs.

Exhibit 6.1   Status of Quality in the United States

Q: *What is the status of quality in the United States?*
A: About 75 percent of U.S. companies report they are involved with some form of quality assessment and improvement endeavor. The gap between what people say they do and what they really do is probably wider than most would admit. The quality area is no exception.

Q: *That's a lot of effort. It's turning out okay, isn't it?*
A: Most people and organizations are being carried along by the steadily growing stream of quality programs. Whether they get in the quality boat, sink or swim, or eventually reach their destinations depends on their vision, mission, goals, and their values. Values are their genuine belief that quality and all that it means are important. The commitment and supportive efforts of senior management, particularly their CEOs, is vital.

Q: *Where do we go once we get in the boat?*
A: Let's start by using boats, crews, uncharted waters, and a captain in our analogy. First, the river is uncharted. Second, there are no maps. Third, there are many tributaries leading away from the big river. Fourth, after a while, you'll know where you've been. You'll never know how far you have to paddle, because your journey is endless.

Q: *Can you even guess about how long it will take to improve quality?*
A: It really depends on how well you have planned for the journey and how many people are going. When people paddle together, it always takes less time. It could take five to ten years or more.

Q: *How will I know when I'm there?*
A: You won't. The path to quality is really a continuous journey with detours and many obstacles. You don't really know where you will end up or whether you will get there.

Q. *Is it really worth it?*
A: Without quality, you can't stay in business for long.

Q: *How long have people been concerned about quality?*
A: Since the beginning of time. Aristotle wrote that, "Quality is a habit." You know about survival of the fittest, adapting to your changing environment, and all that. The pyramids and museum treasures of the world survived because of quality.

Q: *That's interesting. What about recent times?*
A: Islands of quality always exist. You have to find them. Proctor & Gamble has produced quality products for over 160 years. IBM has provided quality products and services for over 85 years. Motorola's longstanding company-wide efforts are well known and respected.

Other younger, proven companies are some of the Malcolm Baldrige National Quality Award winners for service: 1990—Federal Express; 1992—Ritz-Carlton Hotel (in Atlanta) and AT&T for its Universal Card Service in Jacksonville, Florida. The AT&T Network Systems Group/Transmission Systems Business Unit in Morristown, New Jersey received the award for manufacturing in 1992. Its Power Systems divi-

Exhibit 6.1 Status of Quality in the United States (continued)

sion in Texas won a third Baldrige Award in 1994.

Q: *Is there a secret to success like this?*
A: There are really no secrets. Good planning, hard work, and patience are vital. One way is to stay in touch by listening to what people in the organization are saying to you. If you see someone doing a good job, tell them so. Using free and open communication and timely, relevant, constructive feedback can work wonders. Clear mission statements and goals and leaders who generally do most of the right things really help.

Q: *What about Total Quality Management, or TQM?*
A: People interpret TQM in many ways. Results of TQM efforts directed to the organization's culture, customers, and processes range from glowing to unsuccessful. Empowerment, clear quality goals, a supportive environment, and management support from the CEO on down are vital. TQM is a tool. How well people and organizations work with tools depends on their overall skills and on many unpredictable organizational and environmental factors. TQM is not the only tool in the quality area. Some believe it is.

Q: *How can I measure quality?*
A: Quality is difficult to describe and even more difficult to measure, particularly in the service area. It is easier to measure quality when you define it in precise terms that people understand. Managers have a very hard time defining quality, but if they asked their customers, they would find out.

Q: *How will I know if I have quality?*
A: You will recognize it when you see it. If you have specific standards for quality, like 99.99 percent customer satisfaction, one defect per 10,000, or something similar, you can measure what you have. Then, compare it with the standards you want to achieve.

Q: *How much will it cost?*
A: No one knows.

Q: *Will I get a payout on my investment in quality?*
A: Yes. Quality always pays in the long run. One of the major goals of quality efforts is cost savings.

Q: *What happens if you do something wrong or make a false start?*
A: Admit you were wrong, and start all over again. People around you will soon catch on if you keep doing things wrong. You may even lose your customers.

Q: *Any advice?*
A: What you do and how you do it should support the mission and goals of your organization. Your captain must have vision and be able to anticipate what may be ahead. Captains will need to chart a course and pretty much stick to it. You also need strong, supportive, well-informed officers who are not afraid to make a commitment to their crew. Once in a while they will have to admit they were wrong. A highly visible, empathetic, knowledgeable captain and a supportive infrastructure are musts.

Q: *Where can I turn for help?*
A: To everyone around you, including everyone on the boat. You've heard

Exhibit 6.1   Status of Quality in the United States (continued)

many times before that people are the most valuable resource any organization has. Start by asking those doing the paddling. They will know what to improve and how best to improve and maintain quality.

Q: *Anything else I should know?*
A: You should be prepared to change boats or completely change your captain, crew—really, everyone on the boat. You may even have to be careful when you get to shore. Always be on your guard.

Q: *Why?*
A: The captain and even the captain's crew can appear to be supportive, but do nothing. Eventually, you may have to change the boat, how things are done, and even the whole crew and the captain.

Q: *Is this really done?*
A: Yes. The captain and crew work best when they understand their own jobs and also what those around them are doing. They also need to know how the crew's jobs fit together so the boat runs smoothly. They will want to be appropriately paid for their performance. It you closely match pay with performance, the crew will be satisfied and motivated. If not, you may have mutiny.

Q: *Could you sum up this whole discussion in a few sentences? I need to take what I'm learned back to my boss.*
A: One, a clear vision about what quality means inside and beyond the organization. Two, a value system based on hard work, patience, good communication, and strong, positive, committed leaders. Three, listen to your work force, customers, suppliers, even partners. They know what you should be doing and how you should do it. If they like what they see, they will buy from you. However, they must need your products and services, and they must be competitively priced.

Customer satisfaction, non-conformance to standards, and meeting specific quality standards for products play major roles in determining quality. The cost of quality, or the price paid for non-conformance to standards, is critical in product-based or materials-processing industries. Producing excessive scrap and non-standard products is costly and can literally destroy a company's reputation.

5. Customer-focused quality is "...continually increasing customer satisfaction with products and services through attention to performance and conformance issues."[7]

Quality is meaningless unless it is built into products and services. Quality must also be reflected in the mission, strategic plans, and goals of the organization. Companies like Motorola, Disney, Nordstrom, and others incorporate quality into every facet of their business.

IBM recognizes the value of the customer interface involving customers and non-customers. The IBM users groups encourage customers and business partners to try out software being developed. At IBM, customer expectations play a major role in the company's strategic planning efforts.

Pockets of excellent customer service are growing. The philosophy that "the customer is king" is growing. Companies like McDonald's know who their customers are and treat them accordingly. Their cornerstones of business are customer service, quality, value, and cleanliness.

Quality is determined in the marketplace. There are times when quality is based on perception instead of fact. Customers simply want the product or service and disregard the fact that quality is poor or questionable.

Knowing what quality is and achieving it are two different things. There is often a mismatch between what people do and what they expect. They mix goals, tools, programs, and methods. Who would play football on a baseball diamond? There must be a carefully researched quality program, not a "program of the month." Programs must be tailor-made to meet the specific needs of various departments, units, even groups of people. One program does not fit all.

The goals of a specific level of quality can be achieved only when the organizational structure is set up in a way that allows change and improvement. There must be a receptive group of workers, knowledgeable and supportive of top management, and a supporting infrastructure.

Is quality here to stay? Will it disappear? Will it be transformed into yet another change and improvement process? No one knows the answers. However, there should be a genuine commitment to make things run well in the organization or simply help people do their jobs better.[5]

Brief History of Quality

W. Edwards Deming's concept of TQM is a "philosophy for management." Major factors are to strive for continuous improvement in satisfying customers and reduce the variation in products and services. Deming was 93 when he died in 1993, after having spent over 70 years working in statistical process control and quality in general.

Joseph M. Juran incorporates quality planning, quality control, and quality improvement through quality management into his approach to quality. Active for over 50 years in the quality field, he believes in using a "quality planning road map" to plan, coordinate, and integrate a concern for quality into all operations of the organization.

In the 1950s, Armand V. Feigenbaum[8] introduced the concept of "total quality control." This process focuses on quality development, quality maintenance, and quality improvement efforts. The goal is to provide full customer satisfaction at the most economical level.

The massive international study done jointly by Ernst & Young[7] and the American Quality Foundation yielded 1.5 million pieces of information. Data are based on a comprehensive study of management practices of over 500 companies in the automotive, banking, computer, and health care industries in Canada, Germany, Japan, and the United States. Major areas covered were employee involvement, customer focus, strategic planning, and improvement. Japan still leads the United States in all areas.

Benchmarking

This major tool of TQM is often used to identify process improvement opportunities that ultimately lead to quality improvement. The benchmarking process involves assessing competitors and/or companies in industries that demonstrate high-level performance or achievement of quality in the same area, for example, and then comparing one's own performance to theirs.[6]

Processes and services benchmarked do not have to be in the same industry. Much can be learned from unrelated industries. Many work processes are the same, no matter what the output is. Essentially, quality is where you find it. Companies that are often benchmarked are L.L. Bean's billing system, Federal Express's tracking system, and Toyota's manufacturing processes.

Standards for Quality

The International Organization for Standardization (ISO) federation was founded in 1946. The technical committee of the ISO developed the standards. Currently, this committee consists of hundreds of experts from around the world. ISO 9000 series certification is a very important yet controversial quality standard.

The sole purpose of ISO 9000 is to guide the creation of a stable measurement process. ISO 9000 is based on two phrases: "Say what you do and do what you say." Given an opportunity, customers prefer doing business with manufacturers and suppliers that have met ISO 9000 quality assurance standards for products.

The existence of quality awards, like the Malcolm Baldrige National Quality Award and the growing number of spin-off awards, and ISO 9000 Series standards has raised awareness of the need for and benefits of constantly measuring and improving quality.[24]

Goals for quality can never be less than 100 percent. Achieving and maintaining quality should always begin at the top of the organization and be strongly supported by upper management, particularly the CEO. Quality planning, quality control, and quality improvement are major issues. Quality and productivity are inseparable[2] or two sides of the same coin. As you may have discovered, the concepts that underlie productivity and quality permeate this manual.

3. Effectiveness

Effectiveness applies equally to people and to organizations. Broad definitions are adequate, practical, and useful. A prime definition of effectiveness is producing the expected outcome or accomplishing the purpose intended. Being effective is a matter of degree. People exhibit different levels of effectiveness, depending on the type of job performed. Ideally, the gap between expectations and achievement should be as narrow as possible. Measures of effectiveness are commonly compared with standards for quality or usefulness, like achieving goals or finishing a project on time, hopefully under budget.

Standards, or guidelines for comparison or measurement, are very important. Without standards, people may believe that what they do is effective and their organizations are effective. The real tests come from standards the customers and end users set in the marketplace. Customers of educational systems, namely students and parents, are becoming disillusioned. Some school systems are using private companies to provide instruction. Trends toward subcontracting, privatizing, and outsourcing are steadily increasing.[13] The ultimate goal is to increase effectiveness by enhancing customer satisfaction and decreasing cost.

Two major ways to determine personal effectiveness are numeric and descriptive. Examples of numeric ways are amount of output per unit of time, absenteeism, and turnover. Examples of descriptive ways to represent effectiveness are motivation, leadership, and interpersonal skills. Being effective from the personal standpoint means functioning in a manner that involves reaching the highest level of performance using the lowest possible number of resources.

Organizational effectiveness is measured by the degree to which an organization achieves its goals.[17] Another way to show effectiveness is to create the greatest good with the least input. Effectiveness is shown by good planning and sound operating philosophies that are communicated to all employees. Feedback systems designed for measurement, control, and improvement cycle information throughout the organization.

Organizational productivity can be defined as the ratio of effectiveness with which organizational goals are achieved to the efficiency with which resources are consumed in the course of achievement. Efficiency is represented by labor inputs and effectiveness by outputs.[1]

$$\text{Productivity} = \frac{\text{Effectiveness}}{\text{Efficiency}}$$

In a knowledge worker environment, the effective delivery of a service as evidenced by good planning or attention to detail is emphasized. Effectiveness is defined as providing services that markedly contribute to the organization's achievement of its mission and objectives.

Effectiveness of people is shown through measures of client or customer satisfaction, specifically internal customer satisfaction. Customers often "tell it like it is." Other examples include student evaluations of faculty members and subordinate evaluations of supervisors and peers.

4. Efficiency

Concepts used to define efficiency relate to performing or functioning in the best possible and least wasteful manner. To illustrate, in the knowledge worker area, the key question is, "Is the knowledge that is developed applied, or was more knowledge developed than was needed?"

Another definition of efficiency is knowing how to do something and doing it in a timely manner. A time element is often associated with efficiency. Organizational efficiency does not relate to results alone, but includes how well results were achieved.[1] Specifically, were results achieved in a straightforward, logical manner that minimized false starts and did not waste materials, time, or other resources?

In service-based companies, "doing things right" implies: (1) there is a "right" or "better" way to do a job or provide a service, (2) the person performing the job knows what to do and has the necessary skills and knowledge to do the job, and (3) the person works at an "average" pace under normal conditions. We all recognize efficient service when we see it, whether in a restaurant or a retail store. Automobiles have a peak gas efficiency at a specific speed.

Efficiency in simple assembly-line operations or materials-processing units depends on (1) number of pieces produced per hour, (2) number of units produced on schedule, (3) percent utilization of equipment, and (4) percent downtime, overtime, or labor cost/unit of production.[16]

Increasing the number of times a job is done usually has a positive impact on efficiency until a certain level of performance is reached. Like automobiles, people also have peak efficiencies. Possible ways to increase personal efficiency are to combine separate steps of a job or delegate certain parts. However, we must ask ourselves whether quality or some other aspect, like customer service, is being sacrificed. At work and in our personal lives, we gradually learn to do routine jobs faster or more efficiently, often until fatigue or boredom sets in.

When performance levels off, it is often a matter of motivation and attitude and not necessarily efficiency. Efficiency is often considered part of the broader concept of effectiveness.

5. Value and Value Added

Perception influences value and value added. People differ in how they define and interpret value and value added. Value is measured in numerous ways, some of which are tangible, like reliability in equipment and meeting specific quality standards. Products and services must first have value before they can have value added.

Value

Typical definitions customers use are "looks right" and "always have used it." In the organization, value is purchasing power, replacement costs, estimated worth, and market price, among other factors. From the financial standpoint, value is a fair or proper equivalent in money or commodities for something sold or exchanged. The concept of value is timeless.

Knowledge workers and other white-collar workers may add value, or provide that "something extra," to what they do. This extra value enhances the product or process in some distinctive way so that it appears better than competitors' products. In the service area, value added can be taking the extra step to ensure that customers are satisfied. Customers are the final judges of value. Customers have their own ideas regarding "minimum acceptable value."

In the service area, customer–provider relationships can be more important than cost. Value is created by providing services that excite, even delight, customers and also meet their expectations. However, services and products have value only when needed in the marketplace. Unless there is a demand and people are willing to purchase the service or product, nothing is sold.

It is important to know the minimum acceptable value (MAV) of a product or service. Over a period of time, and as products improve, the MAV line always trends up. Ways to develop a Customer Value Profile[SM] are illustrated by Guaspari and Crom.[11]

Value Added

Superlatives like "something extra" or "excellent" which exceed users' expectations are common definitions. Having a value-added feature means having enhanced appeal, as in making a user's job easier.[22]

A competitive advantage may lie in the area of value added. Suppliers who develop special products or processes to meet their customers' unique needs create a special form of value added for their customers. Similarly, highly skilled editors can take a "better than average" manuscript and transform it into an excellent manuscript. Editors and movie and television script writers stamp their manuscripts with their unique brand of value added.

Value-added concepts, like value engineering, concentrate efforts on adding value to a product or system. This dynamic team approach uses economic analysis to add value to products and systems. When used during the development and design stages in the construction industry, costs that do not contribute to value are eliminated.[25] Customers get more value for their money

Value-added mapping (VAM) is one of many techniques that simplify and improve business processes, systems or procedures in order to lower costs, minimize overhead and/or inventory to produce more profit, increase returns, or achieve additional sales. It addresses the problems of *when, where,* and *what.* The *what* considers what the successful solutions mean to the organization and to the customers. To illustrate, VAM can be used to map current methods used in manufacturing and point out areas and processes that reduce time from the instant the order is placed until the product is shipped to a customer.[12]

Placing priorities on work is crucial. Some work is more valuable than other work. In a black-and-white world, does value-added work become "good" work? Does non-value-added work become "bad" work? No. Rather, it is important to concentrate efforts on helping the work force use time, knowledge, and energy to achieve vision-supporting, mission-driven results.[14]

6. Profit

The prime, or only, indicator of an organization's overall success may be the balance sheet. Profit is often represented in terms of financial data like sales, operating costs, direct and indirect costs, and return on investment. Financial success may be taken more seriously than customer satisfaction or achieving high quality standards. Cost and value of human resources are seldom considered. However, the cost of human resources can be approximated through concepts related to human resource accounting[10] and overhead value analysis.[15]

Various units or profit centers within the organization may be judged using similar financial criteria. Profit and non-profit organizations have standard and unique ways to analyze and represent their financial status.

Of the three major variables—cost, price, and profit—cost is the only one that can be controlled through planning, budgeting, and other forms of control. Price is often negotiated. Net income determines profit. Standard measures of profitability are sales/operating costs, retained earnings, earnings per share, capital investments, growth, and return on investment, among others.

Cost of quality, or perhaps more accurately the cost of non-quality, includes the unpredictable cost of internal and external failures. Typical internal failures are scrap and rework. Common external failures are customer complaints and product liability, like failure due to faulty products. Costs of non-conformance can be reduced by the proactive efforts of appraisal and prevention. In general, the cost of non-conformance can be many times the cost of conformance. Great expense may be incurred in repairing defective equipment after it breaks down rather than replacing a small defective part when a problem is first suspected.

The likelihood of resolving the cost/quality dilemma is remote. Controversy may be more stimulating than agreement. The effects of conflict can bring about compromises or even realistic solutions in some instances.

An example of being proactive "after the fact" comes from Corning. In the February 25, 1992 issue of *Fortune*, it was reported that four years ago Corning found that 35 percent of the drawings used to manufacture prescription eyeglass lenses contained tiny errors of perhaps one digit in a document containing 5000 numbers. Problems detected in the earliest stages cost approximately $250 to correct. However, fixing the problem after production started might cost $20,000 and $100,000 by the time the product reached the customer.

Corning's solution was to train a member of the work group in proof-reading. Errors were further reduced when drafting tables were replaced with computerized work stations which allowed drawings to be transmitted electronically to Corning's plants. When production people were able to look over the drawings in advance, the error rate dropped to 0.2 percent.

It is also possible to analyze profitability by assigning an approximate value or even exact value to time delays. Although there are ways to standardize tasks, like using technology to speed up delivery of services, the cost benefits should be carefully weighed against the negative effect a faster method might have on perceived as opposed to actual quality. Time must always be considered from the customer's perspective. Flowcharts indicating where the service is at any given point in time come in handy.

7. Creativity and Innovation

Specific definitions of creativity include spontaneity, sensitivity, openness to new ideas, and tolerance of risk taking and divergent thinking. The creative thinking process produces innovative, exciting new discoveries that lead to new inventions or new ways to solve old problems. Creativity is also a fresh, new approach that opens up a longstanding problem to new solutions. Creative minds have no limits in and of themselves until limits are placed on them by the organization or by supervisors, managers, or team leaders.

Little is done to recognize and reinforce creativity on the job. Often, the creative person, like the creative child in the classroom, is ignored or criticized (they don't fit the mold, and they seldom conform). True creativity implies divergent thinking and non-conformance to guidelines, results, or standards. Non-creative managers or leaders have a difficult time with employees who have ideas that do not fit the norm.

The number of creative ideas produced in an organization is directly related to the extent to which the organization's climate is supportive and tolerant of risk taking that produces innovation.

Creativity and innovation play central roles in the learning organization, as discussed in Chapters 2 and 5.

8 Quality of Work Life

Most quality of work life (QWL) programs focus on people's ability to make judgments about what is or is not desirable in the workplace. Many QWL programs relate to the degree of psychological and physical comfort people experience on the job.

Workplace environments encourage empowerment, teamwork, and collaboration. The open atmosphere encourages constructive feedback and the free flow of information. In high QWL environments, the work force feels secure about their jobs, are valued as people, and perform meaningful, challenging work.

Interest in QWL fluctuates. The current focus on quality may have temporarily redirected efforts away from QWL efforts.[5]

The growth rate of service industries is increasing. Never before have customers had so many choices. A question to ponder is asked in the title of a 1986 article: "Will Services Follow Manufacturing into Decline?"[18]

6.1

Develop personal and organizational operational definitions for quality and indicate how you plan to measure quality. Specify whether you work primarily in the service or product area or in a crossover area. Where does the customer fit in? Where do suppliers, vendors, and others in the supply...delivery chain fit in?

6.2

List and describe five major criteria that you feel could be used to judge your own productivity. How do you plan to use them to evaluate yourself? How will you document results? Solidify your ideas about productivity as it relates to you. How does the overall concept of productivity fit into your personal equation?

SUMMARY AND CONCLUSIONS

1. Of the numerous ways to define organizational productivity, use definitions that most closely fit the vision, mission, goals, and philosophy or culture of your organization. The vital issue is defining productivity in terms that people understand and lead to measurement. Without measurement, there can be no standards and, therefore, no way to compare pre- and post-quality change and improvement efforts.

2. Definitions are often associated with measurement, but measurement shows only what is currently happening. It cannot show the energy people use to do their jobs or reveal how to do them better. Definitions, like the bylaws of some professional organizations, need to be updated from time to time. It is not necessarily a job that people stand in line for, but it is very important.

3. Definitions of organizational productivity can be used to develop standard descriptive or qualitative measures and numeric measures. These measures become mileposts on the road to goal achievement. It is important to have a standard, agreed-on measuring device as a baseline to which later measurements can be compared often over varying time intervals.

4. Product-based and service-based organizations may have common areas. Table 6.1 is designed to show differences, not similarities. Some categories do overlap.

5. Value added is probably one of the most dynamic, insightful ways to express productivity. Value must first exist before there can be value added. This "something extra" will definitely be like a breath of fresh air in our currently underserved approach to reaching customers.

PRACTICAL APPLICATIONS

1. Proactive views of work involve anticipating and preventing problems. Proper planning, carefully monitoring processes and products, and continuous quality improvement apply to both product-based and service-based industries.

2. Separating services from product-based industries may allow a simple form of benchmarking or analysis. Much can be learned by examining excellent processes, selecting the "best" methods, and applying them to new areas. Methods that work in one area could be a clue to solving problems in another.

3. Reverse analysis can be done by starting with the input and working backwards, step by step, to the beginning point. Problems, or "disconnects," may be determined. The product or process can be redesigned using the new information. Throughout this process, feedback is essential.

4. Every month or so, a new competitive weapon appears in the field of productivity, marketing, advertising, and product or service design. The current rage is "value added." Will customers pay for more value? The answer is it depends.

5. Key issues in increasing productivity are to develop a quality culture and communicate quality and quality standards within and beyond the organization. Quality can be achieved by: (1) training, (2) changing company culture, (3) using variable compensation programs or alternate reward systems that tie remuneration directly to team results based on a specific quality improvement, and (4) recognition programs to promote employee loyalty and improve internal quality management.

REFERENCES

1. Bain, David. *The Productivity Prescription*, New York: McGraw-Hill, 1982.

2. Christopher, William F. "How to Measure and Improve Productivity in Professional, Administrative, and Service Organizations," in *Issues in White Collar Productivity*, Norcross, Ga.: Industrial and Management Press, 1984, pp. 29–37.

3. Crosby, Philip B. *Quality Is Free*, New York: New American Library, 1979.

4. Crosby, Philip B. *Let's Talk Quality*, New York: McGraw-Hill, 1989.

5. Danjin, Dick and Cutcher-Gerschenfeld, Joel. "Will TQM Go the Way of QWL?" *Journal for Quality and Participation*, July/August 1992, pp. 94–97.

6. Eccles, Robert G. "The Performance Manifesto," *Harvard Business Review*, January–February 1991 pp. 131–137.

7. Ernst & Young. "Best Practices Report," Cleveland, Ohio: American Quality Foundation, 1992.

8. Feigenbaum, Armand V. *Total Quality Control: Engineering and Management*, New York: McGraw-Hill, 1961.

9. Feigenbaum, Armand V. "Quality Education and America's Competitiveness," *Quality Progress*, September 1994, pp. 83–84.

10. Flamholtz, Eric G. *Human Resource Accounting*, San Francisco: Jossey-Bass, 1985.

11. Gauspari, John and Crom, Steve. "Ultimately, There Is Just One Issue: Value," *Journal for Quality and Participation*, July/August 1993, pp. 6–9.

12. Hall, Robert K. "Value-Added Mapping," *American National Can*, January 1991, pp. 1–11.

13. Handy, Charles. *The Age of Unreason*, Boston: Harvard Business School Press, 1989.

14. Helton, B. Ray. "More of the Right Stuff," *Quality Observer*, September 1993, pp. 5, 14.

15. Neumann, John L. "Overhead: Five Challenges to Conventional Wisdom," *Management Practice Quarterly*, Fall 1986, pp. 5–9.

16. Phillips, Jack J. *Handbook of Training Evaluation and Measurement Methods*, Houston: Gulf Publishing, 1983.

17. Price, J. L. *The Study of Turnover*, Ames: Iowa University Press, 1977.

18. Quinn, James B. and Gagnon, Christopher. "Will Services Follow Manufacturing into Decline?" *Harvard Business Review*, November–December 1986, pp. 95–103.

19. Schwartz, M. H. "What Do the Words 'Product' and 'Service' Really Mean for Management?" *Quality Progress*, June 1992, pp. 35–39.

20. Siegel, Irving H. *Company Productivity: Measurement for Improvement*, Kalamazoo, Mich.: W.E. Upjohn Institute for Employment Research, 1980.

21. Sink, D. Scott. *Productivity Management: Planning, Measurement and Evaluation, Control and Improvement*, Somerset, N.J.: John Wiley and Sons, 1985.

22. Smith, Elizabeth A. "Value Added: Perception vs. Expectations vs. Reality," *The Quality Observer*, in press (proposed publication date July 1995).

23. Smith, Elizabeth A. *The Productivity Manual* (2nd ed.), Houston: Gulf Publishing, 1995.

24. Spitzer, Richard D. "The Only Source of Competitive Advantage," *Quality Progress*, June 1993, pp. 59–64.

25. Stevens, Craig A. and Wright, Karen. "Managing Change with Configuration Management," *National Productivity Review*, Autumn 1991, pp. 509–518.

26. Thomas, Philip R., Gallace, Larry H., and Martin, Kenneth R. *Quality Alone Is Not Enough*, New York: American Management Association, 1992.

27. Tinkham, Mary A. and Kleiner, Brian H. "New Developments in Service Operations Management," *Industrial Management*, November–December 1992, pp. 20–22.

28. Tinkham, Dale. "Measurement of Work in the Service Sector," *Industrial Engineering News*, Vol. XXVI, No. 2, Spring 1992, pp. 1, 3.

THE NATURE
OF WORK

PURPOSE

- Examine the overall importance of major work activities and results
- Compare and contrast the major characteristics of work performed in an organization
- Contrast work performed in product-based and service-based industries
- Evaluate the roles of internal and external customers

INTRODUCTION

The shape of organizations is changing. Positive and negative forces inside and outside the organization affect the quality of work and how much work is done. Individual differences, organizational culture, work environment, technology, and numerous other factors each affect performance in many ways. Continued growth in the service industry and steadily increasing customer demands challenge the work force.

Could productivity and quality be increased if more effort were directed toward understanding how work is performed? Would a closer match between what people are capable of and what they currently do at work make a difference? Are there realistic alternatives to using "bottom-line" financial data to evaluate the quality and type of work performed? Answers to these questions appear in this chapter.

Studying work efforts is one way to reveal relationships with peers, supervisors, subordinates, and internal customers. Outside the organization, relationships between external customers, partners, suppliers, and vendors are extremely important. The need to look beyond our jobs and outside the organization grows daily.

We cannot work with someone much less understand him or her unless we have some feel for the work he or she does. Only then is it possible to help or encourage the person do his or her job better. Competent, knowledgeable people who are willing to share their expertise can become the catalysts of change.

This chapter covers (1) examining and classifying work activities, (2) role of internal and external customers, and (3) major types and characteristics of work.

EXAMINING WORK AND CLASSIFYING WORK ACTIVITIES: LOOK AT YOUR JOB

Work activities can be considered processes or work "in action" or in progress. Results are specific achievements, end points, or tangible accomplishment, like output. Chapter 8 discusses processes and results in more detail.

Being aware of the numerous factors that make up and affect work processes and results makes it easier to understand the work others perform. When we describe our job to others, we develop a better grasp of not only what we can do, but of the importance of various parts of our job.

Some see a drinking glass that is half filled with water as *half empty*. Others see it as *half full*. Similarly, the same work activity may be interpreted in different ways. What appear to be meaningful activities to some, others may consider to be "busy work." Biases also enter into how we feel about our own jobs and how we evaluate work done by others inside and outside our organization.

Increasingly, work is done by groups or teams. Being a "lone ranger" is giving way to cooperative work relationships based on sharing information, authority, and responsibility. Having an established, acceptable identity as a team member may take precedence over being a solo performer.

The information in this section adds to methods you can use to develop your personal equation. Your base was built in "Relevant Ideas or Factors" in Question 4.1. In this chapter, you will develop a better understanding of the unique factors of your job and how your job affects others. The role and importance of internal and external customers are discussed.

Two ways to obtain information on your job are outlined next. The first is open-ended. The second method is structured and requires specific information about your job and how you do it.

Major Sources of Information

Most information comes from the people doing the work. Most information can be grouped into hard (quantitative) or soft (qualitative) data.

Hard, or numeric, measurements, such as cost, cycle time, amount of output, and measures of quality, are often presented as rational, undisputed facts.[15] These data are relatively easy to collect and document. They are often used as measures of success or as indicators of productivity.

Soft data are based on observations, interviews, various documents, appraisals of self and others, and numerous other sources, including thought processes (visions, attitudes, values, and feelings). This subjective information can be a stand-alone source or can be combined with quantitative data. Soft (qualitative) information and hard (quantitative) data are used to support and/or validate each other.[17]

Other information sources include subordinates, supervisors, peers, team members, internal and external customers, partners, vendors, suppliers, and stakeholders. The politics and dynamics of asking peers for information about a close work associate are unclear, as results are mixed.

Open-Ended Method

Can you separate what is being thought from what is being said? Draw a line down the middle of a blank sheet of paper. Write your *thoughts* about your job in the left-hand column. This column represents the mental processes that may or may not be related to what is written down in the right-hand column. Write what actually *happens* in the right-hand column. This column represents reality or concrete, describable events.

You can work from left to right or right to left. Items written in the right-hand column may jog your memory about what to write in the left-hand column, or vice versa. You can also choose to write down everything in one column before starting on the other column. It will take time and patience to determine how to balance both sides. After a while, the sides will come closer to balancing.[1]

Another method that sounds simple but takes some effort is to compare what people say with what they do. Espoused theories are what people say. Their mental models are their guides to action. A prime concern of this manual is mental models that can be developed and used to guide actions.

Structured Method

If you were to examine your job and do it better, what should the best possible end results of your job be? Question 7.1 examines major work activities performed in the course of a week. It is important to know what results are expected and the range of work standards that apply. Differences between expectations and achieved results should be taken into consideration. If the gap is wide, it will be important to look at standards, type of job, even perceptions. While it is not always realistic to rate jobs on the basis of their contribution to the bottom line, it is one way to see how they fit into the overall scheme of things.

An alternative to the "bottom line" is to: (1) concentrate on things that make a difference. Other guides are: (2) tasks that only you can do; (3) aspects that add value, and (4) creative, innovative methods that have far reaching effects. Decide whether the "bottom line" or any of the four proposed alternatives can be used to judge your job.

Classifying Work Activities

Work can be grouped or classified in various ways. Groupings differ between various departments in the same organization and also between different organizations.

Do not confuse activities (steps taken to achieve results) and results. Steps and results should each be clearly defined. A separate time frame needs to be specified for activities and results. Typical questions are, "How well did we do it?" "What should we do now?" "What should we do in the future?" In today's highly competitive environment, the main thrust should be on streamlining efforts, reducing costs, enhancing productivity, and increasing all bottom-line results. Current efforts to improve quality are steps in the right direction.

Work activities can be classified according to:[10]

1. Range or scope of the work refers to repetitiveness or the cyclic, routine nature of work. Group or individual effort is involved. The range can be narrow on the one hand or broad on the other. Some work is cyclic, or comes around once a week. Other work may be routine, like reading reports, having meetings, and other standard operating procedures.

2. Structure of tasks fluctuates between fixed and changeable. Tasks can be highly structured or hard to change. Job descriptions may be very precise and guidelines for doing the work equally precise, as in developing a computer program for a highly technical project.

3. Control or amount of freedom of choice or discretion in planning how and when work is performed.

4. Cognitive effort or reasoning is required to solve work problems. Level of cognitive reasoning is different in various professions and disciplines. Effort can range from very limited to very substantial.

People at Work

Type of work, content of work, and level of difficulty in product-based and service-based industries may differ widely. Assembly-line activities are product based, whereas computer programming is primarily process based. However, both have tangible products and internal and external customers with varying needs and priorities.

Internal customers may help support you and your job, or they may play an indirect role by conveying, processing, and analyzing information. Some will perform a value-added function by interpreting or transforming your information, even your work output, into a different type of product, like a report or brochure.

Most jobs revolve around work done by a wide range of people who work anywhere and do a variety of jobs. Some are self-employed, or entrepreneurs. Others work outside a traditional setting or pursue unique part-time careers as writers or artists or engage in other meaningful endeavors.

The number of white-collar workers grows steadily. By 2000, this number may grow from approximately 70 percent today to 90 percent of the work force. They work at all levels of the organization. With the rapid growth of the service sector, many white-collar workers are, for the first time, in direct, near continuous contact with customers. Some can be classified by their skills.

Types of "workers" and characteristics of work performed presented in Table 7.1 range from clerical to professional.[18] Clearly separating professional from clerical or support work is not easy. These categories are not meant to be all-inclusive, but rather illustrate and describe selected types of work activities from the whole spectrum of work.

Activities listed in Table 7.1 also provides baseline information for developing operational definitions. The listings will help you relate to your own job and determine how it interfaces with jobs others perform. When more is known about types of workers and characteristics of work, it is easier to relate to your own job and determine how it interfaces with jobs other people do.

The term "white-collar work" may be outdated or misused. This manual is based on what you do and not on whether your work classification fits into Table 7.1. The table is a simple guide that illustrates common types of workers and characteristics of work.

Most people you work with regularly include professionals, specialists, support and clerical workers, "knowledge workers," those independently employed or self-employed, volunteers, and former "blue-collar" workers.

Table 7.1 Major Types of White-Collar Workers
and Characteristics of Work Performed

Professional Workers: Knowledge Worker, Manager, Coordinator, Executive,
Specialist, Administrator

Characteristics of Work:

- Routine
- Tasks are fixed
- Short feedback cycle
- Low level of complexity
- Outcome can be measured

- Output is a prime factor
- Objectives are specified
- Relatively easy to define
- Activities can be described
- Repetitive, cyclic in nature

Support Workers: Clerical, Assembly Line, Factory Worker

Characteristics of Work:

- Non-routine
- Discretionary
- Non-repetitive
- Hard to measure
- Difficult to define
- May be ambiguous
- Requires coordination
- Requires self-management

- Has technical and non-technical parameters
- Based on cognitive effort
- Has a long feedback cycle
- Changes hard to anticipate
- Has a "value-added" quality
- Process as important as task
- Produces ideas and information

Types of Work Performed

Work can be grouped or classified in various ways. Groupings differ between various departments in the same organization, as well as between different organizations.

1. Specialty Area. These include education, concept development, market research, idea generation, design and evaluation for areas such as manufacturing, and management. As always, planning precedes learning.

2. Routine vs. Non-routine. The structures of systems need to be flexible in non-routine work. This flexibility implies changing the decision-making body when the subject matter changes, as attorneys make decisions about legal matters and not about sales. Also, long-term groups can be formed around knowledge acquisition, as in doing research and writing grant applications.

3. Process vs. "Content" Issue. Process is associated with intangible efforts, or throughput. Content relates to tangible products, like output. This unclear relationship between input (ideas) and output (new products or services) is difficult to describe, define, measure, and work with in general.

Work processes in many organizations are similar, although the end results (products vs. services) are different. There are more similarities in white-collar activities across organizations, even countries, than many people believe. In a similar vein, jobs throughout the world have similar content. Standard activities, like processing information and communicating with others, are performed regularly, regardless of what you do and where you work.

Guidelines to separate activities, or processes, from results are:

- Define each concept operationally and make comparisons. When work processes and results are clearly defined, it is easier to compare them.

- Identify variables, like input, throughput, and output, wherever possible. Often, what can be easily identified and described turns out to be results.

Starting with results may make it easier to describe jobs. You may find that most of your work is somewhere in the "in between" or process area. If you are in a highly specialized profession, work results may have a narrow range but great depth. An example is research in a specialized area in biochemistry.

4. Direct vs. Indirect Work.   Direct work concentrates on activities and processes related to meeting customer needs for products and/or services on a minute-to-minute basis. Direct work adds value when it directly contributes to the completion of the "vital few" as opposed to the "insignificant many" tasks. The origin of direct work was in the factory.[12]

Making sales and completing projects are easy to report in numeric terms. Critical direct work is basic to survival and to continuous operations. Intra-firm organizations and management in general are common sources of imposed direct work.

Indirect work concentrates on productive potential and reflects the amount of group or organizational time spent on work that is not mission driven. Examples include requests for information, status reports, clerical tasks, maintenance, supervision, attending meetings, and returning favors.[12]

When the amount of indirect work is lowered, superfluous demands are reduced, along with liaison and coordinating activities. This has good and bad points, as coordinators are also prime sources of information on a range of issues. If indirect work depends on following a sequence, as in project management, the leverage points for reducing cost or increasing quality, for instance, are along the path.

Doing more direct work could increase your productivity—but how? Steps are:[12]

1. Clarify your vision of the business and align your organization's mission to this vision. Mission-driven outputs are indispensable, as they are the reason the organization exists.

2. Sort through your work to identify tasks. Involve people who are in any way responsible for these tasks.

3. Estimate how much time is spent in each task over a week. If possible, do a time log.

4. Define each activity as direct or indirect work according to whether the task is absolutely vital to complete the mission-driven outputs and outcomes.

5. Determine the total number of direct and indirect tasks and compute a ratio or percentage. The amount of direct tasks may range from 40 to 70 percent. If direct work is low, estimate how much time you spent on each indirect task. Involve internal and external customers in helping you decide the type of work that no one needs to do. Reduce time spent on marginal tasks, streamline processes, and minimize procedural demands.

It is also possible to improve the quality of direct work by changing the frequency, amount, or level of quality and/or making substitutions. Redistribute the work force to improve the match between people and the resulting work. As always, remeasure, readjust, track processes, and then start all over again. These steps create an endless cycle of change and improvement.

In general, the more direct work the better, unless the job is in the area of providing indirect work. Helton[11] illustrates ways to compare the ratio of direct work/indirect work. It may not be surprising that the ratio in the United States is less than one.

5. Time Frame.   Freedom of choice in planning and in developing long-range timetables or milestone for accomplishment is often greater in research and development activities than in many other areas. However, time frames in manufacturing can be very short.

6. Length of the Feedback Cycle.   Feedback on short-term and intermediate-term results, like a three-month to six-month time frame, is a good substitute. Knowledge of *any* form of results at *any* phase of the work cycle is vital.

7. Level of Cognitive Effort.   This depends on the type of profession and specific requirements of ongoing projects. Cognitive effort may be more subjective and a process or throughput variable.

Professional and Specialist Work

This group performs non-repetitive, non-routine, discretionary work.[2] They collect, process, analyze, and disseminate information in mass media, education, finance, and computer-related fields. Level of work ranges from high-level, complex activities to simple, routine clerical activities.

Work done by professionals and specialists is challenging, involves a major amount of cognitive effort, and in general is not usually repetitious. Differences between specialist and professional work are more a matter of degree than content of work performed. Specialist work emphasizes considerable individual cognitive effort, is often ambiguous, and has long feedback cycles. Unstructured information from external sources is commonly used to solve problems. The complex nature of many tasks, such as research, makes it difficult to find clear-cut solutions. Specialists and professionals depend heavily on the output of support workers or work teams.

Knowledge Work

Knowledge workers, a term Drucker[5] coined, include professionals, managers, human resource development staff, sales staff, administrators, and executives. Knowledge workers are white-collar workers, but not all white-collar workers are knowledge workers.[2] Knowledge workers make up 30 to 40 percent of all employees.[6] Most white-collar workers have a college degree(s) and/or special-ized training. Hereafter, the broad term "white-collar workers" includes knowl-edge workers.

Knowledge work has technical or quantitative and non-technical dimensions, yet is subjective, hard to define, and difficult to measure. Much work goes on in people's heads. This work is illusive and intangible in nature. It is often embedded in the heads of specialists.[14]

A considerable amount of work performed by knowledge workers consists of new, forefront types of activities having few, if any, guidelines. Knowledge work is frequently defined by results and not necessarily by cost or quantity.

Most knowledge workers make contributions that materially affect the organization's capacity to perform and obtain results. They own the "means of production," which is their knowledge, but they still need the tools of produc-tion, such as equipment, technology, and a place to work.[6]

This group performs diverse types of value-adding work for internal and external customers, vendors, suppliers, and partners. As mentioned in the defi-nitions of productivity, value is added when another person or knowledge worker converts ideas, knowledge, or information into realistic, useful outputs. To illustrate, a literature survey or numerical report has little or no value until a trained or knowledgeable person interprets and presents the information in a useful format using terms people requesting the survey or report understand.

Ownership, or self-management, implies self-direction; self-monitoring and empowerment are often a major part of white-collar activities. A great deal of this work involves self-assessment activities that stress analyzing one's own accomplishments and the accomplishments of others.

Monetary investments in knowledge workers are high. The capital investments in knowledge workers' tools, like computers, libraries, and laboratory equipment, may already exceed that of manufacturing workers' tools. Also, the social investment in a knowledge worker's education is larger than the investment in a manual worker's education.

Because of the purported intangible nature of some parts of their jobs, knowledge workers may not have a clear idea of their unique contribution to overall organizational efforts. Work environment are often uncertain and results rarely predictable or quantifiable. Because of the long feedback cycle, being patient and tolerating ambiguity are a way of life.

For example, many research scientists are unable to predict the results of their efforts.[13] They may work in loosely structured environments or on their own.

The production rate of knowledge work depends on a complex interaction of intelligence, creativity, and environment. Knowledge workers have almost total authority in matching their own individual work methods to the varying tasks they perform. Their work efforts and accomplishments affect substantial numbers of people inside and outside the organization. The value of many products and services, including information, is increased by knowledge workers.[8]

Major characteristics of professional, specialist, and knowledge work are summarized as follows:

1. Work is often non-repetitive, non-routine, and performed on an as-needed basis. Activities may overlap, but few people will do exactly the same thing. Customers, clients, or end users may be different.

2. The throughput stage is difficult to clearly identify. Much work is "process" and consists of intangible, cognitive activities like thinking, reasoning, creating, and innovating.

3. Work has technical and non-technical parameters, as the level of work and the mental processes and skills required to perform it range from simple to complex.

4. Activities and outcomes are hard to define and difficult to measure in precise job-related terms. A common belief is that work cannot, perhaps should not, be precisely defined. The (erroneous) assumption was that if work could not be defined adequately, it could not be measured.

5. Work requires self-management, coordination, patience, and often many years of study. Direct supervision is seldom required, but work activities may be monitored. To illustrate, once professional training is com-

pleted, (re)licensing and/or certification examinations and requirements for continuing education help maintain competence, specifically for physicians, attorneys, certified public accountants, and airplane pilots.

6. The feedback cycle is long, ranging from months to no end in sight. The majority of work is long term, like research projects requiring many years or perhaps even a lifetime to complete. Professional educators, inventors, writers, artists, computer programmers, and concert performers often have dual careers.

7. Certification, licensing, or some predictable, standardized method to assess skills and competence may be required. Some professional groups, like nurses, doctors, and teachers, require continuing education in order to meet relicensing or recertification standards.

8. Work may have a value-added component, which is often the sole "invention" of the person doing the job. This "extra touch" is something that the person either does spontaneously or thinks of on his or her own because it relates to the job. Examples are providing an unexpected benefit or special services that keep customers coming back.

    Creativity is involved in developing value added. No one can be certain how to produce concepts or ideas that customers or clients feel are truly value added. This illusive concept may be in the eye of the beholder.

9. Processes associated with work may be as important as the task. When people prepare reports or master new computer programs, the trial-and-error learning experience that lasts weeks or months is invaluable. The acquired knowledge is added on to the existing store of information and enhances and improves overall competencies.

10. Solitary work, like acquiring information, may be done by one person and shared with work groups, or individuals may make a formal presentation to management based on findings of their task force. The knowledge of the team resides in the individuals in the group and in their relationships, even in the synergy between group members. Reassigning this team can produce disastrous results. People who usually work in teams say that it takes several years to build a good team.

Support and Clerical Work

The major characteristics and descriptions of work done by support and clerical workers are listed:

1. Support and clerical work is primarily skill based, repetitive, or routine. The same or very similar types of work may be done repeatedly, with few if any variations. Several slightly different jobs may be done hourly or daily or may be rotated on a regular basis.

2. Feedback cycles are usually short, as in direct interaction with customers or responding to telephone inquiries. In assembly-line work, tasks may be performed in sequence, as in passing work from one person to another.

3. Data gathering and record keeping, or "feeding the administrative systems," may be involved in sales and accounting areas.

4. Tasks are specialized and have fixed objectives. Many use readily available information, as in processing customers' mail orders.

5. Objectives are specified, as in a job description, within the unit or department where the work is done. There will usually be procedures to follow or manuals that set out the objectives and how the job is to be done.

6. Support workers may have college degrees, higher education, or specialized training. The focus of work can be knowledge intensive, as in project teams, or day-to-day procedural, as with clerical workers.[10]

7. Speed, accuracy, and use of current technology, like computers, often characterize this type of work.

8. Job descriptions will be relatively complete. Skills required and other abilities needed to perform the job will be set out in simple terms.

9. Activities often depend on cooperative efforts, as in working in assembling or packaging products or in data processing.

10. Specific procedures or manuals will set out the objectives and how the job is to be done.

It is important to sequence activities and encourage cooperative endeavors and teamwork that enable professional, specialist, and support workers to perform their jobs in an effective, efficient manner. Those who become prisoners of their own fascination may neglect the organization's major mission. Work for the sake of work can be a cyclic, never-ending endeavor. Going into things more deeply than is necessary can be costly to the organization and not provide any specific intellectual or positive gain for the individual. While the bottom line should not figure into every effort, it is important to have a balance between what is essential and what may be extra but not necessarily add value.

The following is an abbreviated example of possible skill areas for engineers and mechanics.[4] Engineers and mechanics would agree that there is some overlap between the work each performs.

Engineers	Mechanics
Design	Maintenance
Materials management	Servicing
Administration	Materials handling
Problem solving	Repair
Evaluation	Quality control
Safety	Planning
Training	Health and safety
Quality control	Welding
Leadership	Detailing

7.1

List five major work activities or jobs you perform during a typical week. Estimate the percent of time spent in each activity. Jot down results you expect to achieve and the results actually achieved. Estimate and then rank (1 is low...7 is high) how much each major work activity affects the "bottom line." You may want to operationally define each of the seven points on the rating scale.

Major Work Activities	% Time Performed	Results Expected	Results Achieved	Rank of Importance to Bottom Line
1.				
2.				
3.				
4.				
5.				

7.2

Did you combine activities and results when you answered Question 7.1? If so, could feedback or knowledge of results help separate activities from results? If your job has few tangible results, you may find that using activities as a source for feedback gives meaningful information.

Major work activities are the heart of your job. You either perform these activities regularly or are expected to perform them consistently. Depending on the nature of your work, it may be difficult to determine and describe these activities in clear, concise terms. In some instances, your activities may be similar to your organization's key result areas. Various people in the organization (internal customers) may depend on your output or your contribution to the regular flow of work. When someone further up the line is late getting a report to you, what happens further down the line if your report is late?

Most types of work performed depend on the profession (e.g., engineer, researcher, computer programmer, accountant, manager, or salesperson). The majority of activities will likely be within your own profession, but may relate to supervision, coordination, or other forms of group activities.

Estimates of time should total between 50 percent to 75 percent. Otherwise, either the activities listed are not representative or your job is not predictable on a week-by-week basis.

Some "dream goals" may have been "visioned" into your present job. When you know your goals, it is possible to achieve then, one small step at a time. Small steps, as we all know, do add up and really do make a difference.

Expected results are the goals and objectives of your department, organization, etc. and may be based on personal or organizational goals or mission statements. Knowing your goals, what kind of business you are in, and who your internal and external customers are is very important.

The extent to which each major objective listed contributes to the bottom line could be a tangible measure of productivity. For jobs that have intangible output or long-delayed results, as in research and development areas, judging only on the basis of bottom-line results is not logical. Stressing processes, or effort rather than only output, may be more appropriate in jobs where end results are not easy to describe.

Examples of surface activities are seeing people attend meetings, work on reports, etc. Inner, or "depth," activities are processes, like communicating, evaluating, and thinking. People assume we are doing these things, but may not know *what* results we have achieved or *when* or *how* we achieved them. Sometimes even we are not sure of our own progress, particularly when involved with long-term projects where definite accomplishments are not easily determined.

Some professions are far removed from the results or direct impact of our work, as in research, designing products, or teaching. However, feedback from various sources, including fellow scientists, production engineers, students, and customers, helps pinpoint results. Being part of a continuous flow of paperwork may also distance people from the real sources of problems and solutions.

Work in Service-Based and Product-Based Industries

As discussed in Chapter 6, a steadily growing number of organizations provide services as opposed to products. However, increasing numbers provide both, like home supply stores such as Home Depot. Sometimes it is the services which accompany the products that attract us and sometimes the exact opposite occurs.

Questions 7.2 and 7.3 ask for information about your job, your work group, and your customers in service-based and/or product-based industries. This information forms the base for your personal equation. The focus can be on both individual and group accomplishments and on a customer orientation.

Product-Based Industries

Descriptions of work in product-based industries include amount of output from production-type operations, manufacturing, and laboratories, for example. Output is measured by number of units produced, assembled, or designed, either by humans or through various automated procedures, including robots. Efforts are directed toward working with suppliers, partners, and others who provide raw materials or equipment used to make products. Control of processes and quality and monitoring costs may be major parts of the job. Definitions will be tangible and concepts used in the definitions relatively easy to describe and measure.

Industries producing tangible, measurable products start with raw materials. Many activities are associated with the flow of production. This includes scheduling, checking maintenance scheduled, monitoring inventory, acquiring raw materials, and similar activities. Rework, cycle time, cost, and employee motivation are also major areas of concern.

Product-based areas are easier to understand. The form of input and output is usually tangible, like food, textiles, or constructing roads or buildings.

The emphasis is on quality control over raw materials, such as monitoring and inspection, and work in progress. Work families could be broadly classified as quality control, quality improvement, productivity, etc. Names of groups or work families may be the same or similar to those used in job descriptions. Getting the product out in the shortest cycle time possible is emphasized.

In product-based activities, major contact is with internal customers who also help design and create products. In car manufacturing, the external customer is the buyer who may live far from the assembly line. Close customer contact occurs when the product is manufactured or repaired on site, as in replacing worn out industrial equipment in a plant or fixing brakes on your automobile.

Service-Based Industries

Descriptions or definitions of work in service-based organizations could be similar to those above. Definitions can include (1) input, like energy, ideas, and creativity; (2) throughput in the form of motivation, coordination, facilitation, and empathy; and (3) output, including innovative or cost-effective services. Definitions may be difficult to create as they will be based on concepts such as sharing ideas, working together, or producing creative products.

The best definitions in the service area could come from customer responses to surveys and questionnaires or face-to-face contact. However, most survey information uses numeric rating scales, which lack the value-added element of the customer's own words. Unless each point on the rating scale is operationally defined by the developer of the scale and the customer, agreement on exactly what a rating of "5" on a 7-point scale really means may be open to question.

The customer's own definition of excellent service or recommendations for improvement are vital to improvement efforts. A customer's definition could be to "provide the service when and where I want it at a cost I can afford."

In service industries, customers often dictate the type of service they want. Unfortunately, many service-based organizations appear not to have been originally designed with customers in mind. Jobs performed will vary from direct, daily, face-to-face contact with customers to developing new services for your "best" customers in another part of the world. All work or work family descriptions will have a customer orientation.

Work differs in terms of amount of customer contact. In service areas where customer contact is high, tasks are communicating, coordinating, monitoring, or supervising customer or end-user services. Training to improve customer services may be emphasized. Teaching in a university is a high customer-contact area. Customers are students, other faculty members, committee members, deans, and associates in other universities with whom information is shared. The diverse work families could be referred to as administration, teaching, and research.

In high-contact areas, customers become partners in designing and testing new services and products. Often, services are developed to complement the products that were originally produced.

A good example of a customer orientation comes from IBM. Its customer service departments are built around the delivery and support of their own products. IBM employees can describe their work efforts in terms of what customers want and need, but most of all in terms of satisfaction.

In medium customer-contact service areas, attention to customers, supervising staff, and training and development will be balanced. Work families include activities like assembling information, providing needed resources, and other forms of liaison activities which connect customers with those who develop, as opposed to directly provide, the services, as in product development.

In low customer-contact service areas, such as research, a work family could simply be "research." Most work is done entirely in the lab. The customer may be an invoice number on a billing statement.

Products and services in "excellent" organizations are being benchmarked by others to determine "best" practices for a given industry, profession, product, or process. Benchmarking also provides baselines for making comparisons and ways to develop standard information for sharing, perhaps throughout the world.

7.3

If you have not mentally defined the type of work you do in product-based and service-based industries, develop your definitions now. The frame of reference you use in this chapter can be used in the remaining chapters.

Definition in product-based industries:

_____

_____

Definition in service-based industries:

_____

_____

7.4

Review your answers to Question 7.1. Select one product-based and one service-based area. Indicate the approximate percent of time or effort spent with customers, typical contact areas, or problems. Specify ways to improve the products/services provided to increase their value and/or satisfy internal or external customers, end users, suppliers, or partners. Could personal productivity be improved by increasing the direct/indirect work ratio?

Product-Based Area	% Customer Contact	Typical Problem Areas	Ways to Increase Value/Satisfaction
___	___	___	___
___	___	___	___
___	___	___	___
___	___	___	___

Service-Based Area	% Customer Contact	Typical Problem Areas	Ways to Increase Value/Satisfaction
___	___	___	___
___	___	___	___
___	___	___	___
___	___	___	___

Roles of Internal and External Customers

Your company policy may specify how internal and external customers are to be handled. If you are fortunate, you may be empowered to do what works best right on the spot. Both types of customers can exist in the same setting. Internal customers of a research lab, for instance, would be peers and lab associates. External customers down the hall or around the world use the services or products the lab produces.

One view is that if you are not reaching external customers at all times, you are too far away from the action. The opposite view is, "Serving internal customers sounds like a good, solid practice, but in reality it is dangerous."[9]

A middle-of-the road view is that both internal and external customers are important. Providers must know what internal and external customers need and want and how both can be served adequately.

Internal Customers

These customers may share your office, use your reports, or work for another company half a world away. They are your peers, supervisors, subordinates, and a myriad of service providers in data processing, human resources, and marketing.

Internal customers in the form of data-processing services provide valuable support functions. They also represent a layer of management whose function is passing along information or transforming your raw data into a formal report.

The prime concern is whether organizations still have the luxury of subsidizing an internal chain of individuals who serve and support the next link in the process. These jobs and the functions performed are buffered from external customers. Harari believes, "If you are not serving the customer, you had better be serving someone who is."[9]

A way to reduce the cost of serving internal customers is to charge them for their services, namely to form profit centers. Internal customers can be encouraged to scan the marketplace for better or cheaper products and services.

External Customers

These customers are easy to identify. Some stand in front of counters, making purchases. Others phone, write, or fax, even actively help design and improve products or new customer services.

For instance, accountants who go on sales calls learn more about the realities of the marketplace. They could work with engineers throughout a product development cycle in order to ensure a cost-effective, timely product, or they could pool resources with the training department to create and deliver a curriculum for teaching how to be cost effective and responsive.[9]

Jobs and functions that are not core priorities of the organization can be subcontracted. Also, people in traditional support functions can reconfigure their jobs to help serve the external customer directly.

It is vital to be in close contact with your external customers. Getting closer to the customer is done by joining self-managed, interdisciplinary project teams that work on reducing some facet of expenses, time, or other critical areas.

7.5

Do you provide different quality of services or products for your "best" customers?

Identifying your "best" external and internal and customers should not be difficult. The number and range of internal customers identified may surprise you. If most customers are external, determining who your best internal customers are will take thought.

You may be unaware that customers themselves may have set the high standards. You simply comply.

For any number of reasons, "best" in your mind could mean customers who are easy to work with because they are easily satisfied, or their standards could be low. "Best" may also mean they are partners and provide valuable information or much-needed resources. Before you stop thinking about your "best" customers, think about the biases you wrote down in Chapter 3

Input from all types of customers is a valuable source of information. Many customers are eager to provide information. If you ask them, you will be both pleased *and* surprised with the results.

7.6

Refer to major work activities listed in Question 7.1. How many were performed for internal customers and for external customers?

The number of activities performed for internal or external customers is influenced by the amount of direct contact a person has with customers.

How can you increase external customer loyalty? Measures of loyalty are retention rate or share of purchases, or both. Revenue grows as a result of repeat purchases and referrals. Cost also declines when it simply costs less to maintain efficient systems to serve experienced customers. Having a brief history of needs, expectations, and dislikes of longstanding customers is a good aid in providing them with specialized services. When customer loyalty is high, employee retention may increase due to job pride and satisfaction, which in turn creates an endless loop that reinforces customer loyalty, etc. etc.[16]

SUMMARY AND CONCLUSIONS

1. The sharpened focus on quality and the growing emphasis on effectiveness and productivity literally force us to learn more about work itself and the workplace. We need to start looking within ourselves and our work environments. We are our own best resource!

2. "White-collar work" performed in the organization is tempered by shifting forces within the organization and by an external environment of continual change. The precise nature and scope of these work activities must be identified and defined before ways to measure quality and productivity can be developed and improved. Teams and "sharing" resources, recognition, and rewards challenge the traditional way work is viewed and performed.

3. How people perceive their jobs or want to perceive their jobs has a major impact on how they relate to others. Having a thorough understanding of exactly what is to be done is critical. Job descriptions are used to serve this purpose. However, the changing nature of jobs makes job descriptions not only difficult to write, but difficult to keep current. Professional-level people seldom have a precise job description, or any job description at all. However, it is possible to know how people's jobs overlap or interface with other jobs. Just observe and make it a point to ask others about their jobs.

4. The organization, the work setting, technology, and many other factors play a role in how people function, as discussed in Chapter 5. Typical factors that influence work activities within the organization are procedures and policies, such as the reward system, information system, quality efforts in process, climate for cooperation, and many other influences. Organizational design could become the basis for gaining competitive advantage.[7]

5. Innovations in technology depend on knowledge workers. All forms of technical and support workers are responsible for building the equipment and "installing" technology. It is essential to keep up with competition, both local and global. A company's capacity to absorb, adopt, and transfer technology is increasingly becoming the key to business strategy.[3]

6. In knowledge work, it is important to maintain an optimum balance between using critical knowledge that is developed and giving underutilized areas the attention they deserve. For instance, it may be necessary to redesign or streamline processes like inquiry, deliberation of content needed, and application in order to make better use of knowledge workers and their special talents or abilities.

7. Internal and external customers play important roles in service-based and product-based industries. Forming partnerships with suppliers and a wide array of end users to help develop new products and services is becoming increasingly common. Wise use of technology as a tool for

streamlining work and enhancing quality is vital in our increasingly competitive, cost-conscious world.

8. Putting a priority on work, and deciding that one type or level of work is more important to the bottom line, helps put your job in perspective. Focusing on direct work will help keep the major mission and goals of the organization in full view. Not all work done individually or in groups is vital to the total success of an organization; some work helps support the infrastructure, as with indirect work.

PRACTICAL APPLICATIONS

1. Do high-performing people have secrets? Are secrets disguised as careful planning, setting the right goals, and working hard? Probably. My personal observations are that most productive people are proactive, as they plan ahead and anticipate problems. They separate direct work from indirect work. They are efficient and effective. They work quickly and generally do things right the first time. Given the opportunity, high performers provide quality products or services that customers value. The profit motive may be high either for themselves or for their organizations. They use their talents to the best advantage.

2. If work activities of a wide range of people working in organizations can be described and measured, there will be overlap among jobs. This opens up the opportunity for cross-training, job-sharing, and other co-operative endeavors which allow people to do more of what they do best. Increased job satisfaction and productivity are logical end results.

3. As much effort as possible should be directed toward the growing number of part-time or temporary workers. Reportedly, they comprise a very large sector of the work force. An editorial in the March 1994 issue of *Quality Progress* discussed the role of part-time or temporary workers. Manpower, the largest of the nation's 7000 temporarily help agencies, has more than 600,000 employees. This is 200,000 more employees than General Motors and 345,000 more than IBM.

    These workers undoubtedly perform well on clearly defined and well-documented tasks. Unfortunately, they know little about the history, culture, and logic of the companies for which they are working. It is often the memories and methods of checking how things are done that are so important to customers—and simply to staying in business. These temporary workers lack the organizational memory and experience that long-standing employees possess.

Current literature reflects that part-timers and temporary workers feel physically and emotionally separated from the organization. Their pay and associated benefits are below the standard for full-time workers. Loyalty and commitment to the organization may be low, just as the organization's commitment to contract workers is low.

4. It may be necessary to redesign or streamline inquiry processes to see where systems or processes can be redesigned to make better use of knowledge workers and their special talents and abilities.[14]

Knowledge scan looks outside the organization to see what is available or will be needed and at the inventory of what is currently available in the system. The gap between what is known and what is needed creates an agenda for augmenting knowledge resources.

Deliberation analysis reveals variances in the way knowledge is handled. The major area of focus is to clarify how the design of the system and the behavior of individuals within it influence which knowledge is given weight and which is discarded.

Knowledge application audit examines factors that influence which knowledge is actually applied to the tasks undertaken. The prime area of concentration answers the question, "Did we apply most of the knowledge we developed, or did we develop much more knowledge than we needed?"

5. Many people at all levels in the organization perform similar activities, like entering data into the computer, searching for information, preparing reports, etc. Sharing or outsourcing some of this "core" or basic work could increase efficiency and effectiveness. These aspects are discussed in subsequent chapters of this manual.

REFERENCES

1. Agryris, Chris. *Reasoning, Learning, and Action: Individual and Organizational*, San Francisco: Jossey-Bass, 1982.

2. Belcher, John. *Productivity Plus+*, Houston: Gulf Publishing, 1987.

3. Branscomb, Lewis M. "Does America Need a Technology Policy?" *Harvard Business Review*, March–April 1992, pp. 24–28, 30–31.

4. Denis, Joe and Austin, Bruce. "A Base(ic) Course on Job Analysis," *Training & Development*, July 1992, pp. 67–70.

5. Drucker, Peter F. *The Effective Executive*, New York: Harper & Row, 1967.

6. Drucker, Peter F. "The New Society of Organizations," *Harvard Business Review*, September–October 1992, pp. 95–104.

7. Galbraith, Jay R., Lawler, Edward E. III, and associates. *Organizing for the Future*, San Francisco: Jossey-Bass, 1993.

8. Gregerman, Ira B. *Knowledge Worker Productivity*, New York: AMACOM, 1981.

9. Harari, Oren. "Internal Customer, R. I. P.," *Management Review*, June 1993, pp. 30–32.

10. Helton, D. Ray. "Will the Real Knowledge Worker Please Stand Up?" *Industrial Management*, January–February 1987, pp. 26–29.

11. Helton, D. Ray. "Achieving White-Collar Whitewater Performance by Organizational Alignment," *National Productivity Review*, Spring 1991, pp. 237–311.

12. Helton, B. Ray. "More of the Right Stuff," *The Quality Observer*, September 1993, pp. 5, 14.

13. Kelly, Robert E. *The Gold Collar Worker*, New York: Addison-Wesley, 1985.

14. Pasmore, William A. and Purser, Ronald E. "Designing Work Systems for Knowledge Workers," *Journal for Quality and Participation*, July/August 1993, pp. 78–84.

15. Phillips, Jack J. *Handbook of Training Evaluation and Measurement Methods*, Houston: Gulf Publishing, 1983.

16. Reichheld, Frederick F. "Loyalty-Based Management," *Harvard Business Review*, March–April 1993, pp. 64–73.

17. Smith, Elizabeth A. "The Role of Qualitative Information in Productivity Measurement," *Industrial Management*, March/April 1991, pp. 14–18.

18. Smith, Elizabeth A. "Operationally Defining Quality of White Collar/Knowledge Work," in *Proceedings of the European Organization for Quality*, Helsinki, Finland, June 14–18, 1993, pp. 286–291.

19. Smith, Elizabeth. "Value Added: Perception vs. Expectations vs. Reality," *The Quality Observer*, in press (expected publication date July 1995).

8

A SYSTEMS VIEW
OF WORK

PURPOSE

- Outline reengineering and business process analysis
- Discuss systems from various perspectives
- Present and illustrate subsystems and their importance
- Discuss uses and applications of systems approaches

INTRODUCTION

Methods or tools primarily associated with a systems approach are used to examine work. A systems approach demonstrates relationships between various input, throughput, and output variables associated with work in general. Feedback plays a critical role in change, improvement, and control.

Input and especially output variables are well-known, readily accepted concepts. However, processes and connections or throughput are really the glue that holds separate activities together. Unless these interfaces, or "joins," are in good working order, perfectly good processes and products can literally come apart.

People reinforce many of these strong connections as well as cause the "disconnects," or gaps, in the logical flow of products, processes, and services.

Processes are the intangible activities that fall between inputs (energy, capital, materials, labor) and outputs (products, services, tangible accomplishments, etc.). Processes are especially important in the service industry, which accounts for 70 percent or more of the gross national product of the United States.

Content of this chapter includes: (1) an introduction to business process analysis and business process reengineering, both applications of systems approaches; (2) history, systems models, and subsystems, including feedback and cycle time; and (3) practical applications of systems approaches.

INTRODUCTION TO BUSINESS PROCESS ANALYSIS AND BUSINESS PROCESS REENGINEERING

Business process analysis and business process reengineering are new names for techniques Henry Ford used in 1910. Business process reengineering represents a systematic approach to accomplish breakthrough performance. Business process analysis goes hand in hand with total quality management. It concentrates on getting the best from people.

Business Process Analysis

Process-based management takes an overall view of the main business processes. Customer involvement, communication, and product development are focal points. This process follows the customer along various paths that meet customer needs, but opens up a whole new way to view and relate to customers.

Process management concentrates on the actual horizontal flows of operations and empowers employees to improve their own work processes, namely getting the best from people. When companies organize around key processes, organizational units are created for each key process that produces a result for internal and external customers. Outputs are tied to job satisfaction and to motivation.[19]

The stated purposes of business process analysis (BPA) are to improve the effectiveness and efficiency of a process, yet stay within the specified budget. BPA is one of the prime elements of total quality management. Changes are often brought about through team efforts that identify how to achieve performance gains in cycle time, quality, and efficiency, yet maintain deadlines agreed to by division management.

Team efforts are directed toward: (1) understanding methods to be used,

(2) using effective communication, (3) developing and attaining clear and congruent goals, and (4) commitment to the project.

Managing the "white spaces" on the organizational chart is another way to portray BPA. Rummler and Brache[13] discuss the various work processes and white spaces that must be effectively and efficiently managed in order to achieve cost, quality, and speed, along with good leadership.

Business Process Reengineering

Business process reengineering (BPR) was defined in Chapter 4. Business processes are collections of activities that transform business inputs into business outputs.[7] A prime concern of BPR is achieving customer satisfaction in order to achieve business objectives.

Major purposes of BPR are to: (1) seek performance breakthroughs by using radical and discontinuous improvements instead of incremental improvements; (2) pursue multi-faceted improvement goals concurrently, specifically, quality, cost, flexibility, speed, and accuracy; and (3) assimilate and adopt the perspectives of the business.[7]

BPR is a top-down, holistic effort that impacts every aspect of an organization's business—work flow, information systems, policies, procedures, and resources. Likely candidates for BPR are finance, human resources, and engineering, as each function crosses many organizational boundaries. Errors and misinterpretations can occur at each "connect." In some instances, short-term efforts can bring about quick gains.

Stages of BPR are:

1. Prepare and/or train those performing the reengineering efforts. Develop a specific game plan.

2. Identify activities that add value, and develop and understand customer-oriented process models of the business. Prepare a process map of the organization.

3. Develop a process vision by which breakthrough performance can be achieved. State the new process vision and define changes required.

4. Specify the technical and social dimensions of the process. Describe and plan standards and procedures and staffing, recruitment, education, and training requirements needed to implement the new technology.

5. Begin a pilot program using continual change mechanisms.

The need to critically evaluate and eliminate any current practice that does not work is the driving force behind BPR. Areas of concentration ranges from narrow to broad. If most processes throughout the organization are the target of BPR, a paradigm shift may be necessary. It is impossible to function in the 20th or 21st century with 19th century maps.

A SYSTEMS APPROACH

A system is an assembly or combination of parts forming a whole. Systems approaches classify concepts and demonstrate relationships between a wide range of personal, organizational, and environmental variables.

Systems techniques can be applied to all levels of work throughout the organization and beyond. Each part of the system is arranged in a particular order or design. Systems methods provide a formal perspective by focusing on input, throughput, and output and on associated feedback and control processes. Feedback loops circulate valuable information back into the system within specific time periods. Adequate, timely feedback for correction, change, and control leads to continuous improvement.

Knowledge of results, or feedback, is basically a communications process that monitors, regulates, and ultimately impacts parts of the system. Feedback is a vital factor in all types of systems and ties separate parts of the system together. It reflects changes and keeps the system dynamic and current.

At work, there are few clear-cut opportunities to give and receive immediate feedback. Activities (inputs and throughputs) and results (outputs) are often complex and difficult to identify and describe precisely. Operationalizing concepts and variables associated with input, throughput, and output used in Chapters 6 and 7 helps clarify meanings and develop a common framework for analyzing white-collar work.

The broad scope and diverse nature of knowledge work, for instance, makes separating work processes into step-by-step units difficult. Often, one work process flows into the next process or overlaps with those around it.

Major uses of systems are to help identify problems and provide formats to generate thoughts and ideas to solve problems. Systems approaches structure and integrate human activities around various technologies, professions, or personal areas of expertise, like engineering or management. Systems approaches are applied to business, specifically management, economics, and computer systems. Systems methods are often used in the fields of transportation, health care, education, communication, biology, physical and social sciences, and many other areas.

This section: (1) presents a brief history of systems approaches, (2) discusses individual and organizational activities in a systems format, (3) provides methods that can be used to build a systems model of work activities, and (4) outlines major advantages of systems approaches.

Historical Perspective

Darwin used a systems approach in his *On the Origin of Species*, published in 1859. Barnard's[1] *The Functions of the Executive* was one of the first management books to describe and illustrate the use of systems. Many of the basic concepts of "general systems theory" were set forth by biologist Ludwig von Bertalanffy.[20,21] Additional contributions to systems theory were made by Churchman and associates[2] in management and by Homans[5] in sociology.

Other applications have been in gestalt psychology and field theory. Gestalt is a German word for configuration or pattern. Early gestalt theory proposed that the sum of a system's components was greater than the sum of its parts or separate components. Synergy results when separate activities, thoughts, or energies combine to produce a new, enhanced result.

Lewin,[9] developer of field theory, viewed personality as a dynamic, constantly changing system influenced by a person's environment, or life space. People perceive and react to their life spaces in different ways. The social field, or the forces around a person (namely the work environment, peers and supervisors, and family and friends), affect a person's behavior. A person moves in his or her social field, or social environment.

From a broad perspective, any national economy can be described as a system of mutually interrelated industries or interdependent economic activities. The economic activities are represented by a more or less steady stream of goods and services which directly or indirectly link all sectors of the economy to each other.[8]

Systems View of an Organization

Assumptions underlying systems approaches are that goals and objectives of the unit, organization, etc. are useful and correct and have the potential to deliver the required outcomes. All systems have a purpose. Very simply stated, inputs, like information, energy, or materials, are allocated according to an operational plan which results in output.

In general, a systems approach functions as a valuable analytical framework that can be used to explore the dynamic or constantly changing nature of human and organizational activities. With the appropriate use of feedback, systems methods are sensitive enough to detect changes in other parts of the system. Information on the internal status of the organization, like a temperature reading on a thermometer, measures what goes on throughout the organization.

Theoretically, no view of a system is complete until all visible and/or describable parts of the organization are seen and evaluated. Then, systems can be grouped into a whole based on a logical or cause-and-effect relationship. To illustrate, managers will interpret variables and systems in terms of their professions and group them in ways different from engineers, physicians, and others.

A systems approach is one way to examine how diverse and separate parts of a whole in a large organization, for example, relate to other parts of the same system. Organizations are made up of literally hundreds of systems, some as large as divisions or departments and others as small as a work group. Each group may be comprised of people who belong to other groups, or subsystems, such as task forces or cross-disciplinary teams. One person may do his or her own job, yet have specific assignments in several other groups.

As an illustration, groups facing the same or similar problems may use the following methods to diagnose problems:

1. Specify major input, throughput, and output variables that either are problem areas now or could be problem areas in the future.

2. Consider how input, throughput, and output affect each other, or assess cause-and-effect relationships.

3. Systematically determine the kind of output needed, namely evaluate amount, quality, customer appeal, time, market share, cost, and many other factors.

4. Determine how best to change or modify input to get the desired output.

5. Evaluate feedback as often as possible to locate and remedy problem areas.

6. Systematically change input and continue to monitor the whole system until the desired results are achieved.

As illustrated above, systems approaches provide an excellent framework on which to build a wide range of diagnostic and measurement techniques to detect changes occurring over varying periods of time.

Systems Approach to Organizations

Table 8.1 presents the standard input variables of capital, labor, energy, and materials, which represent organizational activities. These four broad areas also apply to work people perform, or output.

In service areas, transformation processes are not easily identified. Most are value-added types of activities performed by a wide range of people. In product-based industries, throughput is tangible, like assembly-line operations where units of production, such as car parts, have a specific size and shape.

Output in product-based areas will be tangible, measurable, and countable.

Table 8.1 Simple Systems Representation Showing Input, Throughput, and Output in Product-Based Industries

Input	Throughput	Output
Resources	Processes	End Result
Capital	Transformation process of	Profit
Labor	monitoring, measuring,	Units constructed
Energy	adjusting, improving,	Services provided
Materials	creating, innovating, etc.	Products produced

In service areas, output often relates to providing customers with a range of services (financial, health...food). Many services are used on the spot.

Logically, by improving the quality of input, quality of throughput and output should improve. However, this happens only when people and processes used in all parts of the model are appropriately monitored and feedback is circulated throughout the entire system. In simple systems, efficiency should increase with successive repetitions. The more often something is done, the more smoothly and/or quickly it can be done the next time.

Close monitoring is required to initially produce a high-quality service or product. Once methods are developed and streamlined, less and less direct monitoring is required.

Think about the three typical input, throughput, and output operations in your organization. Do they represent your organization's main mission, goals, and purpose? In most instances, they revolve around the broad groupings of capital, labor, energy, and materials. However, your efforts may be directed entirely toward internal and external customers.

A SYSTEMS MODEL

Systems theory applies to people and to the organization. In interactions with their respective environments, organizational systems are either closed or open.[6] The concepts of "closed" and "open" are often a matter of degree, as few systems are totally closed or totally open.

Closed systems have gradually moved toward a state of equilibrium. No energy or work is transformed. Feedback has little or no effect on closed systems. Models used in management science, for instance, are usually closed in the sense that they consider only variables that can be quantified or measured, as illustrated in mathematics and the physical sciences. Variables that cannot be described and measured are left out of closed systems.

All parts of an open system have a dynamic relationship with their own environment. Despite continual contact with a constantly changing environment, the organization strives to achieve a "steady state," or dynamic equilibrium, while retaining its capacity to transform energy or do work. Boundaries around the separate subsystems are not clearly defined. Information on feedback passes easily between boundaries.

There is considerable support for an open system.[4,12] Most organizational systems are open. The concept of sociotechnical systems proposed by Emery and Trist over 40 years ago is considered to be outdated.

An organization's system is made up of five subsystems: (1) technical, (2) psychosocial, (3) structural, and (4) goals and values held together by the (5) managerial, the core subsystem. Each system interacts with other systems and with the environment in a special or unique way.

Technical Subsystem

The technical subsystem includes the knowledge needed to perform tasks and the techniques necessary to transform inputs into outputs. Technologies influence the types of inputs into the organization, how the transformation process occurs, and how the specific outputs of the system are shaped. The technical system affects the organization's psychosocial system and its structure. To illustrate, the technical subsystem of a university is not the same as that of a hospital.

Psychosocial Subsystem

Individuals and groups working together make up the psychosocial system. This system determines how effectively and efficiently technology is used. Similarly, people employed in each area or subsystem use their talents, tools, and technology to perform their jobs. Some groups will have overlapping memberships and functions, as in a multidisciplinary team assigned to study and improve quality.

Structural Subsystem

At one extreme, the structure of the organization is formal, or well defined. The opposite extreme is unstructured, or loosely organized. Structure ties the technical and psychological systems together.

Formal structure is often set out in organizational charts. No two organization are exactly alike, as policies, procedures establishing authority relationships, communication, and work flow all differ slightly.

Informal structure is the white space on organizational charts, or essentially the opposite of formal structure. Informal structure gradually evolves when people interact and work together to achieve goals. Most informal structure is not planned or documented, like open communication channels that facilitate horizontal and vertical communication throughout the organization.

Goals and Values Subsystem

The goals and values subsystem is extremely important, as the organization acquires many of its values from the sociocultural environment. Functions the organization performs for society are assumed to conform to social requirements and fill a need, like supporting educational projects in schools and universities.

Managerial Subsystem

The managerial subsystem interacts with the whole organization and connects the various subsystems. It performs the core functions of relating the organization to its environment; designing the structure; developing goals, operational plans, and mission statements; and establishing and maintaining a control process.

Management is not in full control of all factors of production, but is affected by numerous environmental and internal forces created by all other subsystems—structural, psychosocial, technological, and goals and values subsystems. Managers function in networks of mutually dependent relationships, where ambiguity and uncertainty are the rule rather than the exception.[14]

In complex organizations, the three subsystem levels in the managerial system of complex organizations are operating, coordinating, and strategic. The operating subsystem is involved with actual performance of tasks. The strategic level pertains to the activities of the organization and its environment. The coordinating system integrates strategic and operating activities vertically and horizontally. A major management responsibility is to keep systems balanced and know when they go out of balance. Efficient management systems have compatible component parts to minimize the duration of "out-of-balance" periods.

Configuration management (CM) is one way to effectively cope with organizational change. "CM ensures that changes affecting the physical characteristics of specific critical systems are identified, controlled, approved, and documented over the life of the system."[17] CM provides checks and balances to maintain quality, prevent oversight, and in general keep things running.

In conclusion, open systems have the characteristic of equifinality. This means that objectives may be achieved with varying inputs and in different ways.[6] More simply stated, no two people do the same job the same way.

Composition of a Systems Model

A systems view of work activities enables users to separate and examine information obtained from: (1) input—individual differences of workers and the broad scope of the job, (2) throughput, or processes, like creativity, perception, and reasoning, and (3) output—how people's achievements relate to the overall accomplishments of the organization.

Table 8.2 illustrates typical input from data processors, a supervisor of customer services, a faculty member, an internal auditor, and a foreman in a manufacturing plant. Examples of input, throughput, and output are given for each of the five examples. The sequences of input, throughput, and output should not be read directly across, as, for instance, customer service representatives may perform any number of throughput processes that are nearly impossible to document. Output, however, is more predictable.

Table 8.2   Input, Throughput, and Output from
Clerical, Knowledge-Based, and Manufacturing Areas

	Input	*Throughput*	*Output*
Data Processor	Data	Monitor	Reports
	Accuracy	Compare	Charts
	Effort	Concentrate	Diagrams
Supervisor of Customer Services	Knowledge	Trust	Good role model
	Integrity	Empathy	Profitable unit
	Enthusiasm	Flexibility	Positive attitude
Faculty Member	Experience	Communication	Patents
	Knowledge	Reasoning	Publications
	Effort	Creativity	Capable students
Internal Auditor	Pleasant	Cooperation	Cost analyses
	Analytical	Synthesize	Ideas
	Persistence	Trust	Recommendations
Foreman in Plant	Procedures	Inspect	Completed units
	Specifications	Change/control	Scrap
	Automation	Motivate	Defective units

Input, throughput, and output are addressed and illustrated through descriptions and illustrations in the following sections.

Input

In the positive sense, input is any effort used to produce desired results or output or to achieve goals. Input can be working long hours until an idea becomes formalized, as in creating something new. However, not all input is positive, as negative employee attitudes can literally destroy an organization.

Examples of tangible and intangible input are presented next. Intangible input is often more closely related to the provision of services than the creation of products.

Tangible Input.   Input, throughput, and output are easier to describe and quantify in product-based industries than in service-based industries. Input is represented by equipment, buildings, land, physical plant, and similar tangible resources required to produce products or provide services. Raw materials to be transformed into marketable output are also tangible. Specifications for making this transformation, like quality standards, master schedule controls, written specifications, and visual inspection, among others, are clear and unambiguous. When the focus is on defect prevention, proactive inspection efforts and various forms of control eliminate as much scrap at the output side as possible.

To illustrate, a mail-order house normally handles customer requests or input by telephone or by written requests for merchandise. Employee input is effort used to send customers their orders and provide follow-up services such as handling substitutions and refunds.

Intangible Input.   Creative, innovative energies used to design new services, as in advertising a new product, are intangible. The creative process is a rapid series of thoughts that may lose their impact and meaning when put to paper. Incubation is a vital part of creativity. An example of intangible input is documenting the financial investment in human resources in only number of hours of training per year. This may sound fine, but output measures of retention of material learned in training are rarely if ever done.

Examples of human input include energy, expertise in a high-demand area, ability to understand and use technology, and special skills, abilities, or experience. Operational definitions can decrease some of the ambiguity associated with human input and allow efforts to be documented in a meaningful manner.

Organizational input variables include policies, philosophies, culture, strategies, established communication channels, leadership, culture, stage of life cycle, or number of years established, to mention only a few.

Standard input financial variables cover investment in human resources, technology, inventory, and numerous other costs of doing business. Often, numbers used are estimates and not *real* numbers.

Throughput

Process variables or throughput transform input into output, but not in ways readily described or defined. The presence of process variables is usually inferred from output. In service organizations, output is much less tangible than in organizations that provide products, as discussed in Chapter 7.

Throughput, also known as an intervening variable, is difficult to visualize. Most levels of work are process, or the *how* as opposed to the *what* of doing things. Throughput often provides clues for identifying and solving problems. A close examination of throughput may reveal, for instance, that people do not know what the real goals of the organization are or the best method to delegate or empower others to maximize results. "Disconnects" that result from misunderstanding the customer can be discussed in a follow-up telephone call.

In manufacturing or materials-processing areas, transformation processes can be seen and documented, as in sequential or step-by-step processes that gradually shape raw materials into final products. When some form of quality control is used, each step is monitored using specific quality standards.

Intangible Throughput.   Although much throughput is intangible, processes associated with people are particularly difficult to document and study. We assume people are motivated because they appear to be working hard, yet we have no specific proof of their efforts.

Throughput can be behavioral, attitudinal, motivational, or perceptual. These intervening variables reflect the internal state and health of the organization and reveal how people feel. Examples are employee loyalties, performance, and perceptions and their capacities for effective interaction, communication, and decision making.[10]

It is possible to get feedback on the existence of factors like attitude and loyalty by using interviews and surveys. However, these results represent only the status at a given point in time. A person having a good day will reflect optimism in responding to a survey on attitude and motivation. In a similar vein, being worried or preoccupied is likely to produce a number of negative responses.

A systems analogy provides a brief outline of the creative process:

1. People think about what was seen, heard, read, or assimilated over a period of time (input).

2. They explore their information or database in order to understand and create the new product or service (throughput).

3. They act on the resulting ideas or concept and achieve the purpose intended (output).

Creative people spend a great deal of time processing information or "muddling through" activities that ultimately produce an idea, an inspiration, or some other type of creative output.

Is intellectual property part of throughput? The jury is still out, and may be out for an extended period of time, on how to protect intellectual property of organizations when employees change organizations or set up businesses on their own. The crux of the matter is to whom intellectual property belongs. Does it belong to the owner or to the organization for whom a person works? Or does it belong to "everybody" after it is shared, or put on an information and/or computer based network?

Output

Historically, output is tangible and measurable. Products or units produced or services provided can be counted and described. Other examples are quality, cost, dependability, and frequency of repair, among many others.

Tangible human accomplishments produce measurable items like reports, patents, publications, drawings, accounting data, software packages, and various services for customers. Services, such as health care, insurance, transportation, and others, are not easily described, but customers are real enough. Output also can be the number of employees mentored, task forces led, or accomplishments in general.

In engineering fields, output may be technical reports or recommendations for any type of effort. Final output may be a longstanding contract or commitment to provide ongoing maintenance, update equipment, and revamp support services.

Outcomes, one step beyond output, range from immediate to far removed. Outcomes are directly related to output. The role of outcomes is presented in Chapter 9.

Feedback

The main role of feedback is to provide a way to achieve equilibrium within a system or organization. Feedback comes from all subsystems as well as the environment. Management interprets the feedback and uses various control mechanisms or adjustments to correct imbalances or irregularities in the subsystems or overall system. Feedback can range from positive to negative.

The role of feedback cannot be underestimated. Information in the form of feedback guides future plans, behaviors, and actions. Feedback is changed in numerous ways and fed back into a system at different points along the way. Feedback does not always circulate back to input, but may re-enter at any place in the system. Information that is cycled and recycled throughout the system changes. It may emerge in a totally different, perhaps unrecognizable, form.

Most traditional forms of feedback relate to various types of individual and organizational performance data—efficiency, productivity, cost savings, or number of customers served. Measures establish feedback loops, which are the foundation of organizational learning. Only through learning can people and organizations alike consistently deliver value in an ever-changing world.

The major types of feedback are adopt, maintain, and grow. When information is realistic, logical, and fits needs, it is often readily adopted. Other types of feedback primarily serve to maintain operations or actions at their current rate, as in meeting quotas, deadlines, or other forms of guidelines or controls. Feedback that is used to change, expand, improve, or other types of activities fits the classification of growing.

In any feedback process, what is going on, or assumed to be going on, is usually compared against some standard. The majority of standards are based on carefully documented information. Automobile speedometers indicate how fast we are going so we can determine whether we are exceeding the legal speed limit. Examination results provide feedback for students. Colleges and universities could not be accredited without feedback from accrediting agencies.

The concept of "robustness" is the brainchild of Genichi Taguchi, a Japanese consultant. The set of statistical techniques he developed was used to reduce the number of experiences (repetitions) required to greatly improve manufacturing processes. To illustrate, when a specific level of improvement is made, results are fed back to design engineers and then recycled through the system. Strengths and weaknesses of the process are taken into account in product designs. Results prompt more changes and improvements. Over time, a "robust" design or product with as few weaknesses as possible is created.

Many standards exist in organizations, namely, control mechanisms, such as financial control. Although there are standards or acceptable results for many forms of output, the real impact of standards comes from tightening them, extending them, or changing them for the purpose of improvement. Feedback expedites this process. As a final reminder, the presence of feedback *and* the appropriate interpretation and constructive use of feedback produce positive change in the form of improvement or adjustment.

The analogy of an automobile illustrates the uses of feedback. Automobile *performance* is judged by miles per gallon of fuel and acceleration rate, both output variables. How the automobile performs and where it goes depend on input variables of the driver (management), the roads (vision, mission, and goals), passengers (workers), frequency of repair (human and technological breakdown), and environment (organizational culture). The entire focus is on what is happening now in terms of miles per gallon of fuel used and acceleration. No other baselines for comparison appear to be important. The real issue is to make the automobile (organization) run well at all times rather than just for one quick spot comparison.

Once a system is understood, feedback helps put cause-and-effect relationships into perspective. Close analysis may reveal interesting, unexpected relationships. A slight change in tolerance of one piece of equipment produces out-of-tolerance, substandard products that must be sold for less. Saving pennies in the input stage may cost hundreds or thousands of dollars further down the line, not to mention customer dissatisfaction and possible loss of longstanding contracts.

Time

Time is a vital variable in the feedback process, as in cycle time in process flow, reaction time, time to produce a unit, and customer waiting time. In many "white-collar" activities, feedback may be intermittent or delayed unpredictably. Feedback cycles may occur once in a while, with frequency measured in years. On the other hand, college students get written feedback from examinations and assignments at least five to ten times a semester. Athletes and concert performers get immediate feedback.

Total Cycle Time

This measure represents the total amount of time required to perform a specific process or achieve a desired result or output. Every cycle and subcycle affects total cycle time. It is especially important to coordinate the efforts of individuals, teams, and others involved in specific projects in order to minimize cycle time and maximize results. Because most processes are more complicated than people generally expect, assigning specific numbers to cycle time can pose problems.

Feedback on time pinpoints every part of the business cycle. Resulting feedback indicates ways to eliminate unnecessary actions and improve or simplify processes and other efforts. The overriding purpose is to reduce cycle time to maximize effort.

The two major types of business cycles are the make/market loop and the design/development loop. Since these loops are interdependent and intertwined, some cycles of activity have a place in both loops.[18]

The make/market loop includes all customer-related activities. This loop begins when a customer expresses an interest in a product or service and ends when the customer pays for what was requested.

The design/development loop encompasses all activities associated with introducing new products or services. It begins when managers identify an opportunity and ends when the product or service reaches the market.

When cycle time is changed, cycles of learning are also changed. Feedback can further reduce cycle time. When cycle time is shortened, costs and overhead usually both decrease. Feedback used to reduce cycle time does not require spending money or adding resources. Eliminating unnecessary or non-value-adding steps reduces cycle time.

Cycle time can also be reduced by using thought processes basic to the creative process: (1) inspiration, (2) identification, (3) information, (4) implementation, and (5) internalization.[19]

Inspiration involves alerting people to the need for change or creating awareness of the need to reduce cycle time, simplify programs, learn more quickly, and follow through on those efforts. Inspiration must flow downward from top management.

Identification means that the person making the improvement accepts, "owns," or "buys in" to the entire process.

When changes caused by reducing cycle time permeate the organization, certain parts of the culture must adjust and change. Information tailored to overcome skill shortages or meet deficiencies in training must be available throughout the life of the total cycle time effort. It is vital that information on change and improvement be accurate and timely.

Information is needed throughout the life of any total cycle time effort. This vital phase includes understanding and charting processes, recognizing and removing barriers, and working effectively in cross-functional environments. Information may come from a wide array of sources, as in skills training. The information component occurs concurrently with implementation and internalization.

Implementation should begin as soon as the company has accepted the challenge of reducing cycle time. At first, people will attack overcomplicated processes and non-valued-adding steps. Implementation will be incomplete unless feedback is used properly and relevant measurements and controls are applied.

Internalization of the purposes and activities associated with reducing cycle time may take years. It takes a long time to break old habits and to begin to change an organization's culture. Change may be accelerated by using the new principles of cycle time, customer satisfaction, and other related factors to evaluate employees. Employees may change their behavior in order to more closely conform with or adopt the gradually changing culture of the workplace.

Proper management of time enables companies to reduce costs, increase number of product lines, cover more market segments, and upgrade the technological sophistication of their products. These companies are time-based competitors. Time is considered a basic business performance variable. However, management rarely monitors time with the same rigor and precision as accorded sales and cost. Time is a more critical competitive yardstick than traditional financial measurements.[16]

Cycle time can be applied to nearly every task and project people work on. The concept of time-based manufacturing focuses primarily on shortening production runs. To reduce time, manufacturing functions for a component or product should be located as close together as possible. This process minimizes handling and moving of parts from one activity to the next. Also, employees are "empowered" to make more production control decisions on the factory floor without waiting for management approval.

The following three points of discussion on work measurement and methods focus on time.[??]

1. Reasonable standards of time should be set for completing projects. Only a few workers will ever exceed 100 percent of a daily work standard. Others will feel that the standard is the shortest time and that they can take more time to complete the job. Unless management provides some form of time standards, workers will use the estimated hours from the current guide for cost standards. They will assume that if they meet these standards, they have also met management's expectations. Newly hired workers, poorly motivated workers, or workers with marginal skills may not even meet the low estimates.

How people are paid affects their rate of work. Those paid a standard rate whether they work slowly, quickly, or not at all will seldom achieve or exceed the expected standards. When pay is based on bonuses, the expectation is that extra pay is received for equaling or surpassing the "average" or standard. Bonus systems based on work rate are, like many aspects already discussed, time consuming to develop and implement. It is possible to achieve an optimum balance between management standards and what workers are capable of and willing to do. It simply takes time and a great deal of effort.

2. Time standards should be updated when improvement methods are implemented. Basic steps include (1) analyzing tasks, (2) selecting typical methods, and (3) measuring time for each task. Standard data have an unpredictable "shelf life," as they do not remain good forever. Two factors are critical. First, there must be a methods description connecting the standard data and the process description. Second, someone must be trained and available to keep the data current.

3. Time studies use pace or effort ratings to determine the normal time taken to complete a task. Usually, the "best" method is installed before the time study is conducted. Only average-trained operators are studied in order to get an "average" result. Weighted factors may be used, but when skilled operators perform two tasks at the same time, determining the "best" weighting can be a real problem. Another area of concern is that workers can perform the same task any number of ways. Should standards or "averages" continue to be used, or should the method that is least costly be used? It's a judgment call.

Time is one of the variables often cited as a competitive weapon. For many, time equals money. Streamlining work efforts, working "smart" or "smarter," and "doing things right the first time" all help add a few more minutes or hours of usable time to people's work days.

Example 1. Atlas Door, a 14-year-old U.S. company, produces a broad array of industrial doors in varying widths, heights, and materials. Because of the wide variety of products, most doors can be manufactured only after the order has been placed. Order-entry, engineering, manufacturing, and logistic systems were structured to move information and products quickly and reliably. The time required to fill a customer's request decreased from four months to several weeks. Atlas prices and schedules 95 percent of its incoming orders while the callers are still on the telephone.[16]

Example 2. Northern Telecom, a 100+-year-old company, moved from a cost-based approach to a time-based approach to management. They used to ask themselves, "How much will it cost to deliver a quality product, and how long will it take?" Now they ask, "How quickly can we deliver a quality product, and how much will it cost?"

In early 1985, change efforts were begun. Because not all parts of the organization could change at once, six core businesses were named: new product introduction and change, procurement practices, manufacturing process improvement, operations planning and scheduling, product delivery costs, and installation–field service. Each business was to make time-based improvements in all areas.

In the spring of 1986, the core program was implemented, beginning with manufacturing process improvement, new product introduction and change, and procurement. The first step was to introduce total quality control. Supervisors and manufacturing line operators were trained in quality control. They were empowered to shut the line down when they saw a problem.

In the following three years, the new product introduction interval in some divisions was reduced by 20 percent in some areas and by 50 percent in other areas. One division cut its receiving cycle time by 97 percent, or from three weeks to four hours.

A "pay for skill" program was adopted at Northern Telecom's Santa Clara, California plant. Pay increases are given for each new task a worker masters. Workers who normally performed a narrowly defined task now can perform many different tasks. This process reduced the number of jobs from 25 to 5.[11]

Time in a Systems Approach

Time, a non-compressible, inelastic resource, ties separate subsystems together. Effective use of time and the amount accomplished in a specific time period are ways to measure performance. When what is happening is "freeze framed," it is possible to take stock and consider what has happened so far. Then, standards for comparison can be developed. When what happened at two or more different time intervals is compared, changes can be detected.

Without a baseline for comparison, changes may be identified in any part of the system, but the reason for change may not be known. Without standards for comparison, changes detected during a time period may not accurately represent what happened.

For instance, the transformation process can be rapid, as when catalysts are added to speed up a chemical reaction. On the other hand, the transformation process for scientists doing research may be very long.

A national preoccupation is with (immediate) output, particularly when it can be seen, described, and measured. First, it is a way to compare output over varying periods of time. Second, output can be benchmarked or compared with output from others producing the same or similar types of output. However, viewing individual and organizational output alone means that other even more important input and throughput variables were likely ignored or simply left out.

BUILDING A SYSTEMS MODEL
OF WORK ACTIVITIES AND OUTCOMES

One of the first steps is to evaluate the broad scope of work—range, cycle, flow, complexity, structure, and people's unique skills, abilities, and knowledge. Work has many overlapping facets, levels, and dimensions. Therefore, this is no easy job. A logical sequence of steps is outlined.

1. Critically examine the broad range and scope of work using methods that may already be in place in your organization. The type and quality of work performed is affected by the location and work environment where work takes place, for example a research lab.

2. Identify major personal and job-related variables. Personal variables are people's unique skills, abilities, and knowledge. Job-related factors are obviously those required to perform the job. White-collar work has overlapping facets, levels, and dimensions. Information may come from flowcharts, task force reports, surveys, questionnaires, or from specific areas of concern throughout the organization.

What is *not* said may be even more important than what *is* said, which is the "iceberg concept." Information "below the surface" could become a critical issue when you least expect it—so be prepared. Once hidden areas are known, numerous scenarios using various levels and types of input can be developed (i.e., "best" and "worst" case scenarios).

By looking at the desired output, or results, it may be possible to work backwards, as in reverse scenario building, to determine possible throughput and then input.[3] This proactive approach helps identify a feasible range or group of input variables, like level of training and introduction of new quality endeavors, among others. When the whole sequence or range of activities is explored in detail, and input, throughput, and output variables are named, described, and possibly quantified in some logical manner, it is then possible to compare all systems and select the "best" one to suit your purpose.

3. Identify typical input, throughput, output, and associated feedback processes. Feedback loops circulate valuable information throughout the system within specific time periods. Time ties separate units together. Feedback from monitoring is used for correction and control for the purpose of improving processes and products. The passage of time, as in months...years, and what major events or changes occur are equally important.

4. Operationally define major input, throughput, and output variables listed in Item 3. Consider services, products, customers, partners, suppliers, end users, control or monitoring agencies (government or regulatory bodies), and the community. Influencing factors, like environment, technology, and organizational culture, affect the content of your model and how it functions.

5. Group major input, throughput, and output variables into categories. These categories may represent progressively higher levels or hierarchies of complexity, effort, involvement, etc. The process of developing hierarchies is another way to place a priority or value on variables. Grouping and classifying variables will be used again in Chapter 10 when working with the Core-Unique-Expanding model.

Figure 8.1 shows typical input, throughput, and output variables which occur in most daily work activities in areas where considerable time is spent communicating. Input, throughput, and output are listed as examples only. As in Table 8.2, specific input does not necessarily produce only one type of throughput or output. For instance, initiating (input) could result in reflecting (throughput), which results in verifying (output).

Figure 8.2 illustrates a systems approach to supervision.[15] This representation shows various input, throughput, and output variables associated with supervision. Feedback can occur at various points in the system. Time and environment play major roles.

INPUT	THROUGHPUT	OUTPUT
Initiate — — — — —	Analyze — — — — —	Respond
Speak — — — — —	Reflect — — — — —	Understand
Show — — — — —	Assimilate — — — —	Describe
Question — — — —	Explore — — — — —	Verify

Figure 8.1. A Simple Representation of Systems in Communication

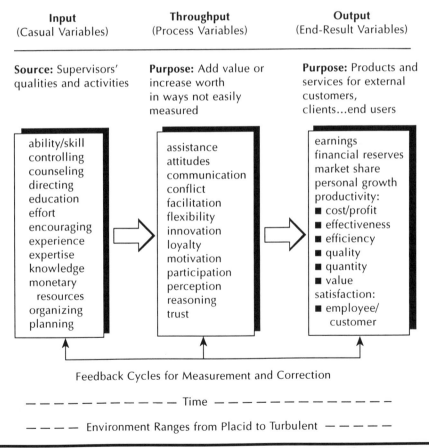

Input (Casual Variables)	Throughput (Process Variables)	Output (End-Result Variables)
Source: Supervisors' qualities and activities	**Purpose:** Add value or increase worth in ways not easily measured	**Purpose:** Products and services for external customers, clients...end users

ability/skill
controlling
counseling
directing
education
effort
encouraging
experience
expertise
knowledge
monetary
  resources
organizing
planning
	assistance
	attitudes
	communication
	conflict
	facilitation
	flexibility
	innovation
	loyalty
	motivation
	participation
	perception
	reasoning
	trust
		earnings
		financial reserves
		market share
		personal growth
		productivity:
		■ cost/profit
		■ effectiveness
		■ efficiency
		■ quality
		■ quantity
		■ value
		satisfaction:
		■ employee/
		  customer

Feedback Cycles for Measurement and Correction

— — — — — — — — — — Time — — — — — — — — — — — —

— — — — Environment Ranges from Placid to Turbulent — — — — —

Figure 8.2 Systems Approach to Supervision (Source: Smith,[15] p. 30)

Examples of input include supervisors' qualities, or abilities, skills, or other talents used in supervision or related activities. Commonly performed activities include organizing or planning. Feedback cycles are used for measurement and correction.

The continued success of the organization and the systems and subsystems within it depends on knowing when and what to measure and when and what to correct. We all have horror stories about correcting the wrong thing too late to do any good, as when people misinterpret what is happening but keep on doing what they have always done, thinking that it will turn out alright.

Use of systems methods implies that variables being studied change—sometimes regularly, other times unpredictably. Discussing concepts related to ideas, processes, and outcomes "in motion" requires tolerance to change. However, when systems are used to view and evaluate services and products, cause and effect variables need to be identified. When this is done, change becomes both more meaningful and acceptable. After all, change is a way of life.

WHERE DOES CHANGE FIT IN?

What happens when change disrupts the status quo? Change can affect all levels and all systems in the organization. Many people have trouble accepting the fact that "nothing is so constant as change." Initially, change efforts begin with the most influential input variables that everyone understands. Without a modest level of understanding, change efforts will be marginally if at all successful. One logical first step is to increase understanding of the proposed changes.

Many effective change efforts begin with a consistent, coordinated effort to change the entire management system of the organization. If this is done, change must have the support of top management. It is imperative to have a common, unitary focus and follow through with what was planned, as when introducing employee involvement or continuous quality improvement initiatives. When change is not implemented from the top down, the ground swell will be from the bottom up. Management is seldom prepared to handle ground swells.

8.1

List at least three typical input, throughput, and output operations in your organization. Examine each to be sure those listed represent your organization's main goals and purposes.

Input	Throughput	Output
1. _____	1. _____	1. _____
2. _____	2. _____	2. _____
3. _____	3. _____	3. _____

8.2

Critically examine information, data, and activities listed in Question 8.1 to see how input, throughput, and output flow into one another and affect each other. A flowchart, for example, monitors and shows changes, as when input is changed for the purpose of improving throughput and output. Can a flowchart adequately represent input, throughput, and output in your job?

8.3

List and briefly describe five or six steps that you would take to build a systems model representing your job or specific work performed in your department or unit.

8.4

Use the information from Question 8.3 to develop your own systems model. Use two major variables from each input, throughput, and output area. Diagram or describe how they all fit together. Show how changes in input affect output. Use feedback loops to connect the appropriate parts of the model. Include time as one of your major variables.

8.5

If you used a product-based model in Question 8.1, respond using service-based model here, or conversely. Consider the broad range of operations in your own organization...work group. Select major activities and identify:

- Input in service industries

- Input in product-based or materials-processing industries

- Throughput in service industries

- Throughput in product-based or materials-processing industries

- Output in service industries

- Output in a product based or materials-processing industries

---

8.6

Describe how systems approaches could be used in your organization or work group.

8.7

Select two major areas of your job. Indicate input, throughput, and output variables for each area.

ADVANTAGES OF A SYSTEMS APPROACH

General advantages relate to providing a wider view of the entire work effort, the organization, and the external environment. On-the-job uses include ways to represent, monitor, and measure work-related activities in a way that leads to understanding.

Systems can be expanded to cover critical forces outside the organization, like competition, technology, economy, politics, regulation, community involvement, and other areas discussed in Chapter 5.

Specific uses and applications of systems approaches are: (1) develop the personal equation or conceptual model for work processes and results, (2) implement change and improvement efforts, (3) diagnose problems in product-based areas, (4) diagnose problems in service-based areas, and (5) identify and describe organizational problems.

Use in Personal Equation or Conceptual Model

1. A method to thoroughly examine work accomplishments, from one person to a multinational company employing tens of thousands of people. However, careful study of selected variables known to influence personal and organizational behavior provides the structure or framework needed to gradually build a systems model that comes alive before your very eyes.

2. A way to focus on specific concepts or variables and determine how they are related, namely through cause and effect. Resulting information helps make decisions, allocate resources, and provide a way to study and compare alternative courses of action. By changing the amount or quality of input (independent variable), changes are brought about in output (dependent variable). For example, improving quality of training should bring about changes in processes (throughput) that improve quality and increase number of services provided or products produced.

3. Combine systems methods and operational definitions in the same setting, as in reaching group consensus on certain issues or problem areas. Operational definitions clarify meanings of major areas of concern or disagreement. When agreement is reached on terms and concepts, the "givens," or input, can be specified. It is then possible to gradually work toward a logical, cost-effective solution, or output. Several scenarios can be developed to reach the desired output, each with its own allocation of human and material resources, costs, and time frame.

Implementing Change and Improvement Efforts

4. When major variables associated with input, throughput, and output are identified, a wide range of information is accumulated. Speaking from a basis of fact or simply knowing how a system works is very powerful. Information sources can show how all parts overlap and interact and how feedback mechanisms function. This makes it possible to trace how changes in one part of the system affect other parts of the system.

5. Feedback that serves specific purposes, like monitoring and control, is essential to improvement. Nothing can be changed or improved unless existing information is used appropriately to make comparisons. One example is the slow, steady process of using customer feedback to modify input in order to improve results.

6. By concentrating on improving the quality of input, the quality of throughput and output should similarly be improved in general. To illustrate, by changing input variables, like leadership, decision making, supervision, compensation, coordination, and evaluation, changes in throughput and output can be determined. For instance, training to bring about changes in attitudes, abilities, or cognitive skills must be compatible with the system of management in which that training is to be used.[10]

7. When difficult-to-measure throughput processes, like assimilating and improvising, are thoroughly examined, each can be divided into smaller steps or units which can be operationally defined and measured. This process increases overall understanding of throughput, often considered to be an unknown and unmeasurable part of the productivity equation.

Diagnose Problems in Product-Based Areas

8. Systems methods are frequently used in production-type operations. Charting the flow of work people, not machines, means identifying a different set of factors, although the process remains much the same. Production operations and clerical and specialist work both require people to think about the sequence of activities performed and the intended results. Careful inspection of the order in which tasks are performed may reveal common elements in what initially appear to be unrelated jobs. Efforts could result in streamlining the process or finding a "better way" or optimum sequence. Examples include designing new products, getting approvals or sign-offs on projects, and processing paperwork.

9. Using output to diagnose input is done regularly in product-based industries, where inferior or substandard products can be traced back to poor machine design, operator error, or any number of possible causes.

10. When one part of the system is systematically changed, it is possible to determine how changes are brought about in other parts of the system. By optimizing designs, changing scheduling, or streamlining designs, costs and cycle time could be reduced.

Diagnose Problems in Service-Based Areas

11. In the service area, it is possible to work backwards through various processes until specific input is identified. This means "playing detec-

tive." For instance, by working backward from the crime committed (output), clues (throughput) that may help solve the mystery are identified. It is possible to identify possible motives (input). This reverse systems analysis can be used to trace the root causes of numerous problems, like bottlenecks, locations where performance or output is substandard, how much certain processes cost, etc.[3]

Identify and Describe Organizational Problems

12. Systems methods can identify the most critical or important parts of the organization or unit where people work. Areas of concern can be matched up with the mission statement and the goals of the organization. Areas showing the most promise, or those in the greatest need of fixing, can be considered from a broad perspective, and consistent methods of analyzing and presenting information can be developed.

13. It may be difficult to obtain reliable, valid measures to compare ratios or other data at specific points in time, but it is possible to get some idea of efficiency and effectiveness of energies or efforts at the input, throughput, and output stages. For instance, if results of employee surveys of morale were very high when a project was first assigned (input stage) and decreased dramatically midway through the information gathering and analysis process (throughput), the logical assumption would be that something went wrong in the throughput process, such as change of leadership, mergers, and intense competition.

SUMMARY AND CONCLUSIONS

1. The organization is viewed as an open, sociotechnical system made up of a number of subsystems. Organizations transform inputs of energy, information, and materials from the environment into outputs, which are returned to the environment. The organization shapes and integrates human activities around various technologies. Typical subsystems of the organization include psychosocial, managerial, technical, structural, and goals and values.

2. When a systems approach is applied to a continuous process of work activities, each can be separated into input, throughput, and output. Although these three groupings may at first appear to be "force fit," overlap is assumed. Careful examination of input, throughput, and output allows each person's activity or effort (input) and intended result (output) to be examined in depth. Feedback at critical time intervals provides meaningful information on what is currently happening.

3. Feedback on all levels of work should be used to make constructive improvements and channel people's efforts and resources. Without continuous feedback in the form of direct communication, monitoring, and updating, it is impossible to determine whether change in the form of improved quality and increased productivity has occurred. Once feedback mechanisms have been tracked and useful facts or information determined, the separate parts can be reassembled or synthesized into an integrated whole. As is true in systems theory, due to synergy, the sum of the separate parts is greater than the whole. There will, however, be a few parts that may not fit.

4. Grouping work activities and results into input, throughput, and output is not easy. However, this method encourages individuals and groups who work together to think seriously about the flow of work, namely how each part affects the whole. When the entire sequence of work activities is known, many problems may be anticipated and handled in a manner that reduces conflict, confusion, and even downtime. These techniques are used in efficiency studies to automate systems, streamline work efforts, and redesign jobs.

PRACTICAL APPLICATIONS

1. Business process reengineering is more likely to be used in older companies as a way of examining and challenging the effectiveness of established methods. On the other hand, younger companies, like Federal Express, Microsoft, and General Motors' Saturn, change and reinvent themselves continuously. However, some feel that business process analysis deals with the symptoms instead of the real problems. Like many change and improvement efforts, it depends on how initiatives are introduced and what the expected results are vs. what is actually achieved.

2. Process management may be confused with business process reengineering. However, process management, a prime tool of total quality management, is geared toward the horizontal flow of information.

3. Combining the precision of operational definitions with the broad scope of systems approaches has numerous uses. Drawing up customer–supplier contracts or partnership agreements, where it is very important to "do it right the first time," is a cost-effective application. A proactive

tact allows terms like quality, cost, amount of time required, skill level of personnel, and other pertinent variables to be clearly defined and agreed upon at the beginning of contract negotiations. Also, the precise nature and frequency of feedback critical to the success of negotiations can be specified. Feedback may come from areas ranging from the shop floor to clients and customers, and perhaps even from competitors.

4. A systems view can be used to identify major factors, place them in perspective, and follow them through the inevitable sequence—input, throughput, and output. Reverse scenario building can clarify the whole scope and sequence of activities and results expected. Constructing scenarios provides a range of "what if" and "best" to "worst" case possibilities ranging from simple verbal communication to complex computer models. A caution is to balance cost with benefits. These scenarios will work well in a learning organization where various types of results can lead to the redesign or reinterpretation of work processes. "Reinvention" efforts should be designed to bring about desired results.

5. Systems are used to isolate and assess the negative impact of variables standing in the way of efficiency, like outdated work methods and poor communication, among others. The ultimate goal is to provide better services and products at a competitive price.

6. From a production standpoint, the number of errors or rejects in product-based industries can be minimized. Step-by-step documentation allows data to be accumulated and compared. Then, it is possible to determine whether costs have been reduced or quality improved, as a minimum. It is seldom possible to rely on guesses and estimates.

7. Many efforts to enhance overall productivity of the work force still use the industrial model that puts people who deliver service to customers last. The paradigm shift is beginning to put customers first and design systems and products for them.

REFERENCES

1. Barnard, Chester I. *The Functions of the Executive*, Cambridge, Mass.: Harvard University Press, 1938.

2. Churchman, C. West, Ackoff, Russel L., and Arnoff, E. Leonard. *Introduction to Operations Research*, New York: John Wiley & Sons, 1957.

3. deGues, Arie P. "Planning as Learning," *Harvard Business Review*, March–April 1988, pp. 70–74.

4. Emery, Fred. "Participative Design: Effective, Flexible, and Successful, Now!" *Journal for Quality and Participation*, January–February 1995, pp. 6–9.

5. Homans, G. C. *The Human Group*, New York: Harcourt, Brace, and World, 1950.

6. Kast, Fremont and Rosenzweig, James E. *Organization and Management: A Systems Approach* (2nd ed.), New York: McGraw-Hill, 1974.

7. Klein, Mark M. "IEs Fill Facilitator Role in Benchmarking Operations to Improve Performance," *Industrial Engineering*, September 1993, pp. 40–42.

8. Leontief, Wassily et al. *Studies in the Structure of the American Economy*, New York: Oxford University Press, 1953,

9. Lewin, Kurt. *Field Theory in Social Science*, New York: Harper, 1951.

10. Likert, Rensis *The Human Organization*, New York: McGraw-Hill, 1967.

11. Merrills, Roy. "How Northern Telecom Competes on Time," *Harvard Business Review*, July–August 1989, pp. 108–114.

12. Rice, K. *The Enterprise and Its Environment*, London: Tavistock Publications, 1963.

13. Rummler, Gary A. and Brache, Alan P. *Improving Performance: How to Manage the White Space on the Organizational Chart*, San Francisco: Jossey-Bass, 1990.

14. Sayles, Leonard. *Managerial Behavior*, New York: McGraw-Hill, 1964.

15. Smith, Elizabeth A. "Training Supervisors to Work Effectively with a Changing Workforce," *Industrial Management*, July/August 1992, pp. 30–32.

16. Stalck, George Jr., "Time—The Next Source of Competitive Advantage," *Harvard Business Review*, July–August 1988, pp. 41–51.

17. Stevens, Craig G. and Wright, Karen. "Managing Change with Configuration Management," *National Productivity Review*, Autumn 1991, pp. 509–518.

18. Thomas, Philip R., Gallace, Larry H., and Martin, Kenneth R. *Quality Alone Is Not Enough*, New York: American Management Association, 1992.

19. Tomasko, Robert M. *Rethinking the Corporation*, New York: American Management Association, 1993.

20. von Bertalanaffy, Ludwig. "The Theory of Open Systems in Physics and Biology," *Science*, January 13, 1950, pp. 23–29.

21. von Bertalanaffy, Ludwig. *General Systems Theory*. New York: George Braziller, 1968.

22. Williams, Dale. "Work Measurement and Methods Engineering," *IE News*, Vol. XXVII, No. 1, Fall 1992, pp. 1, 4.

9

HUMAN FACTORS AND WORK PROCESSES AND RESULTS

PURPOSE

- Present the role of human factors or individual differences in work processes and in results
- Use a systems model to examine various work processes and results
- Introduce assumptions of the Core-Unique-Expanding model

INTRODUCTION

People's talents make up who they are, how they think, what they can and will do, and how they see and judge others. Some people are totally in tune with their talents. Others are still waiting to find themselves. A good many work in areas in which they are trained. No matter where people work, all want a challenging, rewarding job with a future.

Occasionally, hidden talents are discovered or emerge when working in a totally new area. Success stories abound of people who discover dormant talents and have successful second and third careers. Instability in the job market has increased the number of people who have to make job and career changes.

When knowledge, skills, and abilities are effectively used on the job, people are challenged by their jobs and satisfied with the work they perform. Among other factors discussed in previous chapters, performance is greatly influenced by pay. There is a large discrepancy between "what we pay" and "what we get." When individual talents more closely fit job content, overall productivity and job satisfaction are enhanced.

The Core-Unique-Expanding (C-U-E) model provides a framework and a method which enables people to examine their current jobs, assess their talents and achievements, and streamline and focus their efforts in order to improve job satisfaction and productivity.

HUMAN FACTORS

Sir Francis Galton is the acknowledged father of the study of individual differences. Galton's book *Hereditary Genius*, published in 1869, was based on the theoretical and empirical study of individual differences.

The discipline of human factors has its roots in experimental psychology and engineering. Other major contributors are sociological factors, technology, and the environment.

Human factors is a scientific, applications-oriented discipline. It brings together behavioral sciences and engineering, as in the "real-world" development of equipment and systems. Systems provide views on methods to accomplish organizational work and indicate how the organization should be structured in order to optimize work flow and accomplishment. As discussed in Chapter 8, systems are used in decision-making processes.

Programs are often oriented around: (1) factors affecting behavioral designs, (2) equipment/human relationships, (3) development of a human performance database, (4) relationships between human performance and systems output variables, and (5) improvement in methodology.

Comprehensive handbooks on classifying, describing, and applying human factors include those by Boff, Kaufman, and Thomas,[3] Salvendy,[14] Meister,[12] and Booher.[4]

Every person is unique, or special. Each uses his or her talents in different ways. No two people do the same job in exactly the same manner. Each individual has a slightly different set of talents. There is a continuing need to recognize these differences. It is also important to be able to go one step further and see how these wide-ranging skills can complement each other. Recognize individual differences, but make use of ways to combine abilities in order to accomplish work or work together in mutually beneficial ways, as in project groups and cross-functional teams. Working together cooperatively and sharing are the name of the game in today's world of teams.

People's talents are determined using methods ranging from guesses to highly structured measurement and evaluation techniques used in assessment centers. Assessment centers, which are activities as opposed to locations, use management games, in-basket exercises, mock interviews, and leaderless group discussions to evaluate prospective managers.

Typical sources of information or data on individual differences are educational accomplishment, results of tests and measurements, job experience, and self-assessments, among others. Throughout school and college, the average individual has taken aptitude, ability, interest, college entrance, and possibly graduate school entrance tests. In general, tests show areas of competence and points of weakness. However, unless people are *interested, motivated,* and appropriately *paid for performance,* job satisfaction and performance will be low.

Time spent thinking firms up concepts, ideas, theories, beliefs, and values. Silently mulling things over and consolidating certain areas allows intangible processes to take shape. When our thoughts gradually become more clear, we can write them down on paper or tell them to others.

Flexibility and the opportunity to be creative need to be built into how jobs are set up and resulting performance is assessed. All people in the organization have unrecognized creative potential. In most organizational, there are few ways to recognize and appropriately reward creativity and innovation.

Some important major factors which affect human performance not considered in this chapter are age, aspiration level, energy and health, expectancy, intelligence, learning style, lifestyle, motor skills, personality, and temperament. Each area is described in brief by Smith.[16]

Knowing more about your special abilities, interests, motivation, how you perform, and how you impact work efforts of others is a logical first step. This chapter discusses human factors from the standpoint of systems in which people function on a daily basis. Assumptions about how work is done are also presented.

Assembling Information

There are three ways to think about jobs: (1) where you want to be, or "visioning," as in Chapter 1; (2) fact based to establish the major or core activities performed, as in this chapter and in Chapter 10; and (3) overall broad look in order to reevaluate, redesign, reengineer, or change the focus, as in outsourcing, developing partnerships, or developing any number of customer–

supplier relationships. You will be involved in all three for the rest of your working life.

Jobs must first be analyzed before any of the three above-mentioned methods can be used to obtain detailed information. One method is to look at separate components comprising the job, as will be discussed in the next section.

Tasks that make up jobs can be examined in two different ways. The first is to analyze the separate components that make up the job. The second is to examine the tasks that need to be learned, or the learning components required to be able to perform the job or achieve mastery.[5]

To identify the stimulus (input) and response (output) requirements to per form each element of a task. Then determine how each of the parts of a specific task is related to the other. Methods to break something down into smaller parts and see how each part relates to the whole are presented by Gagné[5] and Kaufman.[5]

The systems approach explored the relationship of input, throughput, and output. Process variables, or throughput, are further discussed in this chapter. As such, processes play a critical role in most work activities. As previously stated, processes are difficult to define, describe, and measure. Nevertheless, processes like creativity and innovation can literally change the shape and function of organizations and the entire nature of work.

Processes, like the concepts used to explain them, are in transition. It is impossible to stop a process from changing. Before starting to build a model, verbal building blocks or concepts should be examined.

A concept is an idea of something formed by mentally combining character-istics and particulars about what is being studied or described. Concepts that are put into action achieve a specific goal or accomplish a purpose and provide value. The cognitive processes of reasoning, recalling, evaluating, and synthe-sizing all underlie the creative process.

The following section involves thinking about and describing work pro-cesses in meaningful terms. Your thoughts and actions will help you build your conceptual model for your job.

Examine Your Own Skills and Abilities

We define what we do, how we do it, and numerous activities and events using our own terms or concepts. We can often define our jobs in precise terms using words we understand and have used before. Also, our own systems of beliefs, frames of reference, attitudes, and values show through when we explain our concepts to others.

The following section is a small start in documenting your talents. This information can grow into a theory of knowledge about you, your job, and those around you. Having an intact, viable theory of knowledge about work in general *and* about yourself and your job in particular will place you ahead of your competition. This manual explores and expands your unique theory of knowledge. As knowledge of your talents grows, your ability to face the current challenges of your job and your future will also grow.

First Steps in the Model Building Process

We first build a mental picture of ourselves and of jobs. Remember your vision of your dream job? When we think of what we really want, our ideas start to take shape. Then we can describe them using tangible, job-focused concepts.

We go through an information accumulation and knowledge building process which we select and evaluate what goes into our conceptual model of ourselves and of our jobs. This model, or representation, reflects our many abilities. The physical work environment and the type of work we currently do provide input to this model. With steady input and gradual refinement of information, our models will gradually come alive and continue to grow. Then, we can describe, draw, and explain them to others.

The following questions encourage you to think first, form concepts, and then write down your thoughts.

9.1

List the jobs, activities, work, or "things" you like to do. These should be what you really enjoy doing and can do well. They may or may not fit your current job description or what you actually do at work. You may list activities or tasks that require creativity, a special kind of inventiveness, or a fresh approach.

1. _____

2. _____

3. _____

4. _____

5. _____

Answering Question 9.1 requires divergent thinking with no bounds or direct path. This open-ended thinking frees your mind, or leads you down a previously unexplored path. Ideas and events normally in the back of your mind take a giant leap forward. You may even see old ideas in a new light.

Your responses to Question 1.1 were likely directed toward your job or your professional background or training. Did any ideas from Question 4.1 on your personal knowledge equation stimulate ideas for any other questions? Answers to this question and to the driving and restraining forces inside and outside the organization listed in Question 5.1 can be compared. Are answers to Questions 4.1 and 5.1 the same? Responses to both questions required convergent thinking, or thinking along specific lines leading to similar results. In many ways, convergent thinking is the opposite of creative thought or divergent thinking.

The following guidelines will help you get started:

1. Focus on activities around that are easy to document. Think about responsibilities, time commitments, and restraints. Consider the number of people you see each day, week, etc. History has a way of repeating itself and so does work. You may find that what happens one week pretty much represents what happens during a whole month or even a year.

2. Consider the major jobs you do at work that truly represent what you are supposed to do. Some days we feel like we never get to do what we are supposed to do. Consider the mission and goals of your organization. Look at short-term, intermediate-term, and long-term goals of your group, department, and organization.

3. Determine if you are part of a multi-stage process that involves passing tangible things like component parts or information along to others. If so, you should consider what occurs before you begin a project or process and what happens after you pass it on. In this instance, you are a liaison person, or someone who "connects" with others.

4. If you are part of a process or sequence of events, and nearly everyone is at some time or another, first think about your unique contribution. Then, think of how your special knowledge or input could affect, and hopefully improve, the process or product *before* it reaches you. On the other hand, consider how something you could do right now might be a plus for a person or group down the line. These "beyond the call of duty" efforts add value or worth. Such benefits accrue in the form of saving time and enhanced internal or external customer satisfaction.

5. If you are a "troubleshooter, or are temporarily assigned to difficult projects, writing down what you do may take effort. Although your job focus may change, you will do the same or similar things over a specific period of time, say a month. These common work activities can be grouped into the same general area, or "work family."

6. If you have just changed jobs or have added new dimensions to your current job, it will take time to see which activities occur over and

over again. It may not be easy to decide on exact job content. Also, relationships with team members, peers, supervisors, or people in other department or outside clients and customers may be quite unpredictable. Nevertheless, in all jobs, there is a certain amount of routine. Doing jobs in an assigned order takes time, but it can also save time. A minute or two invested in the flow of a process can save someone down the line both time and frustration.

Input

Common, broad types of input are human and organizational resources, energy, capital, and labor. In our "human systems" approach, input is an individual's talent, energy, enthusiasm, attitudes, beliefs, frames of reference, and many other special human factors. Many research studies on human achievements explore areas directly related to skills, abilities, and knowledge.

Skills

Verbal or numeric skills, manual dexterity, or musical talent are often inherited. Aptitude tests assess innate or acquired capacity or talent in a specific area, like mathematics, music, mechanical aptitude, and others. Aptitude tests often are used in prediction. Many people have the verbal or numerical aptitude to do various jobs. They simply apply or transfer their aptitudes to do work they have never done before. Also, having a set of skills in one area makes it easier to perform jobs in similar areas.

Word-processing or computer skills, writing skills, and the ability to speak and write various languages can be learned. In junior high school you probably took basic skills tests—verbal, mathematical, clerical, manual dexterity, mechanical, abstract, space, and spelling, among others.

Achievement tests measure present performance in some important task, like language or clerical proficiency. They also assess level of learning, or status of specific skills, such as computer literacy, manual dexterity, etc. Such tests are often taken throughout school and college. At work, they are used to screen, select, and place prospective job applicants and guide career planning.

For example, a skills matrix lists skills, behaviors, and training required for each step in a career plan. People interested in performing the job can compare their skills with the skills that are reported to be needed for successful performance.[19]

A sequential approach to evaluating and using skills is to: (1) assess current skills, (2) use vision and mission statements to select and set realistic goals, (3) plan or match current skills against future job(s), (4) implement plans or follow the proposed plan to apply skills on the job, and continuously develop new skills.[19]

Abilities

Abilities are the power or capacity to do or to act—mentally, physically, or in other ways. Innate abilities are present at birth but are further developed and refined, through study, training, or on-the-job experience. Ability often refers to competence in an occupation or activity, as in being a competent engineer, accountant, attorney, or professor.

Ability tests, also known as performance tests, measure what a person is likely to do in a given situation or in a broad class of situations. Performance tests are used to help predict how a person's interests or personality will affect what is done on the job and how the person relates to others around him or her.

When tests of cognitive or reasoning ability are combined with either assessment center results or standardized personality tests, the validity of predictions of job performance is increased.[7,8] In most employment situations, reasoning ability is the best predictor of performance.[7] The overwhelming conclusion is that intelligence and aptitude are positively related to job performance.[1]

At work, special abilities, like being a good mediator, can be in great demand. Also, the ability to assimilate complex data or information and present it in a simple, meaningful way is invaluable.

Knowledge

Knowledge is familiarity with facts, truths, or principles. Knowledge is gained through experience in numerous situations through our senses (vision, hearing, etc.). Knowledge can be acquired in an academic setting by any number of methods or by an array of interactive means involving learners or mentors.

Knowledge is also acquired through independent study methods, trial-and-error efforts, and on-the-job experience. Underutilized sources of knowledge are the off-work experiences which occur in groups of all descriptions—academic, sports, community-based, social. Hobbies provide excellent resources and challenging learning opportunities. Last, but not least, the information superhighway lined with computers and software is a rapidly growing source of all types of information. Yet, only we can transform this information into knowledge.

9.2

List at least ten activities or jobs that you perform regularly, either on your own or in a group. You may do them as a member of a cross-functional team or on a temporary basis. Compare them with major work activities you listed in Question 7.1.

Jobs or Activities Performed Regularly

1. _____ 6. _____
2. _____ 7. _____
3. _____ 8. _____
4. _____ 9. _____
5. _____ 10. _____

After reading the following section, look back through your list and indicate which jobs require the use of knowledge (K), abilities (A), or skills (S). Write K, A, or S opposite each activity listed in Question 9.2.

Was anything omitted. What is *not* listed may be even more important than what *is* listed. Missing or hidden items represent the "iceberg" concept. Information below the surface could surface when you least expect it. When "hidden" areas are known and recognized, they can be added to other job functions. Comments from peers are very valuable.

Visualize results of questionnaires, surveys, reports, performance appraisals, accomplishments, flowcharts, recommendations, and any other likely source of information on your job.

Your list of activities in Question 9.2 probably contains about an equal number of jobs requiring knowledge, abilities, and skills. There may be overlap as some blend together. Using all three on an as-needed basis balances performance. In some instances, it is important to upgrade skills in order to make better or more efficient use of knowledge. One example is to acquire a few more basic computer skills in order to run a program that you need.

Your knowledge, abilities, and skills or talents are easier to describe and examine than the processes involved to do those jobs. Describing the end result expected (output) is easier than discussing the processes we used (throughput).

We are all unique and use our special talents in different ways. *How* we do our job, or the activities performed on the job, is often less important than *doing the job correctly.* Meeting management's or end users' standards in a timely, cost-effective manner is generally considered more important than the methods and processes used. However, streamlining processes is a proven way to reduce both time and cost and also benefit suppliers and customers. Theoretically, business process analysis can do this.

If you have ever been in a group that was assigned to observe people, each group member probably had a slightly different set of views and interpretations of the same activity. Diverse results can be attributed to lack of training in what to look for and how to record your observations.

In carefully controlled observations, observers and raters go through rigorous training in order to ensure reliability and validity of results. This level of intensity of training helps people agree on jobs, processes, and performance.

Processes or Activities

In Chapter 8, processes were considered to be throughput, or the somewhat intangible aspects of work. Most "work" is considered output. Most processes are difficult to describe, document, and measure. Output, however, can be described, documented, and measured. Historically, output is more generally accepted as an indicator of accomplishment and/or productivity than is throughput. In a step-by-step process, without throughput there would be no output.

Processes

A process is any method, technique, or procedure that usually serves as a means to a useful end. The organization spends most of its time and resources on processes—communication, legal, supervisory, accounting, marketing, etc.[9]

These often invisible, complex, intangible, and unique processes are rarely well defined or documented and often have no owners. Processes may be similar activities that are performed differently. To illustrate, no two people will perform a literature survey and use the same information for their papers. They will be selective. Processes are not typically measured.[18]

Many people use the word "process" due to the current focus on business process analysis. Processes imply a larger, less clearly defined group of events than do activities. "Activities" mean action or movement. You may already have created your own definition for processes and activities. For our purposes, the concepts processes and activities will be used interchangeably.

Work is often described as a continuous flow rather than separate units being performed in isolation. The systems approach demonstrates the flow of work. Systems analysts in the computer field are trained to find out what is blocking the expected flow, or locate "disconnects." These same procedures could be applied to finding out what is blocking the general flow of work done by people throughout the organization.

At work, the process of mentally preparing for an oral presentation or an interview can literally take all the remaining time available. Clocks, rather than people, usually signal the beginning and end of processes.

Activities

Activities are actions or acts that require physical and mental energy. Activities may involve direct experience rather than textbook experience. Think of the activities you perform each day, week, or month.

Work activities such as supervising, training, coordinating, and mentoring can be observed. People look busy and appear to be actively engaged in doing something. But, you may ask, "Are they *really* busy?" The question is whether you are efficient and effective or productive. Efficiency and effectiveness are prime concerns in describing and assessing processes that eventually lead to output.

When starting most new projects, it is difficult to see real progress. First, there is the information gathering stage, then the getting-to-know-people stage, followed by some trial-and-error activities until you get a feel for what you are doing and where you need to go with the project. Only when you have a vision of where you are and where you need to be with a specific project can you experience or feel a sense of direction and accomplishment.

Key processes are designed around customers, products, services, and numerous other business transactions. Some people don't want to know about activities, much less document them. They believe that activities evolve and change and are, therefore, almost impossible to define. They may even view activities with a bit of suspicion and consider them less important than outcomes. Managers' judgments are based on accomplishments as opposed to the hours spent trying to reach agreement.

One line of thought is that activities represent actions in progress and not necessarily tangible accomplishment. The opposite line of thought is that tangible output can be seen, described, measured, and evaluated. This will be discussed more later.

Output

Processes are the step before output. Output is the tangible result of processes and shows the results of efforts. Many processes are illusive, but end results or output can usually be documented in some form.

As previously discussed, people are usually judged by their output—the "B" on the final exam instead of the "A" on lab reports and assignments and the self-assessed "A+" for effort.

Output can be "hard" data, like number of sales, units produced, or projects completed. However, use of hard data may take precedence over other equally important or even more important "soft" data.

"Soft" data are usually subjective and difficult to define, collect, and analyze. Examples are work habits, feelings, attitudes, initiatives, satisfaction, motivation, etc. Soft data can be rated, grouped, and statistically analyzed.

Output can also be the point at which another process starts. What appears to be output is really transformed into input, perhaps to be recycled through the system and emerge as a different type of output with new or unexpected outcomes. Feedback cycles can build a — from output, back to input, as shown below:

Input → Throughput → Output → Input → Throughput → Output

In another vein, there is much more to work than output, which is the next topic.

Outcomes

The concept of outcomes goes one step beyond output. Outcomes are the ultimate, possibly far-reaching results of output. Outcomes are also the results of consequences. In business, outcomes can be the conclusions reached by a logical process of thinking. Employee reactions to certain policies and management decisions are also outcomes.

Output and outcomes are distinctly different. Output may not be the final event. What people do or produce can be output. The end result of face-to-face contact with customers can be positive. However, the expected outcomes go one step beyond output. A person's impact may go beyond an invention, a book, or an award. Fame, national acclaim, and peer recognition are outcomes.

Outcomes are impacts an organization makes with respect to success, self-sufficiency, self-reliance, perhaps even survival. As an example, organizations can have a positive impact by supporting community efforts and schools and being aware of environmental concerns, among others.[9]

Thinking of your job in terms of systems may be helpful, as in Input → Throughput (Process) → Output → Outcomes. It is seldom possible to visualize and hold processes or concepts in sequence in our minds. We may have to write them down and possibly rearrange them. It is easier to visualize and actually see things happening in sequence in assembly-line jobs or when the flow of paper and information is clear.

Some people seldom think in terms of cause and effect or think beyond their own jobs. These people are often too busy putting out brushfires to think about anything else. Whether you are proactive (anticipate problems) or reactive (fight brushfires) also depends on your job and management style, as well as your position in the organization.

Spending time on outcomes prepares you for Chapter 10, Expanding areas, the third part of the Core-Unique-Expanding model. Expanding tasks are the creative, synergy-producing efforts that literally go beyond the basics and common activities of the everyday world of work.

In the organization, everything a person does has some impact on others up and down the line. For example, front-line clerks who wait on customers have the power and ability to turn their customers on or off or leave them in neutral.

A very positive approach to handling customers is used by the Houston-based Federal Reserve Bank. The best-informed employees answer the phones. If the person answering the phone cannot answer the customer's question, he or she transfers the call to someone who can. The customer definitely wins.

Based on material for laying the groundwork for your personal equation, (Chapter 1); the introduction to people, organization, technology, and the environment (Chapter 5); the descriptions of work activities (Chapter 7); and systems approaches (Chapter 8), we are ready for the next step.

THE CORE-UNIQUE-EXPANDING (C-U-E) MODEL

This model provides a framework and a method for enabling people to examine their current jobs and view their talents and achievements in a logical perspective. One major application is in determining areas that can be streamlined in order to improve productivity.

The C-U-E model evolved over a ten-year period. It began with my basic set of assumptions about people and work processes. Late one evening, in what might have been a sudden burst of insight, three broad categories emerged. Each level was more complex than the one before. They came to be known as Core, Unique, and Expanding. And so they have remained.

These three concepts are described briefly here. The separate parts of the model and how it is to be developed and used are presented in greater detail in Chapter 10.

"Core" represents the basic, routine, repetitive tasks required to keep the organization running. Examples are routine clerical or assembly-line jobs.

"Unique" tasks in the next higher level cover what a person is trained to do and does best. Performing these tasks requires expertise and knowledge based on education and training. Examples are tasks done by accountants, engineers, nurses, teachers, etc.

"Expanding" describes the creative, mind-expanding jobs that employ our talents to the fullest. Many of these tasks at the top of the hierarchy call for expertise or knowledge based on creativity or innovation. Examples are doing forefront research, designing new products or processes, and creative thought processes that defy description.

The C-U-E model is built around active work assignments rather than static job descriptions. The prime emphasis is on what people do at work. Essentially, the model forms the basis of a self-developed portfolio of work accomplishments.[16]

The ten assumptions underlying the C-U-E model provide a way to view, communicate, and understand people and their world of work. This model helps place abilities, skills, knowledge, work-related, and numerous other factors discussed earlier in this chapter into a meaningful whole.[16]

Assumptions reflect my personal equation and are built into the C-U-E model. Neither one is the final word. Ways to develop your own C-U-E model and apply it at work are presented in Chapter 10.

ASSUMPTIONS

Ten general, simple assumptions about work per se and how work is performed form the framework of the C-U-E model and are listed in Table 9.1. They are not listed in any particular order of importance. Each assumption is explained and illustrated in greater detail in the following paragraphs.

Some assumptions are more closely connected than others. Assumptions

Table 9.1   Assumptions of the Core-Unique-Expanding Model

1. Work is cyclic, repetitive, or routine.
2. Major work activities and results can be described.
3. Amount of time spent doing work can be measured.
4. Work level of difficulty ranges from simple to complex.
5. Structure of work ranges from formal to informal.
6. All work has standards.
7. Work is done in a logical sequence or order.
8. Work differs in motivating potential.
9. Work has some form of control.
10. Work has value-added functions.

represent some of the most common, basic findings about work (in my view). Only when the true nature of work is understood can people's talents be matched with work activities in order to achieve a desired output. People change. Jobs change. Obviously, people do many jobs over their lifetimes.

1. Work may be cyclic or follow a given order or arrangement of tasks or activities. Work can be performed for a specific part of the hour, day, or week. It can be repetitive or routine. Routine work done for a relatively long period of time becomes automatic. We don't even think much about what we are doing. Sometimes, we can't even remember whether we did it. This means, of course, that we are not paying much attention.

Mistakes made in assembly-line, routine packaging, or checking routine work done by others, for instance, can be due to lack of attention or low motivation. Monitoring performance using specific standards or sampling output for deviations is very important in both products and customer-related services.

2. Major work activities and results can be specified in basic terms and illustrated by examples. Activities commonly refer to events in progress or transition, like negotiating, thinking, and creating. It is always easier, and often more acceptable, to represent work using "hard" data, or tangible input and output, rather than "soft" or descriptive data.

However, activities or processes can also be depicted in simple terms people understand. Soft data can be assessed or measured and documented using qualitative terms.[15] It is important to use words or operational definitions that people agree on or readily understand. Few people are ever at a loss for words when telling others about their jobs. When you talk about your job, you are committing yourself to words that can be written down.

All activities can be described in some meaningful way. It is important to be objective about our jobs, the people we work with, and the processes we perform, or how we describe what we do, as in developing new ideas or processing complex information.

End results are usually reported in terms of number of projects finished, number of customers served, etc. Measurement is easier when we have job-specific operational definitions of rating scales that describe each point on the rating scale. Such a scale was used in Question 7.1. Rating scales can be readily developed to measure quality, satisfaction, output, cost, time, etc.

Key or main results or output are measured in most benchmarking activities. One way to judge an organization's staying power is how well key results which support the mission and goals statements of the organization are performed.

Some processes may be more in a person's mind. These processes could be ideas for new products or services or creative thoughts that are difficult to write down. However, every process has a stimulus or a beginning and an outcome that can be described in simple terms. If it is impossible to describe something adequately, draw a simple sketch and start to fill it in. Other people may be able to help you add details you did not previously consider or felt were unimportant.

3. Time is an inelastic commodity. An old cliché is, "each of us has the same amount of time every day—24 hours." Time is perishable. Once it is gone, it can never be recovered. Time per se and cycle time, or the time it takes to do a particular job, are now seen as one of the many competitive weapons in the race for quality and leadership.

Time and motion studies date back to the early 1900s. Cycle time is not really a new concept in manufacturing industries, but it is relatively new in the service area.

One illustration of supervisory cycle time is:

$$\text{Supervisory cycle time} = \frac{\text{Number of projects supervised per month}}{\text{Monthly completion rate of projects}}$$

Job-related standards or time guidelines for completing a certain type of job often exist, as in assembly, packing completed products, or processing information. Supervisors should have a good feel for the time required to complete projects. Cycle time is becoming increasingly important in all fields of endeavor. Time is money.

Time overruns can be just as bad as cost overruns. When something is late, customers no longer want or need it and refuse to pay for it. Opportunity and income from the sale are both hopelessly lost, as are current contracts.

4. Work level or difficulty ranges from simple to complex. Similarly, skill levels required to perform work also range from simple to complex. Lower level skills may be used in simple, routine jobs. Consistent with a normal distribution, many skills will be in the middle range and require a specific level of mastery. High-level skills will require college degree(s) and/or specialization and certification, as required in medicine, teaching, and other fields. Level of skill also relates to knowledge, ability, and intellectual specialization, among other talents.

Skills can be examined for depth, vertical level, horizontal level, or a three-dimensional approach. Depth means learning more about the area (greater knowledge) or increased proficiency, as in advanced-level work.

Vertical level implies the use of administrative and leadership skills required for upward advancement in the organization's hierarchy, as required to be a leader or coordinator.

Horizontal level means developing skills in parallel work areas in the company in order to make lateral moves among various jobs. Such skills are valuable in teamwork and in increasing the flexibility of the work force.[10]

What is difficult for one person may not be difficult for another. Each of us has our own concept of difficulty. Difficulty or level of complexity can also be in the eye of the beholder. What is simple to one may be complex to another.

As people develop more skills in a certain area, they soon discover that what was very hard at first is now easier. People move up the learning curve as they add skills and the knowledge that accompanies these skills.

5. Structure or format of the job is the way the job is set up. The order in which separate parts are to be done can affect how well the job is done, and even who does it. Order makes a difference in how quickly jobs can be done. Some jobs, like word processing, follow a logical sequence of steps. Other jobs, however, require input or assistance from others along the way.

Work structure, like the structure of an organization, ranges from formal to informal. Formal jobs, such as those of quality control inspectors, have strict guidelines. Structured jobs require a precise output at a specific point in time, as in passing customers along through a line. Each activity requires a specific, perhaps one-of-a-kind calculation, analysis, or approval.

The more informal the job, the more difficult it is to describe. Job descriptions for writers, researchers, artists, entrepreneurs, and faculty members are few and far between or non-existent. Such jobs may relate to performing work that requires specialized skills similar to those knowledge workers use.

Most people know how structured their jobs are. Some individuals can't stand lack of structure and may build structure in the form of unnecessary routines or standards into their loosely organized jobs. This procedure makes perfect sense to the person doing the building.

Another way to impose order or structure is to work on the routine or fixed tasks at a specific time, like early in the morning. When the structured tasks are completed, individuals who need some structure may be perfectly content to start on the unstructured tasks. Without structure and guidelines, it may be difficult to tell if you have even done your job, let alone know if you did it well.

Some creative, innovative people enjoy, or thrive on, lack of structure. Their minds are not bound to any set course of action or stream of thought. Free-wheeling efforts lead to breakthrough discoveries and inventions. However, there will be a time when some of the things they do will have to be structured, documented, measured, or written up in the form of a report or patent application.

Structure can be set by the person doing the job. It can also be established by the specific unit or company where the job is performed. Some industries, such as automobile manufacturers and insurance companies, also set standards.

6. All jobs have standards or performance guidelines. This is true in school, in sports, in the professional world, in the military, etc. Standards set forth minimums for training, experience, learning, and professionalism, among other requirements. Standards differ in basic type, level of clarity, and cost to implement and maintain, to name only a few considerations. Standards also apply to both products (regulation, inspection, certification, etc.) and services (customer satisfaction).

Standards range from simple, or basic, minimum standards to the very highest possible standards ("perfect" or zero defects). Standards are often set by customers, clients, or partners or by those developing the products or services. Partners often work with developers or manufacturers and suppliers to create and set joint standards. Collaboration results in mutually agreed-upon standards.

Some standards, like safety in the workplace, are enforced. Standards are common in nearly every field of human endeavor, from weights and measures to professional accreditation. Other factors in setting, interpreting, and enforcing standards include your own organization, your peers, supervisors, and team members; regulatory bodies; and industry codes.

Some of the most rigid standards are those we set for ourselves. High standards may lead to disappointment, but often keep us motivated and on target.

Standards can also simply be in the eye of the beholder. If the customer, supplier, or end user says that something is okay, it is assumed that the product or service at least met his or her minimum standards.

7. Most jobs can or should be done in some logical sequence or order. For mind-stretching jobs, this may be impossible. If other people up and down the line depend on you, you will probably do the various parts of your job in a given order. Sequencing allows work to be checked. Also, others see that it has been done. Work that bridges a gap prevents "disconnects" in the flow of events.

In routine jobs, the order will be stipulated in clear terms, such as checklists, verbal orders, a detailed manual, or extremely close supervision.

As jobs become less routine, the person doing the job will have some leeway to make decisions about the sequence in which the job is to be performed. Some people will change the order of the separate tasks within the job to fit the way they like to work—do the simple things first, then do the hard things, or vice versa.

The order in which activities or tasks are performed can be a matter of personal preference. The entire area of human factors suggests that people do things differently, depending on their special talents and interests. Order can also be based on skills or even the needs of those up and down the line. In matters of safety, as in the airline industry, standards are mandated and enforced.

8. Jobs differ greatly in ability to motivate, or motivating potential. Motivation is closely related to personal growth and development. As we know, different things motive different people in different ways. Some people enjoy a routine job with little responsibility. They avoid stress and always leave work on time. Others will want the most challenging job possible so they can learn and grow on the job. Most individuals fall somewhere in between, again as shown by the normal distribution curve.

Interesting, challenging, mentally stimulating jobs that make people think and create have a greater potential to motivate than do routine jobs that require little effort or thought. If people do not enjoy exerting mental effort, they will not be motivated to perform. In such instances, motivating potential has little or no value. To find out what motivates these people, just ask. They will tell you. You can use the information they provide to build motivators, like a challenging job with a future, into their jobs. New motivating potential is thereby created.

New job assignments, rewards, recognition, and cross-training are good intrinsic motivators. Unless people are honestly motivated by the jobs they are performing, their jobs will have no motivating potential for them. Most importantly, satisfaction of needs does not motivate.

In general, the more complex and demanding the job, the higher the motivating potential. This holds true *except* for people who do not want to think too much, work too hard, or be challenged on the job.

The more open-ended and less structured the job, the more likely the person doing the job is to inject his or her own challenges and motivators. This can become the "fun" part of work that people anticipate and enjoy. What excites and motivates people at work depends on an array of human factors too numerous to mention here.

Motivating potential will be highest when the upper three of Maslow's needs are satisfied: the need for belongingness, self-esteem, and self-actualization.[11] Except for belongingness, the workplace does not offer these motivators on any consistent basis. Being in a work group and socializing with peers and other work associates away from the office often satisfies needs for belongingness. Self-esteem and self-actualization are excellent but underused motivators.

People are reported to be well motivated when their chance to succeed is about 50/50.[6] However, a few people are motivated only when they are literally stretched beyond their abilities. Vroom's 1964 landmark book, *Work and Motivation*, integrates the work of hundreds of researchers. His new book covers, among other areas, choice of work, job satisfaction, and job performance.[20]

Motivating potential relates to the job and to job characteristics. A job with high motivating potential, like being an astronaut, a concert performer, a much revered educator, and so on, can be very attractive. The prime questions are, "If the job currently has motivating appeal, will it always have motivating potential? If so, for how long?" Again, satisfied needs do not motivate. The person will have to set progressively higher levels of performance or focus on new, exciting areas in order to maintain level of motivation.

Do people see motivating potential in the same way? No. The old saying "don't judge others by yourself" applies. No two people will interpret the level of motivating potential in a given job in the same way.

Five main concepts are basic to motivating potential: autonomy, task identify, task significance, skill variety, and feedback.[13]

Autonomy illustrates the degree to which people feel personally responsible for their work, like an artist who produces a beautiful, one-of-a-kind painting. Outcomes are the spinoff effects of output.

Task identity includes the effective use of skills and abilities that the person performing the job considers important and believes are valuable. A task has identity when there is a definite sense of beginning and ending to what is being done.

Jobs with high-level task identity are "prestige" jobs, like special assignments. Preparing a status report for your supervisor has high "task identity." Taking your turn driving in the car pool, while important, has low task identity.

Tasks can be divided into short, relatively homogeneous work elements. Each work element can be treated separately or can be combined with a "family" of other similar elements. There may be three or four basic overlapping work families for a specific job. Typical work families in engineering are design procedures, interface with production, and working with team members.

Task significance represents the intrinsic value of the work people do. Tasks contributing something to the overall accomplishments of the organization have significance. The person doing these tasks feels that the tasks are important and not just routine. Motivating potential is high in tasks that people feel are meaningful or contribute value or worth to the workplace.

Skill variety refers to the wide range of skills people possess in order to do their jobs. Jobs that require a number of skills will motivate people who enjoy intellectual challenges. Conversely, high skill variety may demotivate less capable individuals.

Feedback, or knowledge of results, provides information on how effectively people perform their jobs. When feedback comes on a periodic basis or is continuous, there is opportunity to modify and change behavior in order to improve results. Feedback was discussed in detail in Chapter 8.

The following equation illustrates the variables that make up motivating potential.

$$\text{Motivating Potential Score} = \frac{\text{Skill variety} + \text{Task identity} + \text{Task significance}}{3}$$

$$\times \text{ Autonomy } \times \text{ Feedback}$$

Although values could be determined for each of these five variables and the equation solved, the main purpose in this chapter is to illustrate the broad concept of motivating potential. Data for the equation could come from re-sponses to surveys, questionnaires, or possibly opinions. Data will need to be representative and appropriate statistical analyses performed if the results are to be considered reliable and valid.

9. Control has positive and negative sides.   Do jobs control people, or do people control jobs? Generally, when people have control, they feel more com-fortable. Those who are controlled may not know what to expect. Frequently, use of negative control, like withholding important information, is a form of power. Flexibility of thought processes, particularly those involved in creativity, is greatly reduced by negative control.

This is where empowerment comes in. Empowerment means that there is some flexibility or autonomy in how the job is to be done. When authority is delegated, and people are both responsible and accountable, little direct super-vision or monitoring is needed. Nordstrom, the Seattle-based department store, is one of the most decentralized companies ever created. Management control is minimal. The only rule in Nordstrom's employee handbook is, "Use your good judgment in all situations. There will be no additional rules."

Control can be viewed in terms of financial constraints (like budgets), time limitations, reduced work force, rules, standards to be met on a consistent basis, and even the flow of communication through proper networks. Through their very structure, organizations, like bureaucracies, control the way people do their jobs. In this instance, control takes the shape of specific rules and regulations.

One negative form of control is deliberately slowing down the flow of work activities so that everyone down the line is affected. This is a problem of ineffective supervision and not necessarily motivation.

Some forms of control are necessary, as in personal safety, handling danger-ous equipment, or working with hazardous chemicals.

Although control may imply negative aspects, reducing control means au-tonomy in delegation and supervision. Control also indicates that there are choices, as in allocating money at budget time or in meeting goals.

**10. Value-added functions are the pluses that exceed users'
expectations.**   Value added implies "going beyond" expectations or standards, or being "excellent." People know when they see or experience value added. They like being delighted with superb customer service. They also know when value added is not there.

It is necessary to have value before achieving value added. Most often, value added comes only after products and services are seen to have value. (See Chapter 6 for a complete definition of value.)

Like perception, value added can be in the eye of the beholder. The roles played by perception and expectation are extremely important. We all have our own ideas about what types of work we do that have value and value added. Knowledge workers having specialized knowledge in an area and use their unique skills to assimilate information and transform it in a way that adds value for end users. Resulting information can be designed into new products or used to create innovative services or products for customers.

Value-adding services can be the key to business success and longevity. Value added also takes the form of life span, pride, excitement, and high standards.[17] Customers can readily detect products and services that go "one step beyond value."

Managerial and technological competencies, experience, education, and intellectual capital are the major building blocks of value added. When more effort is directed toward developing value-adding human resource management strategies, staff departments can enhance their value to their customers.

People contribute their own special brand of value added. People may set up the circumstances whereby others can add value by taking the product or service one step further than expected. The potential to add value is what forefront designers, developers, marketers, etc. look for. Will the customer be willing to pay for more value added? The answer is to ask the customer.

Value added, like the steady achievement of quality, gets further away the closer you get. As revealed in an interview with General Merrill A. McPeak, Chief of Staff of the. U.S. Air Force, Washington, D.C., when speaking of quality, "It recedes from us at the same rate we walk toward it. That is to say, the Air Force will never get there."[2]

Feedback on value added that comes from customer and end-user input is vital if products and services are to be improved. Feedback is a major key in enhancing value and value added. When value added provided by suppliers is received by customers, everyone wins. Achieving value added impacts outcomes, like goodwill or reputation for outstanding services and products. When value added is known to exist, the normal time lag required for acceptance and recognition in the marketplace is shortened.

Real value-added managers of the 21st century will be innovators, entrepreneurs, and conceptual thinkers who develop new ideas that add value for their customers.

INCORPORATE SKILLS AND TALENTS INTO A MEANINGFUL WHOLE

We all assemble ideas and facts in different ways. Ideas, assumptions, and concepts presented in this chapter may add to your unique frame of reference or collection of attitudes, beliefs, and values. You may now view and evaluate your job in a slightly different manner. As mentioned before, your frame of reference is affected by perception, experience, training, and many other factors. It is a major part of your personality and impacts how you view and perform your job.

The major issue, however, is to (1) understand your own job and (2) know how your job relates to jobs others perform. Operationalizing major concepts or factors lets us develop and use a common language to describe our work and personal world. When those around us use terms we understand, communication problems are greatly decreased. The converse also applies.

SUMMARY AND CONCLUSIONS

1. There is a continuing need to recognize and make the best possible use of human factors. Accepting differences in individuals and building them into the job increases job satisfaction. When people use their own resources, they are likely to develop new ways to do their jobs, perhaps even streamlining them and doing them more quickly.

2. Separating processes and activities from output and output from outcomes is not meant to be an intellectual exercise. Rather, it requires thinking in sequence, or in terms of cause and effect. This type of thinking is not done often enough. There is always a natural flow to events of all kinds, including work, as discussed in Chapter 8.

3. The assumptions basic to the Core-Unique-Expanding model cover a broad range of work activities, processes, and outcomes. These assumptions form the standards or guidelines on which work-related behaviors and achievements can be selected, analyzed and compared.

4. Thinking in terms of systems means knowing what the logical sequence or flow of events really is. This method of thinking encourages people to consider cause-and-effect variables that impact performance or, conversely, keep things from getting done. Considering outcomes, the far-reaching effect of output, is a critical issue in customer satisfaction and, in particular, customer loyalty.

PRACTICAL APPLICATIONS

1. Reviewing work processes, results, and outcomes can be a stand-alone educational experience. Looking at jobs through a new set of eyeglasses often reveals opportunities for change and improvement.

2. Thinking in a logical, step-by-step sequence is a first step in developing scenarios. Scenarios with a full range of input variables and slightly different types of customers can be discussed before putting them down on paper. Carefully developed and well-documented scenarios can provide valuable guides to action.

3. Knowing oneself is purported to be one of the first steps to true understanding. If we do not know our own skills, we will not be aware of areas where we excel or where we may be deficient. If we do not know our own talents, how can we realistically judge the talents of others?

4. Value added is probably one of the most valuable keys to successfully competing in, if not currently winning, the productivity and quality race. In our increasingly customer-oriented world, customers are more and more demanding. In order to attract and keep customers, services and products must be better than those of the competition. Benchmarking provides the tools to determine what our competitors are doing. However, if we just copy our competitors, we are already behind. We must leap ahead and try to remain ahead. Value added has great potential. However, creative abilities of those who develop and produce value-added products and services must be appropriately recognized and reinforced. Otherwise, without a supportive infrastructure, value-added concepts will die on the vine.

REFERENCES

1. Barrett, Gerald V. and Depinet, Robert L. "A Reconsideration of Testing for Competence Rather than for Intelligence," *American Psychologist*, October 1991, pp. 1012–1024.

2. Bemowski, Karen. "The Air Force Quality Flight Plan." *Quality Progress*, June 1994, pp. 25–29.

3. Boff, K. R., Kaufman, L., and Thomas, J. P. (Eds.), *Handbook of Perception and Human Performance* (Vols. 1 and 2), New York: Wiley-Interscience, 1986.

4. Booher, H. R. (Ed.). *MANPRINT: An Approach to Systems Integration*, New York: Van Nostrand Reinhold, 1990.

5. Gagne, R. M. *The Conditions of Learning* (4th ed.), New York: Holt, Rinehart and Winston, 1985.

6. Hampton, David R., Summer, Charles R., and Webber, Ross A. *Organizational Behavior and Practice of Management*, Glenview, Ill.: Scott, Foresman, 1978, p. 264.

7. Hunter, J. E. "Cognitive Ability, Cognitive Aptitudes, Job Knowledge, and Job Performance," *Journal of Vocational Behavior*, Vol. 29, 1986, pp. 340–362.

8. Hunter, J. E., Schmidt, F. L., and Judiesch, M. K. "Individual Differences in Output Variability as a Function of Job Complexity," *Journal of Applied Psychology*, Vol. 75, 1990, pp. 28 52.

9. Kaufman, Roger. "Assessing Needs," In *Introduction to Performance Technology*, Washington, D.C.: The National Society for Performance and Instruction, 1986, pp. 25 39.

10. Landis, Larry J. "Try a Pay for Knowledge Process with a PLUS," *Journal for Quality and Participation*, June 1994, pp. 26–29.

11. Maslow, A. H. *Motivation and Personality* (2nd ed.), New York: Harper and Row, 1970.

12. Meister, David. *Conceptual Aspects of Human Factors*, Baltimore: Johns Hopkins University Press, 1989.

13. Miner, John B. *Theories of Organizational Behavior*, Hinsdale, Ill.: The Dryden Press, 1980.

14. Salvendy, G. (Ed.). *Handbook of Human Factors*, New York: John Wiley & Sons, 1987.

15. Smith, Elizabeth A. "The Role of Qualitative Information in Productivity Measurement," *Industrial Management*, March/April 1991, pp. 19–22, 24.

16. Smith, Elizabeth A. *The Productivity Manual* (2nd. ed.), Houston: Gulf Publishing, 1995.

17. Smith, Elizabeth A. "Value Added: Expectation vs. Perception vs. Reality," *The Quality Observer*, in press (expected publication date July 1995).

18. Snee, Ronald D. "Creating Robust Work Places," *Quality Progress*, February 1993, pp. 37–41.

19. Tucker, Robert and Moravec, Milan. "Do It-Yourself Career Development," *Training*, February 1992, pp. 40–50, 52.

20. Vroom, Victor R. *Work and Motivation*, San Francisco: Jossey-Bass, 1994.

10

THE CORE-UNIQUE-
EXPANDING MODEL

PURPOSE

- Present the Core-Unique-Expanding, fact-based, experience-based, representation model as a way to examine jobs people perform

- Compare and rank major work-related variables along the ten dimensions presented as assumptions in Chapter 9

- Group the ranked, work-related variables into Core, Unique, or Expanding areas in order to determine how much each activity contributes to an entire job

- Provide information that can be used to make decisions to streamline or refocus efforts in order to maximize productivity, quality, and job satisfaction, among other goals.

INTRODUCTION

You have outlined pertinent job-related variables, specified job content, and perhaps operationally defined what you do at work. Any number of human factors, including your system of beliefs, or frame of reference, attitudes, and values, influence not only your performance, but how you relate to others. The content of your model and how you use it is really an individual matter. You and your model truly are unique.

This model is not designed to elicit all the information in a given area. Rather, it provides a framework on which to build and document a history or theory of knowledge of your talents and your current job. Knowledge precedes understanding. Understanding precedes action. A theory of knowledge about ourselves and others that is put into action lets us step ahead of our competition.

The major framework of the model integrates the ten assumptions discussed in Chapter 9. These concepts take the form of theories, knowledge, ideas, intuition, and beliefs about people and how they think and react

THE CORE UNIQUE-EXPANDING (C-U-E) MODEL

The C-U-E model introduced in Chapter 9 examines various types and levels of work skills, activities, or processes and output from any job. The model groups the wide range and type of work performed into three broad areas—Core, Unique, and Expanding. The model is built around work assignments rather than job descriptions.[17]

Purpose

A prime purpose of a model is to provide ways to make comparisons and illustrate order, or logic. Working on any model or artistic creation can be slow and painstaking. Each model contains a specific set of elements. Like people, no two models are exactly alike. Once a model is constructed, it can be used in a variety of ways.

The specific purpose of the C-U-E model is to identify, describe, document, and group skills, ability, knowledge, work processes, and work-related variables into a meaningful whole. Resulting information helps users determine how separate parts of their jobs relate to one another and fit together. The model is really a picture of a person's job. This model, as mentioned before, grows and changes with the individual. It also mirrors work and workplace changes.

When broad-based tasks that people do on a regular basis are divided into smaller parts, each part can be carefully examined. The role each part plays in performance can be evaluated in terms of importance, value, or any number of other important criteria, like quality.

Obviously, the model works best for me. You are encouraged to develop and use your own assumptions to create a model that best meets your needs. On the other hand, you are welcome to give mine a try.

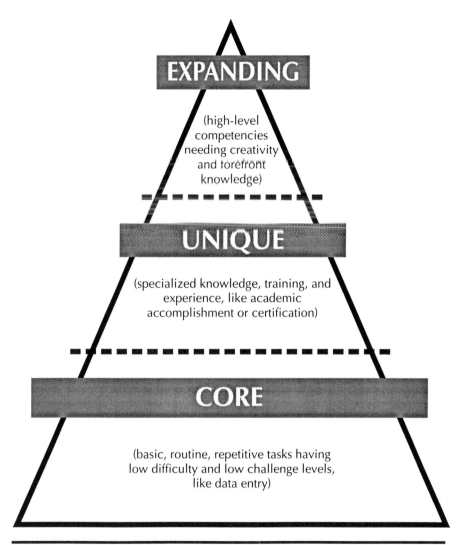

Figure 10.1 The Core-Unique-Expanding Model

The C-U-E model is presented in Figure 10.1. Core is the lowest level and is least complex. Unique is the mid-level and is relatively complex. Expanding is the highest level and is the most complex.

The size of each area is not necessarily proportional to the amount of time spent in it. The relative amount of time people normally spend in each area will change, depending on the type of work they are performing. Allocations of time and time devoted to each level could help make time allocations or possibly (re)assignments.

The dividing lines between adjacent levels are shown as dashed lines. Adjacent parts of the model overlap slightly. Some types of work activities in Core, for example, will be similar to work activities in Unique. The dividing line between higher-level Core tasks and lower-level Unique tasks can move up or down. Most skills will remain where they were first assigned. However, as people acquire more skills, their level in the hierarchy will gradually move up, as from upper-level Core to lower-level Unique, and possibly further up.

This also applies to the line dividing Unique and Expanding. Boundaries are not distinct or permeable. Some job areas will overlap. Clearly separating Unique and Expanding areas may be difficult. Some high-level yet routine job may be at the upper end of the Core area or at the lower end of the Unique area. When skills in one area are increased, or jobs get more complex, this flexible line moves upward toward the next higher level in the hierarchy. Also, as work level and complexity change during the course of a day, people will move back and forth among the three levels.

Core Components

These routine, often basic, simple tasks are relatively easy to perform. These simple operations may consist of technical and non-technical tasks. Most people agree on what Core tasks are. Each job or task has a definite knowledge or information base that can be described and defined.

Core activities revolve around the mission- or vision-driven efforts of the organization. These basic but important tasks are generally understood.

Doing each task involves performing a series of routines. How and when to do them is specified in straightforward, basic terms.

Most Core jobs are organized around a set of projects (for example, maintenance and repair in products-based industries) or around specific aspects of customer service. To illustrate, most superstores that sell computers and video equipment will be involved in repair and customer service.

Core activities, for example, are performed by the line crew at an airport. They fuel the plane, perform required maintenance and inspections, clean out the cabin, restock it with supplies, and do the associated record keeping.

There are common elements in Core tasks in the same or similar industries. Nearly every level of worker in the world does similar Core tasks within the same industry (vehicle repair), similar industries (line crews at airports), or outside the industry (process data). Similarly, many people in the professional world perform the same or similar Core activities, like search for information, supervise others, try to meet deadlines, etc. These and similar aspects relating to negotiable skills are considered under Practical Applications.

Core jobs can be rotated between people performing similar tasks, e.g., data entry or standard assembly-line operations. Job rotation is one way to bring some flexibility to routine jobs and, hopefully, increase motivation and enthusiasm. Job rotation is a basic form of cross-training.

One person's low-priority Core activities may be another person's high-priority Core activities. To illustrate, one person may enjoy the challenge of word processing—learning new programs, increasing input speed, and working alone. Another person may dislike word processing because he or she likes to talk to people and can't sit still for extended periods of time.

Data input clerks, engineers, accountants, medical technicians...pilots all enter data into computers. Clerks may do so for six or seven hours a day, medical technicians for perhaps half a day, and airline pilots for less than an hour a day or perhaps just ten minutes. *All levels of clerical and professional people do exactly the same thing. Time spent inputting data is the only difference.* The skills needed to input data are essentially identical.

A major concern is that unless Core activities vital to an organization's success are performed at least at an "average" level and performed consistently, the entire operation can be put in jeopardy. Essentially, Core tasks are the seemingly small activities that must be done in order to keep the big machinery of the organization in smooth running condition—or simply to stay in business.

Measures of productivity, quality, and use of other standards are based on relatively simple activities and observable, countable output, like number of customers served. Core activities are prime targets for measurement due to their simple, basic nature. Since these routine tasks can be readily described and measured, processes and outputs can be expressed in clear, concise, operational terms.

Existing company-wide or industry standards for performance may serve as a basis of comparison. Handbooks or manuals may also provide guidelines on quality, performance, or numerous important, job-specific standards.

Job aids can be developed for Core work processes and results. The job aids are often written descriptions, like a guide, flowchart, decision table, checklist, or protocol. They are not tools, like texts, audiovisuals, or screwdrivers. Job aids: (1) can be used on the spot or in real time, (2) provide signals to the performer as to when to do something, (3) give sufficient direction on how to perform a task, and (4) reduce the quantity of information required and the time needed to recall information.[6]

Unique Components

These areas are specific to education, training, and/or experience and depend primarily on knowledge, ability, and skill. Unique activities relate to a profession or discipline, like engineering or accounting. Knowledge workers and "white-collar workers" spend most of their time in this area. These specialized activities form the major part of a job and represent what people are educated and trained to do.

Unique skills are not readily transferable, but can be upgraded by study or training. For instance, if you are an engineer, some Core skills could be taught to non-engineers. However, Unique skills take much longer to learn, as they are specialized and more complex than Core skills. Despite training, the person would lack knowledge a traditionally trained engineer has. However, there are standard, competency-based exams in engineering, as in other professions, that people can take to demonstrate competence and become certified or licensed.

When we work in Unique areas, we feel very comfortable because of our training and experience. We readily talk about our areas of expertise. We enjoy working in Unique areas, as they challenge and excite us. Keeping up with the changes in our professions can be a welcome but time-consuming challenge. However, maintaining competence definitely gives us a feeling of satisfaction, if not status.

We also have resources to help support and encourage us in our professions, and in other areas of expertise. Faculty members supported us as students. At work, peers, managers, and professional associates provide information and guidance. Confidence increases when we have a sound base of knowledge from which to make proposals, solve problems, or teach others.

People around the world with the same Unique skills, whether they would admit it or not, do pretty much the same type of work. Examples are architects, physicians, nurses, computer programmers, and administrative assistants. It is often possible to work in different countries of the world without much difficulty, other than certification or licensing and possibly learning a language(s). Exceptions are those who applied their Unique skills in other areas or professions and climbed an unfamiliar, often steep learning ladder.

Some Unique tasks can be restructured or simplified to become Core tasks. Many of the common elements in nearly every job are probably Core tasks. Restructuring work builds skill variety into the job. Skill variety is one of the six parts of motivating potential discussed in Chapter 9. People who normally perform Core tasks most of the day are motivated by a higher-level newly designed job from Unique areas. For example, when people are on vacation or temporarily working in another area, someone with the required skills and knowledge can step in and do the job.

Skills in which people specialize can also be considered Unique skills. The key to productivity in the professional office is intellectual specialization. "A high level of productivity cannot be achieved unless managers and professionals devote most of their time to work appropriate to their level."[15]

When Core and Unique tasks are understood and performed at the appropriate level, as in meeting job-specific standards, it is then possible to move upward to Expanding tasks.

Expanding Components

To stimulate your mind to think "expanding," consider things that you really enjoy doing. Ponder your attributes, interests, and what truly motivates you. Thoughts need not relate directly to work, but to hobbies or other fun things you enjoy but seldom do.

These unstructured activities relate to personal growth and development in a profession or area of expertise. Expanding areas represent "maturity." Tasks are demanding, challenging, and often require creativity and innovation. Expanding tasks approach self-actualization or maximal realization of potential.

Maslow[11] lists self-actualization as the highest of five needs. The order, from lowest to highest, is physiological, safety and security, belongingness and affiliation, esteem and recognition, and self-actualization.

Self-actualization is the desire to realize or actualize one's full potential. Self-actualization is "...to become more and more what one is, to become everything that one is capable of becoming."[10]

Maslow's concept of self-actualization goes beyond the static self to include broad concepts like autonomy; independence of culture and environment; freshness of appreciation, spontaneity, or simpleness and naturalness; and, perhaps most important of all, authenticity and creativity.[12,13]

Authenticity involves selective commitment of energies and freedom to choose what is most meaningful at work and in one's personal life. Involvements are often on a broad, challenging front where there are no real answers. Efforts may be directed toward contributing to the greater good, where results may be years away. People have the ability to take satisfaction in "the fabric of being" and can fit together numerous experiences into a meaningful whole.[2]

Centeredness is the heart of actualization. To illustrate, people who are aware of their choices after recognizing the possibilities open to them, as well as problems and responsibilities, can choose knowingly. They become centered in the activities of the moment without being concerned with the past or fruitless apprehensions of the future. Actualization occurs only in the moment.

Due to human factors, self-actualization in one person can be quite different from self-actualization in another person. Self-actualized people may also be creative, but creativity and self-actualization are not necessarily related.[10]

No one person will have all of the nine traits or attributes discussed below. Further, these nine represent only a sample of the many traits that could be discussed. However, most people have experienced some of these traits or feelings at one time or another. This list will help you enhance your feelings about the nature of Expanding, or self-actualization, concepts.

People who have achieved a level of self-actualization, and who function at that level for a (small) part of their day, have "advanced maturity." This comes only after a certain level of personal mastery has been achieved. These people build and hold deep values and make commitments to goals larger than themselves. Their capacity for delayed gratification enables them to aspire to objectives others would disregard or become too impatient to work toward.

Some of the characteristics of self-actualizing people are as follow.

1. More efficient perceptions of reality and more comfortable relations with it. A keener sense of observation and an ability to think and focus activities in many directions. These people concentrate first on real problems listed or symptoms or what appears to be wrong or out of place. This emphasis may be due to experience in similar areas or an ability to cut through the surrounding fog and go to the heart of the issue.

2. Accept themselves, others, and the realities of life. This overall acceptance comes from knowing one's own abilities and from having to continuously demonstrate competence in specific academic and work-related areas.

Acceptance also comes from knowledge of self, or an ability to reflect on thoughts and feelings. This inner knowledge builds up slowly. Over time, people develop a repertoire of scenarios that they can run through in their mind. They gradually develop a range of acceptable, proven behaviors needed to cope with the realities of their everyday world. Occasionally, there will be an opportunity to use a scenario or set of skills that has worked before in a similar instance.

3. Continued freshness of appreciation. Such "freshness" comes from enthusiasm for and openness to thought and action. Behavior is not set, but rather is flexible. Those having inner standards, or a stable set of attitudes, beliefs, and values, and a frame of reference are able to see and evaluate new ideas, concepts, and ventures with enthusiasm and optimism.

4. Focus on problems outside themselves, or an outer-directedness. Having a clear mission provides direction and stability. The visions and missions of these people are ingrained in their minds, so they don't have to think about who they are and where they are going.

They unconsciously compare what is going on around them with their "inner core of stability." This frees up time and energy to focus on important aspects of their work and home environment other than themselves. This inner core contains the essence of their talents, frame of reference, and experience. It is both ballast and compass.

5. Creativeness and ability to show this potential. Creativity is characterized by originality and inventiveness. Creative people are receptive to new ideas. They are independent in thought and action.

Creative people thrive in an atmosphere that provides for and encourages a genuinely free exchange of information both horizontally and vertically in the organization. Openness to risk and to failure is the hallmark of the creative individual. Errors and failures are accepted as stepping stones in the development of creative ideas. These innovative individuals like to assimilate concepts (input), synthesize, and expand (throughput) in order to create ideas or produce satisfying output that has value.

Risk taking should be a legitimate, necessary, and expected aspect of both individual and organizational behavior. Creative people need the "right to be wrong" and the assurance that failure is as much a part of the job as is success.

The creative process is enhanced when people are allowed: (1) more freedom to manage their own work, (2) leeway to complete a job once undertaken, (3) the latitude to spend part of their working hours on problems of their own choice, (4) opportunity to participate in decision making, (5) freedom to make mistakes and not be held accountable for every action and idea, and (6) opportunity to consult with their colleagues inside and outside the organization.

If creativity is to flourish, managers must be guided in their attitudes and work practices by the basic assumption that almost all individuals are capable of responsibility, considerable initiative, self-direction, and self-control. Employees will direct their creativity toward accomplishing worthwhile objectives.

Example. Creativity, like productivity and motivation, is a very broad field. Creativity in action at Cray Research in Eagen, Minnesota is revealed in its customer policy or mission statement. People from diverse areas in the company are encouraged to express their creative ideas in an atmosphere of open communication. Cray strongly supports individual and group efforts to transform their ideas into quality products for customers.[4]

Creative people are ready to take the next step beyond what is known or traditional. They enjoy applying what they know to new fields. Their vision for the future is on more meaningful, challenging work. Creative people will develop the products or process for which there are "killer applications," design new devices, revamp old ways of doing things, and create fantastic software.

6. Capacity to resolve dichotomies. The traditional "American way," as described in the International Quality Studies performed jointly by the American Quality Foundation and Ernst & Young, revealed that thinking in terms of dichotomies is very common. Everything is "black or white," "good or bad," "right or wrong." This line of thinking takes us to the extreme ends of the normal distribution curve. Chapter 6 revealed that there is much in the middle.

Those who accept and resolve dichotomies literally have the ability to focus on any point on the normal distribution curve. They can move their feelings, ideas, and solutions back and forth in order to resolve the dichotomy. They see the other person's position and meld opposing opinions into an acceptable solution.

7. Strong commitment to ethical and moral standards. These commitments are built into a person's frame of reference. Attitudes, beliefs, and values are formed gradually, beginning in childhood. Much is learned from family, peers, friends, and other important people in an individual's life. Work experience adds to ethical and moral standards. Many people espouse their organizations' beliefs and standards regarding ethics, often as seen in company culture.

Strong commitments and standards produce individuals who are very firm in their convictions. They can seldom be swayed. If they do change their standards, they will need proof that there is a need to change. Their inner beliefs about what is fair and just are so strong that they tend to retain these convictions despite controversy, negative opinions of their peers, and other contradictions.

8. Democratic character structure. Fairness and equitability characterize this group of people. They are open to suggestions, listen carefully, and are basically non-judgmental and non-evaluative. People around them feel comfortable, because they know their beliefs and opinions will be valued. Empowerment and feelings of satisfaction are high in a supportive, democratic atmosphere.

9. Spontaneous, highly desirable naturalness, or an ability to react quickly and enthusiastically. These people are excited about new ideas, methods, and concepts. They are secure enough to be unconcerned about what others think. They do not have to prove themselves on a daily basis.

They believe they have nothing to lose, and much to gain, from being open and natural in relationships with others. Their approach to people and to events is positive. These traits build on, or interact with, other traits listed here.

USES OF THE CORE-UNIQUE-EXPANDING MODEL

There are a number of ideas within each group of uses. Broad areas covered are (1) job placement and assignments, (2) planning and redesign, (3) education and training, (4) motivation, (5) career passport...personal knowledge equation, and (6) analytical tool to measure and enhance productivity and quality.

Job Placement and Assignments

1. Provide baselines for initial job placement to maximize the fit between talents and job requirements. Correct job placement enhances productivity and job satisfaction. When people know more about their own talents, they make informed decisions about their own jobs and the jobs of others. Job assignments can reflect preferences for job content and can be based on proven, negotiable, flexible skills. Placement is also an issue in assignment to teams, project groups, and cross functional groups

2. When people have worked in numerous positions, a roster of talents gradually accumulates. This roster can be used as a basis for making decisions on initial job assignments or placing people in work teams based on expertise or other significant factors.

3. Helps reduce the gap between a person's present level of skills and what is required now and in the future. Rapidly expanding technology requires that people remain competent in their fields.

4. Serves as an aid in understanding and communicating critical job variables, particularly when coupled with uniform ways to create and assess standards, as in performance appraisal or promotion.

Planning and Redesign

1. Scheduling and capacity planning improve handling of work load cycles. This relates to scheduling of people and plant capacity, among other resources, or is directed to areas where improvement would be beneficial.

2. For structuring managerial and support hierarchies at the correct number of layers to provide for positions at the right level of complexity of work. Results of a comprehensive survey of 1000 employees in 20 white-collar or "professional" departments in 5 major U.S. corporations indicated that managers reportedly spend almost 30 percent of their work week on clerical and non-productive tasks, such as word processing, searching for information, filing, and photocopying.[16] The activities described in this study are Core activities. They are not, however, Core activities of busy managers; they are Core activities of clerical workers.

3. Sassone reports that as intellectual specialization uniformly decreases, job levels increase. This is the exact opposite of what is proposed in the model. Managers should not spend time on clerical activities, as costs of

support staffs are driven up because computers require support staff, troubleshooters, and systems analysts. Another false assumption is that support work is not vital to an organization's success. Anyone can and should do it. Immediate cost savings can be achieved by letting the clerical staff go. And it happens all the time.

4. Staffing imbalances also disrupt the logical flow of work. Too many at the top and too few support people slow down the whole process. People often end up doing other people's jobs, but not effectively or efficiently.[16] It is vital to create robust workplaces where people work cooperatively and productively.[19]

Education/Training

1. Training efforts, including literacy training and cross-training, can begin with Core tasks. Core tasks are likely candidates for job rotation if streamlining, simplifying, or consolidating work efforts are the goals. The downside is that continuously performing simple Core tasks may lower motivation and productivity.

2. Reach consensus on Core activities that can be identified and defined and for which common sets of skills can be taught. Results could be used to design a basic skills curriculum. Skills would apply to a wide range of industries. Outcomes could be technology exchange, formation of cross-functional (international) teams, application of military insights to regular educational...business channels.

3. Similar efforts to the above would work with Unique and Expanding tasks, allowing cross-training or cross-functional groups in the same or similar industries. Results also have implications for research and development activities.

4. Apply on the job what is learned in volunteer activities. Wide ranges of leadership skills and many other valuable attributes and talents are used in volunteer groups. Clerical workers may perform leadership functions in a service group. The opposite occurs on church retreats, where executive volunteers perform manual labor. Reversing roles leads to understanding and opens the doors to communication in general.

5. The C-U-E model could help answer the question, "Are training dollars being spent in the right areas?" The increased awareness of the need to focus primarily in Core areas lends credence to the need for basic skills training. Careful analysis of Core activities before and after training

should show that more higher-level skills were used after training. The same could be true for Unique areas when training is in professional areas. Getting value for training dollars spent and being accountable in the workplace are the critical issues.[7]

Motivation

1. Expanding tasks, because of high level demands and diversity, are highly motivational. In areas where productivity and motivation are low, opportunities to perform Expanding tasks will be extremely well received.

   Because Expanding tasks require creativity and innovation, motivating potential is greatest for Expanding, less for Unique, and lowest for Core tasks.

2. Focusing on critical business processes, or Core activities, is essential to the organization's long-term ability to achieve its goals. Intangible areas associated with satisfaction, loyalty, trust, and intrinsic motivators, as demonstrated by Expanding tasks, are now being recognized.

3. Opportunities to do work in Expanding areas can be used as motivators, like Herzberg's intrinsic motivators (personal growth, advancement, achievement, recognition, value of work itself, etc.).

4. Internalizing intellectual and emotional components related to the job is one way to improve performance. Internalizing means total acceptance, or "stamping in" ways to think and react that can be applied to achieving positive results.

5. Facilitates self-assessment of personal accomplishment in order to streamline and upgrade by having less Core and more Unique and Expanding work. This effort would enhance productivity, intrinsic motivation, quality, and self-esteem and provide a sense of accomplishment.

Career Passport...Personal Knowledge Equation

1. Self-analysis is a useful tool, but is woefully underutilized. If forced to judge themselves, most people turn out to be pretty good at it. Most know how well they perform and could reluctantly fill out a productivity scorecard. Increasingly, managers have their employees do their own performance appraisals. But employees never see their managers' self-appraisals. It is a one-way street, with the manager leading the way. It is time to introduce 360° feedback.

2. The passport analogy implies that people have a current, viable passport. Each entry reflects current status or new competencies, interests, and accomplishments. Creating and maintaining your own career passport can be done on your own. These efforts will be interesting and challenging instead of "work."

3. Continuous education reveals crossover skills, as in relationships between what are normally considered to be separate disciplines, like statistics and mathematics. Compare what you know in one professional field with what is known in another field (i.e., intellectual benchmarking that reveals crossover skills)

   For example, Linus Pauling, father of molecular biology, won the Nobel Prize for Chemistry in 1954. He used one science (physics) to explain another (chemistry). In 1962, he won the Nobel Peace Prize.[8]

4. If the learning organization is going to be the preferred organization of the future, we will all be busy. Self-assessment of personal accomplishment is permitted, even encouraged, in learning organizations. Having a good knowledge base and staying current are extremely important. By the year 2000, our current crop of graduates will have many outdated skills, assuming they have useful skills in the first place. They must be encouraged to get involved in continuing education activities as soon as they graduate. This will take some convincing.

5. Self-assessment and self-knowledge leading to self-mastery are logical outgrowths of the C-U-E model. Ultimately, milestones along the self-mastery path could be (1) learn for the sake of learning; (2) prepare for a more demanding career, or "do-it-yourself" career development;[20] (3) master a totally new discipline, as in being "retredded"; and (4) achieve and maintain career resilience over the long haul, or, as "survivors" say, "keep your job while others are losing theirs."

Measurement

1. Efforts to measure productivity and establish quality standards should focus on Core areas where major efforts take place and/or people spend more of their time than they want to. Core activities with common elements can be streamlined between and within disciplines and industries in order to save effort, time, and cost.

2. Unique tasks form the major part of a profession or discipline. Most people enjoy performing them. While developing productivity measures may be somewhat difficult, using operational definitions helps identify

job content. Existing professional standards and benchmarking are used to develop and establish common quality standards within and between professions, like bar exams for attorneys.

3. This model helps illustrate and document the complex nature of "white-collar work." The sequence of define–measure–test–improve increases the scope, precision, reliability, and validity of resulting measures. Results can be used to "free up" people so they can devote more time to performing Unique and Expanding tasks. Both levels have greater motivation potential than Core tasks.

4. Emerging and steadily increasing standards for quality and value can be built into work skills, activities, and outcomes. These standards can be communicated within and beyond the organization, for example to customers, clients, partners, suppliers, and others.

Enhance Productivity and Quality

1. A systems approach and the C-U-E model can be combined. Each part of the model can be examined in terms of systems. They can be compared in parallel fashion, and common areas, including overlapping areas, can be determined. Other comparisons can be with a family of measures, matrices, or standard output/input ratios. These measures should reflect an organization's internal environment (strategic priorities, culture, knowledge base, etc.) and external environment (economy, competition, politics, etc.)

2. Provides a quality vision that has observable and measurable steps along the way. Efforts would support existing total quality management initiatives within the organization, like business process analysis and reengineering, among others. The entire C-U-E model could be built around the concept of quality. Quality standards could be specified for Core, Unique, and Expanding, including ways to reach these standards. One result might resemble Figure 10.2.

3. Factor analysis could be used to determine additional factors in each of the C-U-E areas. Simple or weighted averages reflecting the relative importance of Core, Unique, and Expanding areas could be developed based on percent of time spent in each area. The index could yield one productivity score.[16]

4. Streamlining Core activities that share common elements across disciplines, industries, and even countries can save time. Improving produc-

Job	Activities Performed		
	Core	Unique	Expanding
Author writing a book	Perform computer search of titles Read pertinent literature Proofread manuscripts Rearrange content of chapters	Review articles carefully Summarize important material Write new material Ensure relevance of content	Create excitement and enthusiasm Develop novel practical applications Communicate with business leaders Apply creativity in classroom
Engineering	Examine data Input data into computer Do materials testing Draw schematics	Critique reports Solve daily problems Coordinate information flow Serve on team projects	Create new manufacturing methods Develop patent Present distinguished lecture Write state-of-the-art paper
Accounting	Input pertinent data Gather financial data Maintain records on cash flow Obtain approvals	Perform cash flow analysis Prepare budget reports Analyze status of business units Review corporate budgets	Make long-term forecasts Create annual report Expand operations Plan financial strategies

Figure 10.2 Typical Core, Unique, and Expanding activities for author, engineer, and accountant

tivity and quality measures in numerous types and levels of jobs requires taking many small steps. When carefully planned, these steps will be in the right direction.[6]

5. The C-U-E model can be used to further analyze the specific job content identified by existing methods and models, such as family of measures,[18] productivity management competency model,[14] weighting systems and partial and total factor productivity,[3] and skills matrix at British Petroleum Exploration.[20]

Figure 10.2 illustrates Core, Unique, and Expanding work activities for an author, engineer, and accountant. The author uses words and concepts. Engineers and accountants work primarily with numeric data.

Unique activities performed differ widely in content, areas of expertise, and focus of specialization. An author does not solve daily engineering problems. An engineer does not review and revise corporate budgets. However, the standard mental processes such as critiquing, reviewing, and analyzing information are common to all professions. It is the *content* and focus of work efforts that are used to group people performing Unique tasks, not the mental *processes* and physical effort used to achieve results.

Activities classified as Expanding involve creativity, enthusiasm, and state-of-the-art knowledge. People lacking knowledge and experience in Unique and Core areas seldom perform well at the Expanding level. Taken one step further, only when senior managers recognize and appreciate the diverse nature of Core and Unique work can they begin to understand the value of work performed at the Expanding level.

10.1

Refer to the basic definitions of Core, Unique, and Expanding. Write down your major work-related activities, input, through-put, output, and outcomes that you feel comfortable grouping as Core, Unique, or Expanding.

Core Activities	Unique Activities	Expanding Activities
_____	_____	_____
_____	_____	_____
_____	_____	_____
_____	_____	_____

To prepare your answer to Question 10.2, you may want to refer to Questions 4.1 (first elements in the personal equation), 7.1 (major work activities), 8.1 (systems approach), 9.1 ("things" done well), 9.2 (activities performed regularly), or 10.1, using Core, Unique, or Expanding areas.

Not all dimensions will apply to every task or job. You may rate some jobs on three or four dimensions. Do not rate any job-related area or job variables if the dimensions do not apply. The major purpose is to determine the "average" for each major work-related concept. "Averages" are only approximate. Their sole purpose is to provide a framework or guidelines for grouping jobs or activities into Core, Unique, or Expanding.

10.2

Directions to complete the grid consist of five steps:

1. Select five or six activities or types of work that you do on a regular basis and write them in the columns at the top of the grid.

2. Rate each activity on the ten dimensions of the C-U-E model using the operationally defined seven-point rating scale in Table 10.1.

3. Add the columns for each job category to find out the approximate level of the various jobs you perform.

4. Divide the sum of each column by the number of variables on which it was rated to get an average. If you rated your job on all ten variables of the model, divide by 10. If you used six variables, divide by 6, and so on. This rough estimate of your level of work is only a guide.

5. Group "averages" in #4, above, using the following numerical baselines: Core: 1.0 to 2.5, Unique: 2.51 to 5.5, and Expanding: 5.51 to 7.0.

Table 10.1   Basic Assumptions and Associated Ranking System

	Basic Assumption	*Ranking System*
1.	Work is cyclic, repetitive, or routine	1 = high routine...7 = low routine
2.	Major type of work activities and results can be described	1 = very easy to describe...7 = very hard to describe
3.	Amount of time spent doing work can be measured	1 = very easy to measure...7 = very hard to measure
4.	Level of work difficulty ranges from simple to complex	1 = very simple...7 = very complex
5.	Work structure ranges from formal to informal	1 = high in structure...7 = low in structure
6.	Work standards range from very specific standards set by others to open-ended, or self-imposed	1 = very specific...7 = self-imposed

Basic Assumption	Ranking System
7. Work is done in a logical sequence order	1 = very definite order...7 = very flexible order
8. Work differs in motivating potential	1 = very low motivating potential...7 = very high motivating potential
9. Control over work ranges from low to high	1 = very low control...7 = very high control
10. Work has value added functions	1 = very low value added...7 = very high value added

Grid for Question 10.2

VARIABLE	#1	#2	#3	#4	#5	#6
		WORK ACTIVITIES				
1. Cyclic, routine						
2. Can be described						
3. Time is measured						
4. Difficulty level						
5. Structure						
6. Standards						
7. Logical sequence						
8. Motivating potential						
9. Control						
10. Value-added						
Sum Rankings						
Number of Variables Used						
Average Ranking						
Grouping* (C, U, E)						

•Core = 1.0 – 2.50; Unique = 2.51 – 5.50; Expanding = 5.51 – 7.0

ALTERNATIVES

After Question 10.2 is completed, variations may be useful exercises.

1. Have peers, subordinates, and supervisors or work groups also complete the survey. Results from various sources can be compared in order to enhance reliability and validity and get more comprehensive answers.

2. If you have several jobs, analyze each. Jobs might be a temporary or team assignment or "filling in" for someone else. Comparing two or more jobs could provide meaningful information.

3. Use the model several times a year to see how you and your job change. Naturally, you would like to spend more time in Unique and less in Core. Devoting more time to Expanding would be my ideal. I get to the Expanding parts of my job about 5:00 p.m. or later. The morning is spent in Core, so I can get to Unique after lunch. Most of the time spent writing this book was probably in Expanding—and at night.

4. If you could develop your own job that would make a definite contribution to your organization and/or profession yet motivate and satisfy you at appropriate levels, would it be? Would you do only Expanding tasks? Could you justify this job on a cost or profit-center basis? Be creative. Think positively. You may be able to do your "dream" job sooner than you realize.

Sample work-related activities and results of three jobs are presented in Table 10.2. The following six major items in each of the three categories are meant to illustrate rather than be definitive.

Table 10.3 is a hypothetical estimate of the various types of productivity measures, operational definitions of quality, and estimates of time five different workers spend in Core, Unique, and Expanding areas.[17] These data could be based on responses to Question 10.2. Sample measures based on definitions of productivity and an operational definition of quality show that operational definitions and standards can be added to the C-U-E model.

To explain Table 10.3 more fully, assessments of productivity and quality use information from performance appraisals, group output, peer evaluations, or other feedback mechanisms. Peer review is a possible but seldom used source of first-hand information.

More traditional evaluations of major productivity factors will pinpoint output. They may focus on any number of important throughput or process variables discussed in Chapter 8. The abundance of process variables and the difficulty in obtaining reliable output-based measures of achievement have historically put performance appraisals on shaky ground.

Table 10.2   Illustration of Work-Related Activities
in Research, Engineering, and Sales

Research
1. Examine results of own lab or from labs of colleagues and associates
2. Maintain competence in profession by independent study and presenting papers
3. Communicate with peers and colleagues
4. Perform research
5. Prepare articles for possible publication
6. Supervise lab and/or research personnel

Engineering
1. Problem solving
2. Discuss various projects with other engineers
3. Use resources of others, as in work teams
4. Plan, schedule, and attend meetings with customers, end users, members of cross-functional teams, etc.
5. Meet with others, as in production, design, legal, etc.
6. Independent study to retain competence and/or become registered

Sales
1. Learn product information
2. Understand the client/customer interface
3. Communicate with sales force
4. Seek future clients, do promotions, etc.
5. Develop and maintain communication channels with customers, suppliers, and all forms of end users
6. Further organizational and/or personal image

Can specialized knowledge be turned into common Core knowledge? Yes. When complex or even average difficulty concepts and processes are made easier to understand and perform, everyone will profit. The line between theory and practice is still visible. Only when it disappears will the organization and the people in it begin to share a sense of "oneness" or working together. The real key is to vest the real power in people at the lower levels in the organization.[1] In my mind, this statement applies to work from Core and Unique areas.

Quality standards and guidelines may be covered by professional licensing or certification requirements, quality manuals, or company standards, like Motorola's often-quoted Six Sigma. We know that quality is the illusive entity everyone is searching for. However, just as quality at a given level comes within reach, it is necessary to search out and achieve a new, higher level of quality. The quality journey is endless.

Table 10.3 Sample of Work Activities Using the Core-Unique-Expanding Model

Type of Worker and Activity	Estimates of % Time in			Measure or Definition of Productivity	Operational Definition of Quality
	C	U	E		
Clerk inputs numeric data	90	8	2	Output/input	3 sigma
Accountant does cash flow report	65	25	10	Work output/ Labor hours input	Accurate and timely report
Manager of information systems	55	30	15	Management output/ Management cost	Meets standards
				Actual–Desired/ Desired	Satisfied employees
				Utilization survey	Customers satisfied
Professor teaches engineering	50	35	15	Number of publications, papers presented	Recognition, promotion, "success"
Scientist does space research	15	45	40	Obtain value patents, lead high-level task force	National reputation, publish in ranking journals

When more people work at their level of specialization, the number of current "disconnects" in the flow of transactions and communications is reduced. When work is restructured to reflect specialization, quality of products and services, and possibility job satisfaction and productivity, should be increased.

When people throughout the organization work at a level of capability appropriate to the complexity of the work, performance and satisfaction should be at a high level.

10.3

If you could develop your own job that would make a definite contribution to your organization and/or your profession yet motivate and satisfy you at appropriate levels, what would it be?

Do internal and external customers and end users have any input to your job or make it different from jobs your peers perform? Does working in a product-based or service-based industry make a difference? Some guidelines to answering these questions are:

1. Take a broad look at your work. Write down about ten or twelve jobs or tasks you perform daily. Determine how many times you do them weekly, then monthly. See how they may possibly change over time.

2. Get several people who have jobs similar to yours to do the same thing and compare results. This may mean adding a few areas or consolidating or expanding other areas.

3. Go back to #1 and make a grid. You may be able to group some of your tasks into the same category.

4. Define these categories carefully using operational definitions.

5. See what qualitative and quantitative data you have access to. Don't reinvent the wheel!

6. Check the variables using a systems approach to see if there is a flow and logic to your variables.

7. Look at key results, or end result areas, and redefine them operationally. You should end up with what you do, including a better understanding of your whole job.

SUMMARY AND CONCLUSIONS

The following statements give an overview of the make-up and uses of the C-U-E model.

1. The three-part, hierarchical C-U-E model is used to examine and group various types and levels of work activities and outcomes. This model contains:

   - **Core components:** Routine, often manual operations having low difficulty level. These activities are vital to an organization's success (e.g. data entry, assembly-line work).

   - **Unique components:** Specific to education, training, and/or experience and depend on ability and skills. They are unique to a profession or discipline and form the major part of a job (e.g., medicine, engineering, accounting).

- **Expanding components:** Relate to personal growth and development in profession or area of expertise. They are demanding, challenging, and require creativity and innovation (e.g., perform forefront research and develop new products or services).

2. Subdiving tasks that make up the model is not meant to be reductionistic, but rather ensures that the major parts are not omitted. As before, the whole is greater than the sum of the separate parts. Synergy is created when tasks are reassembled into a new, slightly expanded self-designed model. People always take pride in something they create themselves.

3. The C-U-E model is only one of many ways to examine and assess jobs people perform by using a variety of dimensions they create or select themselves. Users can build factors into the model, such as quality, specific work standards, cycle time, and numerous measures of productivity, for the purposes of comparison.

PRACTICAL APPLICATIONS

1. Create an awareness of the need to think about jobs in a logical manner. Each part of the model is shown and described in a way people understand. When people are aware of their talents, they know that a very small change in the way they perform or organize their job can increase their productivity. It is the small, steady gains that add up and really make a difference.

2. The great mismatch between what people do and how they are paid will never really be resolved. However, better initial job placement would be an excellent start. People cannot be expected to perform well in jobs for which they have little or no training.

3. Increased use of teams and cooperative work efforts means that teams should consist of capable, trained people who have complementary talents.

4. There are numerous opportunities to identify skill or competence areas for purposes of training and development. Methods could be developed to assess pre- and post-training skills.

5. The process of finding a job and/or trying to stay employed places the burden on the individual. Some people carry an up-to-date resume with them, but not all are that proactive. Preparing and maintaining a

list or some form of written information documenting skills, abilities, knowledge, and work and professional accomplishments is increasingly important.

REFERENCES

1. Block, Peter. "Finding Community at Work," *Journal for Quality and Participation*, September 1994, pp. 22–25.

2. Bugental, J. F. T. *The Search for Authenticity.* New York: Holt, Rinehart and Winston, 1965.

3. Chew, W. Bruce. "No-Nonsense Guide to Measuring Productivity," *Harvard Business Review*, January–February 1988, pp. 110–111, 114–116, 118.

4. Galagan, Patricia. "On Being a Beginner," *Training & Development Journal*, November 1992, pp. 30–38.

5. Hampton, David, Summer, Charles R., and Webber, Ross A. *Organizational Behavior and the Practice of Management*, Glenview, Ill.: Scott, Foresman, 1978, p. 264.

6. Harless, Joseph H. "Guiding Performance with Job Aids," in *Introduction to Performance Technology*, Washington, D.C.: The National Society for Performance and Instruction, 1986, pp. 106–124.

7. Jacques, Elliott. "Managerial Accountability," *Journal for Quality and Participation*, March 1992, pp. 40–44.

8. Kaufmann, George B. and Kauffman, Laurie M. "Linus Pauling: Reflections," *American Scientist*, November–December 1994, pp. 522–524.

9. Landis, Larry J. "Try a Pay for Knowledge Process with a PLUS," *Journal for Quality and Participation*, June 1994, pp. 26–29.

10. Maslow, A. H. "A Dynamic Theory of Human Motivation," *Psychology Review*, Vol. 50, 1943, pp. 370–396.

11. Maslow, A. H. *Motivation and Personality*, New York: Harper and Row, 1954.

12. Maslow, A. H. *Toward a Psychology of Being*, Princeton, N.J.: Van Nostrand, 1962.

13. Maslow, A. H. *Motivation and Personality* (2nd ed.), New York: Harper and Row, 1970.

14. Preziosi, Robert C. "Productivity Management Competencies: Differences in Managerial and Organizational Assessments," *National Productivity Review*, Spring 1986, pp. 174–179.

15. Sassone, Peter G. "Survey Finds Low Office Productivity Linked to Staffing Imbalances," *National Productivity Review,* Spring 1992, pp. 147–158.

16. Sassone, Peter G. "Don't Fire the Clerical Staff," *Management Review,* December 1992, pp. 16–19.

17. Smith, Elizabeth A. "A Conceptual Model for Introducing Quality into Measurements of White-Collar Productivity," in *Productivity & Quality Management Frontiers-IV,* Vol. 1, Sumanth, Edosomwan, Poupart, and Sink (Eds.), Norcross, Ga.: Industrial Engineering and Management Press, 1993, pp. 391–398.

18. Smith, Elizabeth A. *The Productivity Manual* (rev. ed), Houston: Gulf Publishing, 1995.

19. Snee, Ronald D. "Creating Robust Work Places." *Quality Progress,* February 1993, pp. 37–41.

20. Tucker, Robert and Moravec, Milan. "Do-It-Yourself Career Development," *Training,* February 1992, pp. 48–50, 52.

AUTHOR INDEX

SUBJECT INDEX